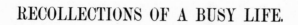

RECOLLECTIONS OF A BUSY LIFE.

KENNIKAT PRESS SCHOLARLY REPRINTS

Dr. Ralph Adams Brown, Senior Editor

Series in
AMERICAN HISTORY AND CULTURE
IN THE NINETEENTH CENTURY
Under the General Editorial Supervision of
Dr. Martin L. Fausold
Professor of History, State University of New York

RECOLLECTIONS OF A BUSY LIFE.

BY

HORACE GREELEY.

Volume II

A NEW EDITION, WITH A MEMOIR OF MR. GREELEY'S LATER
YEARS AND DEATH.

KENNIKAT PRESS
Port Washington, N. Y./London

1 0 9435

RECOLLECTIONS OF A BUSY LIFE

First published in 1873
Reissued in 1971 by Kennikat Press
Library of Congress Catalog Card No: 71-137913
ISBN 0-8046-1481-4

Manufactured by Taylor Publishing Company   Dallas, Texas

KENNIKAT SERIES ON AMERICAN HISTORY AND
CULTURE IN THE NINETEENTH CENTURY

XLII.

FREMONT. — BUCHANAN. — DOUGLAS.

THE popular elections of 1854–55 had made manifest the fact that the Opposition, if united on one ticket, was strong enough to oust the Democratic party from power at Washington; the long and arduous struggle for Speaker had shown that such combination could only be effected with great difficulty, if at all. The "American" party was first in the field, — selecting as its candidates Millard Fillmore, of New York, for President, with Andrew J. Donelson (nephew and namesake of "Old Hickory"), of Tennessee, for Vice-President, — men of decided personal strength, but impossible candidates for the Republicans, because radically hostile to their cardinal principle. The Democrats next held their Convention, and nominated James Buchanan, of Pennsylvania, for President, with John C. Breckinridge, of Kentucky, for Vice-President. President Pierce and Senator Douglas were Mr. Buchanan's competitors, and were wisely defeated, — each of them being conspicuously identified with the Nebraska bill; while Mr. Buchanan, having been, throughout President Pierce's term, Envoy to Great Britain, had escaped all complication in the popular mind with that measure. And, as Pennsylvania was the probable pivot of the contest, it was manifestly wise to present a Pennsylvanian for the first office. The Republicans, meeting last, nominated Colonel John C. Fremont, of California, for President, with William L. Dayton, of New Jersey, for Vice-President. They were strongly urged to present John McLean, of Ohio, then a Justice of the Supreme Court, for the first office, with the assurance that he could secure the bulk of the "American" vote, — at least in the Free States, — and thus probably carry Pennsylvania and Indiana. This assurance seemed to rest on no certain or tangible data, and was overruled, — a mistake (if such it were) for which I accept my full share of responsibility. I felt that Colonel Fremont's adventurous, dashing career had given him popularity, with our young men especially; and I had no faith in the practicability of our winning many votes from those "Americans" who were not heartily Republicans.

Our canvass was very animated, and our hopes, for a season, quite sanguine, especially after Maine had gone for us in September, by 25,000 plurality; but the October elections gave us a cold chill, — Pennsylvania choosing the Democratic State officers, by 3,000 majority, over the vote of the combined Opposition, with 15 of the 25 representatives in Congress, and a majority in the Legislature. Indiana likewise went against the combined Opposition, by an average majority of more than 6,000; and when it transpired that the "American" leaders, rejecting all offers to run combined tickets, persisted in running distinctive Fillmore tickets for Electors in each of these (as in most other) States, it was clear that we were doomed to defeat, — all the States that we could still rationally hope to carry casting less than half the Electoral votes. Yet we fought on with much resolution, though with little hope; giving Fremont and Dayton the six New England States, by clear majorities; New York, by 80,000 plurality; and Ohio, by nearly 17,000; while Michigan, Iowa, and Wisconsin went decidedly for us, as Illinois would have done had there been no third ticket. Pennsylvania and Indiana each gave Mr. Buchanan a bare majority over the two opposing tickets. Mr. Fillmore received the 8 electoral votes of Maryland only; Colonel Fremont had 114 votes, — those of eleven Free States; while Mr. Buchanan was elected by 112 votes from fourteen Slave States, and 62 from five Free States, — 174 in all, or a clear majority. The aggregate popular vote stood: Buchanan, 1,838,232; Fremont, 1,341,514; Fillmore, 874,707. Buchanan's inauguration (March 4, 1857) was swiftly followed by the since famous Dred Scott decision of the Supreme Court, which denied the right of Congress to prohibit slaveholding in the Territories of the Union, and proclaimed it the notion of our Revolutionary fathers that Blacks have no rights that Whites are bound to respect. Mr. Buchanan foreshadowed this decision in his Inaugural, gave it his hearty indorsement, and commended it to general approval.

_____

Kansas had begun to be settled in 1854, directly after the passage of the Nebraska bill, and had inevitably become an arena of strife and violence. Colonies were sent thither from the Free States expressly to mould her to the uses of Free Labor; while weaker colonies were sent thither from the South, to bind her to the car of Slavery. These would have been of small account had they not been largely supplemented by the incursions of Missourians, who, thoroughly armed, swarmed across the unmarked border whenever an election was impending; camping in the vicinity of most of the polls, whereof they took unceremonious possession, and voting till they were sure that no more votes were needed; when they decamped, and returned to their Missouri homes. As the Free-State settlers refused to be thus subjugated, there were soon two Territorial legislatures, with sheriffs and courts to match; and these inevitably led to collisions of authorities and of forces, resulting in general insecurity and turmoil, with occasional sacrifices of property and of life. Congress had tried to end these disorders; but no plan could be agreed upon by the two Houses, and nothing was effected. At length, in the Summer of 1857, the pro-Slavery minority, powerfully aided by the "Border Ruffians," elected a Convention, framed a Pro-Slavery Constitution, adopted it after their fashion, and sent it to Congress for approval and ratification. It was known as the "Lecompton" Constitution, from the place where it was fabricated.

Mr. Buchanan at first hesitated to indorse or be complicated with this procedure; so that there was trouble in the camp;

and it was currently reported that his less scrupulous Secretary of the Treasury, — Howell Cobb, of Georgia, — being asked by a visitor what was the matter, carelessly replied, " O, not much ; only Old Buck is opposing the Administration." Senator Douglas, on the one hand, at first seemed inclined to the side of the Missourians, whose cause he had upheld with signal ability and energy in the preceding Congress ; but he soon demonstrated in favor of genuine " Popular Sovereignty," in Kansas, which was his more natural and consistent position. Reports of this change had preceded his appearance in Washington as a member of the XXXVth Congress ; so that, on his calling to pay his respects to the President, an animated and spicy colloquy on the ruling topic was at once commenced by his host. " Mr. Douglas," said the President, " how are we to allay the contention and trouble created by this strife over the Lecompton Constitution ? " " Why, Mr. President," replied his guest, " I do not see how *you* should have any trouble in the premises. The Constitution says, ' *Congress* shall make all needful rules and regulations respecting the Territories,' &c., but I cannot recall any clause which requires *the President* to make any." Thus the conversation ran on, until the President, waxing warm, saw fit to warn his visitor that his present course would, if persisted in, soon carry him out of the Democratic party. " Mr. Senator," he inquired, " do you clearly apprehend the goal to which you are now tending ? " " Yes, sir," promptly responded the Little Giant ; " I have taken a through ticket, and checked all my baggage." Further discussion being obviously useless, Mr. Douglas soon left the White House, and I believe he did not visit it again during Mr. Buchanan's administration.

The XXXVth Congress, which had been mainly chosen simultaneously with Mr. Buchanan, or nearly so, was decidedly Democratic, and still more strongly pro-Slavery, — the Senate impregnably so, by about two to one, — and yet, so flagrant were the enormities of the Lecompton measure, and so conspicuous the ability and the energy of Mr. Douglas, who led the resistance to it, and threw his whole soul into the work, that the attempt to make Kansas a Slave State under the Lecompton Constitution (which her people were forbidden to change to the detriment of Slavery for several years to come) was fairly beaten; being vitally amended in the House by a vote of 120 to 112, after it had passed the Senate by 35 to 23. The Senate at first refused to concur by 34 to 22; whereupon a conference was had, and an equivocal compromise measure thereby devised and carried through both Houses by nearly a party vote. But, as this measure gave the people of Kansas a chance indirectly to vote upon and reject the Lecompton scheme, such a vote was thereupon had, and the scheme rejected by an overwhelming majority. Kansas thus remained a Territory until after the secession from Congress of most of the Southern Senators, early in 1861, when she was admitted as a Free State, with the hearty assent of three fourths of her inhabitants.

Mr. Douglas's second term as Senator expired with the Congress in which he made his gallant and successful struggle against what I deemed a great and perilous wrong, — a wrong so palpable that the eminent Senator Hammond, of South Carolina, who supported it at every step, afterward publicly declared that the Lecompton bill should at once have been kicked out of Congress as a fraud. It seemed to me that not only magnanimity, but policy, dictated to the Republicans of Illinois that they should promptly and heartily tender their support to Mr. Douglas, and thus insure his reëlection for a third term with substantial unanimity. They did not concur, however, but received the suggestion with passionate impatience. Having for a quarter of a century confronted Mr. Douglas as the ablest, most alert, most effective, of their adversaries, they could not now be induced to regard him in a different light; and, beside, their hearts were set on the election, as his successor, of their own especial favorite and champion, Abraham Lincoln, who, though the country at large

scarcely knew him as for a single term a Representative in
Congress, was endeared to them by his tested efficiency as a
canvasser and his honest worth as a man.   Four years before,
the Whig portion of them had wished to make him Senator;
but the far fewer anti-Nebraska Democrats held the balance
of power, and they decisively said, "You will elect *our* leader,
Lyman Trumbull, or you will not elect at all."   Having given
way then, the great body of the party had fully resolved that
Lincoln should be their candidate now, and that, at all events,
Douglas should *not* be.   So Lincoln was nominated, and accepted in a memorable speech; and the State was canvassed
by him and Douglas as it had never before been, — they repeatedly speaking alternately from the same stand to gatherings of deeply interested and intently listening thousands.
In the event, Mr. Douglas secured a small majority in either
branch of the Legislature, and was reëlected; but Mr. Lincoln's
friends claimed a considerable majority for their favorite in
the aggregate popular vote.   They did not, for a while, incline
to forgive me for the suggestion that it would have been wiser
and better not to have opposed Mr. Douglas's return; but I
still abide in that conviction.

Mr. Douglas was the readiest man I ever knew.   He was
not a hard student; if he had been, it would have been difficult to set limits to his power.   I have seen him rise in the
Senate quite at fault with regard to essential facts in controversy, and thence make damaging blunders in debate; but
he readily caught at and profited by any suggestion thrown
out by friend or foe; and no American ever excelled him in
off-hand discussion: so that, even if worsted in the first stages,
he was apt to regain his lost ground as he went on.   Once,
as I sat with the senior Francis P. Blair and one or two others
outside the bar of the Senate in 1856, he made us the text of
an amusing dissertation on the piebald, ring-streaked, and
speckled materials whereof the new Republican party was
composed; and, passing us soon afterward, he hailed me famil-

iarly with the interrogation, "Did n't I give you a good turn just now?" At a later day, when the Lecompton struggle was in progress, a mutual friend, remembering that my strictures on Mr. Douglas in former years had been of a *very* caustic sort, inquired of him whether he had any objections, on account of those strictures, to meeting me on a friendly footing. "Certainly not," was his instant response; "I always pay that class of debts as I go along." Our country has often been called to mourn severe, untimely losses; yet I deem the death of Stephen A. Douglas, just at the outbreak of our great Civil War, and when he had thrown his whole soul into the cause of the country, one of the most grievous and irreparable.

———

Mr. Buchanan, though born nearly a quarter of a century earlier, survived Mr. Douglas by fully seven years; dying in 1868, when he had long outlived whatever influence or consideration he may once have enjoyed. Alike ambitious and timid, his conduct throughout the initial stage of the Rebellion is yet unaccountable on any hypothesis but that of secret pledges, made by him or for him, to the Southern leaders when he was an aspirant to the Presidency, that fettered and paralyzed him when they perverted the power enjoyed by them as members of his Cabinet to the disruption and overthrow of the Union. That, during those last mournful months of his nominal rule, he repeatedly said to those around him, "I am the last President of the United States," I firmly believe; that he proclaimed and argued that the Federal government had no constitutional right to defend its own existence against State secession, is matter of public record. Though he had spent what should have been the better part of a long life in working his way up to the Presidential chair, I think the verdict of history must be that it would have been far better for his own fame, as well as better for the country, that he had failed to obtain it.

XLIII.

A RIDE ACROSS THE PLAINS.

FROM the hour when, late in 1848, the discovery of rich gold *placers* in California had incited a vast and eager migration thither, insuring the rapid growth of energetic and thrifty settlements of our countrymen on that remote and previously unattractive, thinly peopled coast, the construction of a great International Railway from the Missouri to the Pacific seemed to me imperative and inevitable. I could not deem it practicable to retain permanently under one government communities of many millions of intelligent, aspiring, imperious people, separated by fifteen hundred miles of desert, traversed by two great mountain-chains, beside innumerable clusters, spurs and isolated summits, and compelling a resort, for comparatively easy, cheap, and speedy transit, to a circuit of many thousands of miles. A Pacific Railroad was thus accepted by me at a very early day as a National necessity, alike in its political and its commercial aspects; and, while others were scoffingly likening it to a tunnel under the Atlantic or a bridge to the moon, I was pondering the probabilities and means of its early construction. I resolved to make a journey of observation across the continent, with reference to the natural obstacles presented to, and facilities afforded for, its construction; but no opportunity for executing this purpose was afforded me prior to the year 1859. I then hoped, rather than confidently expected, that, on publicly announcing my intention, some friend might offer to bear me company on this journey; but my hope was not realized. One friend did propose to go; but his wife's veto overruled his not very stubborn resolve. I started alone, on the 9th of May, and travelled rapidly, *via* Cleveland, Chicago, Quincy, and the North Missouri Railroad, to St. Joseph; thence dropping down the Missouri to Atchison, and traversing Kansas, by Leavenworth and Wyandot, to Osawatomie; thence visiting Lawrence and returning to Leavenworth, whence the "Pike's Peak" stage carried me, through Topeka, Manhattan, and Fort Riley, to Junction City, then the western outpost of civilization in that quarter.

We stopped overnight at the said city, and I visited a brother editor, who was printing there a little Democratic weekly, for which he may possibly have had two hundred subscribers; but, if so, I am confident that not one half of them ever paid him the first cent. He was, primarily, as I remember, a Texan; but, having spent two years in California, he gave me the most rapturous commendations of the beauties, glories, and delights of that region. "It is the greatest, the finest, the most attractive country that man ever saw," he concluded. "Then why are you not still in California?" I inquired, glancing around his doleful little shanty. "Because I am a great fool," he bluntly replied. I did not see how profitably to protract the discussion.

We left Junction City on a bright morning late in May, following a new trail, which kept within sight of the Solomon's or middle fork of the Kansas River for the next two hundred miles. The country was, in the main, gently rolling prairie, covered with luxuriant young grass, and fairly glowing with flowers. Antelopes, though shy, were frequently seen at a distance, which they rapidly increased. Streams running into the Solomon, across our track, were at first frequent, and often skirted with trees; but grew scarcer and more scanty as we proceeded. There was some variety of timber in the wet bottoms at first; but soon the species dwindled to two, — Cottonwood and a low, wide-branching Water Elm; at length, upon passing a wide belt of thin soil,

covering what seemed to be a reddish sandstone, both wood
and water almost entirely vanished, save as we descried the
former at intervals in the bottoms of the Solomon, some miles
to the left (south) of us.   The Cayota or Prairie Wolf (a mean
sort of stunted or foreshortened fox) was infrequently seen ;
the bolder and quite formidable Gray Wolf more rarely ; soon,
the underground lodges of the Prairie Dog (a condensed gray
squirrel) covered roods of the ground we traversed, — our
newly located path lying right across several of their " towns,"
which it had not yet impelled them to desèrt.   I refused, at
first, to credit the plainsmen's stories that an Owl and a Rattlesnake were habitually, if not uniformly, fellow-tenants of his
" hole " with the Prairie Dog, though I had already seen many
Owls sitting, as we came near, each at the mouth of a hole,
after the Prairie Dog had barked his quick, sharp note of
alarm at our approach, and dropped into it ; but I was finally
compelled to succumb to testimony that could not be gain-
sayed.   The *rationale* of the odd partnership is this : the
Rattlesnake wants a lodging, and cannot easily dig one in that
compact soil ; the Prairie Dog *does n't* want to be dug out and
eaten by the Cayota, as he quickly and surely would be but
for the protection afforded by the Rattlesnake's deadly fangs.
What the Owl (a small particolored one) makes by the association, I do not so clearly comprehend ; but I suspect the
Hawk would pounce upon and devour *him* but for the ugly
customer presumed to be just at hand, and ready to " mix in,"
if any outsider should venture to meddle with the Owl ; whose
partnership duties are plainly those of a watch-dog or lookout.

Beyond the sterile sandstone belt, we struck a wide stretch
of almost woodless, gently rolling prairie, thickly reticulated
by tortuous buffalo paths, with frequent skeletons and still
more plenteous skulls, — the soil being covered by a mere
sward of the short, strong buffalo-grass ; and soon we came in
sight of galloping, fleeing herds of first three and four, then
twenty to a hundred and fifty, buffaloes, generally running

southward, in their alarm at our appearance, to seek safety in more familiar haunts, — the entire host being at this time in movement northward. Twenty or thirty miles farther on, having reached the summit of a gentle slope, we looked down its western counterpart to the pretty brook at its base, perhaps five miles distant, and thence up the opposite "rise," — the eye taking in at a glance at least a hundred square miles of close-fed velvet glade, whereof nearly or quite half was covered by buffalo, not "as thick as they could stand," but as close together as they could comfortably feed. Say that there were but twenty (instead of fifty) square miles of buffaloes in sight, and that each one had four square rods of ground to himself, the number in sight at once was 512,000. And for three days we were oftener in than out of sight of these vast herds, and must have seen several millions of buffaloes. In fact, we could with difficulty avoid them, — our driver being once obliged to stop his team, or allow it and us to be overwhelmed and crushed by a frightened, furious herd, which, having commenced its stampede southward across our path forty or fifty rods ahead of us, continued to follow each other in blind succession until we must have gone down and rolled over beneath their thundering charge (as an empty stage did a few days afterward), if we had not halted, and so avoided them. A day or two before, an agent of the line, who was riding a horse along the track, unthinking of danger, was borne down by a herd started by some emigrants the other side of an elevation, and instantly hurled to the earth. Though badly hurt, he saved himself from death by firing all the barrels of his revolver at the great brutes careering madly over his prostrate form ; but his horse was instantly killed.

Emerging from the buffalo region, the soil became visibly thinner, and the vegetation poorer and poorer, until — the head sources of the Solomon having been passed — we bore rather north of west across several tributaries to the Republican or main northern branch of the Kansas, which we found here a rapid, shallow stream, perhaps a hundred yards wide by one to two feet deep, rippling over a bed of coarse sand

and gravel, with a very few cottonwoods thinly dotting its
banks at long intervals, — precious little thin, coarse grass
being occasionally discernible. A mule, bitten in the jaw by
a rattlesnake, lying dead beside a station-tent, was one of the
fresher features of this dreary region. A stunted cactus —
which reared its small, prickly leaves barely above the
ground — here began to be manifest. Following up the
dwindling river, we soon came to a "sink," — the entire
stream percolating for fifteen or twenty miles hence through
its gravelly bed far below the surface of the earth, — a team-
ster, who dug through eight feet of sand and gravel in quest
of water for his fainting beasts, being obliged to desist without finding any. Most of the tributaries we crossed on the
Republican were simply broad beds of coarse, loose, dry sand,
into which our mules often sank to a depth of several inches;
though in Winter and Spring I presume these are considerable brooks. Wood here became so scarce that, to supply
one station, it had to be carted sixteen miles. At length, we
left the head springs of the Republican on our right, and
struck, a few miles on, a northern tributary of the Arkansas,
known as the "Big Sandy," which we ascended some twenty
or thirty miles; finally leaving it on our left. Its bed was
dry, of rather coarse sand, and often covered with a white,
alkaline efflorescence; but, occasionally, a small stream ran
gently aboveground, under one of its banks, where the channel had been worn exceptionally deep.

Soon after leaving the Big Sandy, we crossed the head waters of Bijou Creek, which runs northward into the South
Platte. "Pike's Peak," snow-crowned, had for some time
been visible nearly west of us; soon, we found deeper ravines and steeper hills than we had seen since we left the
Missouri, with thin clumps of Yellow or Pitch Pine, — out-
posts of the Rocky Mountain forests, — occasionally covering
patches of their sides or crests: the soil being sterile, and the
grass too scanty to nourish sweeping fires at any season.
After a few hours of this, we descended to the valley of
Cherry Creek, near the point where it emerges from the

mountains, and, following down its east bank to its entrance into the South Platte, saluted, one bright morning in June, after a rough, chilly, all-night ride, the rising city of DENVER.

Denver was then about six months old; but the rival city of Auraria (since absorbed by it), lying just across the bed of Cherry Creek (which suddenly dried up at this point during one night of my brief sojourn), had already attained an antiquity of nearly a year. As there was no saw-mill within several hundred miles, none of the edifices which composed these rival cities could yet boast a ground-floor; but I attended Divine worship the next Sunday (in Auraria) on the first second-story floor that was constructed in either of them. It may at first blush seem odd that a second-floor should precede a first; but mother Earth supplied a first-floor that did very well, while nature has not yet condescended to supply man-made dwellings with chamber-floors.

I suppose there were over a hundred dwellings in the two cities, when I reached them. I judge that they averaged fully ten feet square, though probably the larger number fell short of that standard. In material, none could boast over its neighbors, as all were built of cottonwood logs from the adjacent bank of the South Platte; but some of these were rudely squared on one side, with an axe; while others were left as God made them. I believe there was a variety in roofs also, — some being constructed of "shooks," or pieces split with an axe from a cottonwood log, while others were of cottonwood bark. I seem to remember that all the chimneys were of sticks and mud; but then some were without chimneys; and, while several had windows (I mean one apiece) composed of four to six lights of seven-by-nine glass, others were content with the more primitive device of a rude wooden shutter, closed at night, and during severe, windy, driving storms. Most of these cabins had known as yet only male housekeepers; and nearly half of them had been deserted by their creators and owners, some of whom were off prospecting

for gold; while quite a number — disappointed, hopeless,
homesick — had left for the States early in Spring, convinced
that gold in the Rocky Mountains was a myth, a humbug, or
that (in the vernacular) "Pike had n't got any peak." But
the recent discoveries on Clear Creek had given matters a new
and more cheerful aspect; so that, while two thirds of those
who started for "the diggings" that Spring never went within sight of the Rocky Mountains, — many of them not half-
way to them, — while some barely reached Denver, and then
took the back track, the rival cities were gaining population
quite rapidly during the ten days that I spent in or near
them, and some good families were among the acquisitions.
Cabins that would gladly have been sold for $25 two months
earlier now ran rapidly up to $100; and the market could
fairly be quoted as active and advancing. There were as yet
few or no servants to be hired at any price; but a considerable band of Arapahoes were camped in Denver; and, while
the braves were thoroughly worthless, their squaws were willing to do anything for food. True, they could do very little;
but lugging water from the South Platte was the first requisite in housekeeping, and this they did faithfully. We lived
mainly on bread, bacon, beans, coffee, and nettles, the last
being boiled for greens; but those who were not particular as
to dirt could often buy a quarter of antelope just brought in
by an Arapahoe; or, more probably, killed by the hunter and
backed in by his squaw. Whiskey was in good supply (I
know nothing as to the quality) at a quarter (silver) per
drink. There were several rude bedsteads just constructed in
the Denver House, — the grand hotel of the city, — on which
you were allowed to spread your blankets and repose for a
dollar a night; but mine, being bottomed with rough slats
nearly a foot apart, almost broke my back, proving far less
luxurious than the bosom of mother Earth. Two blacklegs
rented opposite corners of the public room, and were steadily
swindling greenhorns at three-card monte, from morning till
bedtime: one stage-driver, who was paid off with $207 at
noon, having lost the last cent of it to one of these harpies

by 2 P.M. The gamblers and other rough subjects had an unpleasant habit of quarrelling and firing revolvers at each other in this bar-room when it was crowded, and sometimes hitting the wrong man, — by which phrase I certainly do not indicate any of their own number. On the whole, therefore, I soon tired of hotel-life in Denver. It was not dull, — quite otherwise, — but I am shy by nature and meditative by habit, and some of the ways of the Denver House did not suit me. They were unmistakably Western, and I was journeying to study Western character; but, even though distance might not lend enchantment to the view of these mining-region blacklegs and ruffians, I am sure that they can be studied to better satisfaction out of pistol-shot than at close quarters.

"Suppose you jump a cabin?" suggested the friend to whom I intimated my preference for a less popular lodging. I did not understand; but he explained, and I saw the point. Several cabins were still standing vacant, as many had been; and no one knew whither their owners had gone, so whoever wanted one of these empty tenements just helped himself. I at once followed the fashion, and was happy in my choice. I was thenceforth lodged very eligibly till the owner of my cabin, returning from a prospecting tour, put in an appearance. He was evidently embarrassed at the thought that his advent must seem abrupt and unceremonious; but I cut short his apologies by insisting that the cabin afforded ample accommodation for two; and we thenceforth shared it very comfortably for the few days that I tarried in Denver.

While thus snugly and cheaply lodged, I boarded with a widow lady from Leavenworth, who had been keeping a mail-station on the plains, but, tiring of that, had just migrated to Denver, and jumped a cabin. She, with her little son, slept on a sort of shelf nearer the roof than the floor of her single room; while two male boarders, waiting outside while she made her toilet, spread their blankets on the earth-floor of her tenement. At daylight, they turned out, giving her a chance to dress, clear up, and get breakfast, which they duly returned to eat. Such was life in Denver in June, 1859.

XLIV.

THE ROCKY MOUNTAINS. — THE GREAT BASIN.

I MADE a flying visit, directly after reaching Denver, to the then new " Gregory Diggings," on Clear Creek, where is now Central City. A good road, I hear, now winds thither through the mountains, mainly keeping close to Clear Creek ; but that was impossible in 1859 ; as even an empty wagon would have been capsized into or toward the creek at least a hundred times before making the distance. Our route lay across the South Platte, the prairie and Clear Creek (where Golden City has since sprung up), and then right up the face of the first ridge, rising 1,600 feet in a mile and a half, — an ascent so steep as to appear impossible to teams, however lightly loaded ; and even saddle-horses seemed in great peril of falling off and rolling to the bottom. After two miles of level path through an open pine forest on the summit, we had to descend a declivity nearly as steep ; then ascend a second mountain ; and so on, till we camped at sunset, weary enough, seven miles short of the diggings, which we reached about nine next morning ; spending the day and night with the pioneers, and returning to the Platte Valley the day after. I saw enough on that trip to convince me that the Rocky Mountains abound in Gold and nearly all other metals, but that these must be earned before they can be enjoyed.

I bade adieu to Denver about the 18th of June ; having hired an "ambulance," or wagon and four mules, to convey me to the Overland Mail-route at Fort Laramie, on the North Platte, 200 miles northward. I judge that there were twenty considerable streams to cross in that distance, — all then in flood, from the melting snows of the inner and higher mountains. Several of these streams were forded with difficulty by our team, — one of them (the Cache le Poudre) being as large as the Charles at Cambridge. I think we saw four huts on the way, but only three of them were occupied. There was no White person then living within fifty miles of Cheyenne, where the Pacific Railroad now enters the Rocky Mountains; and only a deserted fort or military camp spoke of civilization. Yet most of the region between the two Plattes and the base of the Rocky Mountains — a district equal in area to Connecticut, if not to Vermont — has good soil, is tolerably timbered, grows fine grass luxuriantly, and will yet subsist a large farming population. It is subject to drouth, but may easily be irrigated; and then its product of Wheat, Oats, Barley, and Roots will be immense. I judge that nearly all the larger tributaries of the Missouri traverse a good farming region directly under the Rocky Mountains wherein they take rise. This region lies from 4,500 to 6,000 feet above tide, and hence is subject to frost, hail, and late snow, as well as to drouth; yet I predict its rapid settlement and growth. I wish I could see how to save its Aboriginal inhabitants from sure and speedy extinction.

After waiting five days at Fort Laramie, I took the mail stage (then weekly) which traversed the old Oregon as well as California emigrant trail up the Platte and its northern tributary, the Sweetwater, to that wide gap in the Rocky Mountains known as the South Pass, — the Sweetwater heading on the west side of the mountains, and sending (in Summer) a scanty mill-stream through the Pass. Much of this region is quite sterile; snow lay deep in a ravine of the Pass on the 5th of July; while there is one large swamp, thirty or forty miles this side, which remains frozen a foot or two below the surface perpetually. There are small lakes on this route that look most inviting, yet so surcharged with alkaline minerals that to drink freely of their water is death

to man or beast. There is some Yellow Pine on the hills, with
less Cottonwood and Quaking Asp, mainly skirting, at long
intervals, the streams; but this region is, for the most part,
unless rich in minerals, good for nothing. I learn that bounteous mines of Gold have lately been found here; and I know
that the indications of Gold were quite palpable on the hills
in the Pass, where we camped and spent a day beside a runnel which brings its scanty tribute to the Sweetwater. But,
a few miles beyond the South Pass, where the mountains disappear, and the road to Utah and California diverges from
the old trail to Oregon, and where each begins to descend
toward the Pacific, the country is utterly worthless for at
least two hundred miles; in the midst of which we crossed
Green River, running swiftly southward, in a very deep, narrow valley, which yields a little grass and less Cottonwood.
On either side of this valley stretch dreary wastes of thirsty
sand, shaded only by the two low shrubs, known locally as
Greasewood and Sagebrush, which, together, enclose a thousand miles of the Overland Wagon-route, and probably cover
half a million square miles of the interior of our continent.
Greasewood is a species of Artemisia, and derives its vulgar
name from a waxy or resinous property, which causes it to
burn freely, even while green; but it grows in bunches or
stools six or seven feet apart, with naked, glittering sand between them; and so defies destruction by fire. Sagebrush
exhibits a number of shoots, twelve to twenty inches long,
from a common stalk or stump of about equal height; each
shoot somewhat resembling a stalk of Sage in appearance and
color. There is a Sage-Hen that eats this plant; but who,
unless famishing, would thereafter choose to eat the Sage-
Hen?

Fort Bridger was the first village we had seen since we left
Laramie; like which, it owes its existence to a military post.
It is traversed by a brawling mill-stream (Ham's Fork) which
is rushing to be lost in Green River, and is said to have some
arable land in its vicinity. We were still considerably north
of the present route of the Pacific Railroad, which we had

crossed and left near Cheyenne; but soon, crossing a high divide, we bore southward, and, descending rapidly, forded Bear River, here a swift stream one or two hundred yards wide, but scarcely more than two feet deep. It is unfortunate that the Pacific Railroad cannot follow this river hence to Salt Lake; but the course of the stream is so tortuous and so shut in by mountains and difficult precipices that this may not be. I judge that, next to the Sierra Nevada, already nearly vanquished, the stretch from Green River to Salt Lake — some three hundred miles — is the most difficult section of the entire work. But the route we traversed, leaving that of the railroad far on our right (north), rises easily out of the valley of Bear River, and thence follows down a long, narrow, grassy valley or glen known as Echo Cañon, with steep cliffs on either side, emerges from it to cross Weber River (also a tributary of Salt Lake), and thence crosses two difficult ridges of the Wahsatch and Uintah mountains, whence it winds down a ravine known as Emigration Cañon till that opens into the valley of the River Jordan and of Salt Lake; and soon we roll into the city of the many-wived prophet, the capital of his sacerdotal and political empire, and the most conspicuous trophy of his genius and his power.

That city has so changed since I saw it, — being now probably at least thrice its size nine years ago, — that I will speak of it briefly, and only as to certain permanent phases of its character. My present belief is that, like most strangers, I was more favorably impressed by it than I should have been. Not that its more intelligent people received me kindly and treated me with emphatic hospitality, — I have been thus welcomed to other cities, which nevertheless did not specially impress me. But a thousand miles of parched, mountainous desert (counting from Denver only) on which I had seen no single productive farm, and nothing that could be fairly termed a house but a few cheap structures for officers' lodgings at Forts Laramie and Bridger — no vegetables, no furniture, no beds, — had predisposed me to greet even the ruder appliances of urban life with uncritical satisfaction.   Our civilization, regarded as an end, is faulty enough, and open to objections from every side ; but, considered as a stage in our progress from the *status* of the Esquimaux, the Digger, the Hottentot, I submit that it may be contemplated with a complacency by no means unreasonable.   Soon after leaving the last Kansas settlement, I noted the rounds of the ladder I had descended during the preceding fortnight, and photographed them as follows :—

"*May* 12*th, Chicago.* — Chocolate and morning journals last seen on the hotel breakfast-table.

23*d, Leavenworth.* — Room-bells and bath-tubs make their final appearance.

24*th, Topeka.* — Beef-steaks and wash-bowls (other than tin) last visible.   Barber ditto.

26*th, Manhattan.* — Potatoes and eggs last recognized among the blessings that "brighten as they take their flight."   Chairs ditto.

27*th, Junction City.* — Last visitation of a boot-black, with dissolving views of a board bedroom.   Beds bid us good by.

28*th, Pipe Creek.* — Benches for seats at meals disappeared, giving place to bags and boxes.   We (two passengers of a scribbling turn) write letters to our journals at nightfall in the express-wagon that has borne us by day, and must serve us as bedchamber for the night.   Thunder and lightning, from both south and west, give strong promise of a shower before morning.   Our trust, under Providence, is in buoyant hearts and a rubber blanket.   Good night ! "

I descended somewhat farther afterward, and I did not think of hardship, though the water was often scanty, as well as bad, and the pilot-bread had been so long exposed to the drying air of the Plains that human teeth could hardly penetrate it.   Those who fancy army "hard-tack" dry eating would devour it thankfully, after being rationed a single week on that which I confronted on the Sweetwater and the Colorado.   But hard-tack is wholesome, if not toothsome ; while the bread made on the Plains, of nearly equal parts of flour and saleratus, baked in a frying-pan or spider, and eaten hot, though I ate it with facility, destroyed my digestion, and made me sick, — there being nothing to relish it but poorly smoked pork, except tea and coffee, which I declined. With good water, I could stand almost anything; but this was often unattainable, and I suffered for want of it.

Salt Lake City suddenly restored us to abundance and comfort, — rooms, beds, sheets, towels, vegetables, dried fruits, shade, &c.; while the water was beautiful and good. The Mormons have faults; but they are more uniformly industrious and (after their fashion) pious than any other people I ever visited. I doubt whether there is another city on the continent wherein family worship is so general, and profanity so rare, as in Salt Lake City, so far as its Mormon inhabitants are considered. I must believe the authors of their revelations either knavish or self-deluded; but I have such a liking for solid, steady, *bona fide* work, that the rank and file have my most hearty good wishes. Nowhere else are there so few idlers (Brigham Young assured me that there was none but himself; and he is kept busy in his vocation of prophet and ruler), and nowhere else have so few poor and ignorant people achieved so much that remains to benefit future generations, as in Utah. I cherish the hope that their spiritual vision will soon be cleared, and that they will yet, ceasing to be polygamists, become better Christians, — retaining the habits of industry, frugality, and thrift, which command my hearty admiration. "He builded better than he knew" is a truth of very wide application; and I am confident that the Pacific Railroad, of which Brigham Young is grading the thirty miles next northeast of his metropolis, is destined to work changes which it is well that he does not foresee, and which will render his dominions more populous and his people far less docile to his guidance than they now are. I judge our age inauspicious to prophets and new revelations from on high; and, though the past history of Utah seems to refute my theory, I confidently expect that of the next twenty years to confirm it.

XLV.

UTAH. — NEVADA.

A PORTION of our little army, despatched from Kansas late in 1857 to put down a threatened (or apprehended) revolt of the Mormons, had stopped for the Winter at Fort Bridger, after its trains, following carelessly in its rear, had, not far from the Colorado, been surprised and burned by a Mormon force, rendering its Winter sojourn in that desolate region one of great hardship, especially for its animals; but it finally marched into the Mormon settlements unopposed, — the chief Saints protesting that they had never purposed rebellion against the National authority. The expedition, which had threatened a bloody tragedy, was thus transformed into a most expensive farce; for, though the regulars were hardly more out of place in Utah than they had been in Kansas, they were a far more costly nuisance. Every pound of their sustenance had been hauled across twelve hundred miles of desert and mountain at a cost of $400 or $500 per ton, — or, at any rate, was charged for as if it had been. And, when I visited Camp Floyd, where it was stationed, forty-five miles south-west of Salt Lake City, officers were engaged, under orders from Washington, in selling its heavy trains at auction, at prices possibly averaging one half the actual value of the mules and one tenth that of the wagons, — the bidders being few, and evidently combined to give Uncle Sam the worst bargains possible. Governments are made to be plundered, — at all events, are regularly used to that end. I presume that, when the army was ordered from Camp Floyd to Texas the next year, part of these same wagons were bought back from their purchasers at generous prices, — which by no means implies any generosity on the part of those who bought them of the government and sold them back again.

I spent a day at Camp Floyd as the guest of my oldest army acquaintance, Lieutenant-Colonel D. C. Ruggles, 5th Infantry, whom I had first known in 1835 as a Massachusetts cadet, just appointed to a lieutenancy ; and who, having married in Virginia, afterward became a General of the Southern Confederacy. We dined with the commander of the post, Colonel Albert Sidney Johnston, — a grave, deep, able man, with a head scarcely inferior to Daniel Webster's, — who, less than two years afterward, left Texas overland to take part in the Rebellion, and finally found death on the bloody field of Shiloh or Pittsburg Landing, where he led the Rebel host with a gallantry and soldiership worthy of a better cause. If some wizard had foreshadowed to us the future, as we sat around his hospitable board not three years before, who would have believed him ?

Camp Floyd had been located beside a small but constant stream, with considerable stunted, bushy Cedar covering the low mountains adjacent, whence it issued ; but the stage-route thence to California rose gradually from its valley into a hilly, burnt-up region southwestward ; and thenceforth, till we bore up to strike the Humboldt at Gravelly Ford, some three hundred miles westward, I can remember seeing but three brooks of any account, — neither of those carrying water enough to render it a decent mill-stream ; and neither, I judge, running more than five miles from the clustered mountains between which it was cradled, till the arid, thirsty plain had drank the last drop, and left its shallow bed thenceforth in Summer a stretch of dry, hot gravel and sand. We may have passed a dozen springs in this distance, though I believe we did not. In one place, there was a stretch of fifty miles from water to water, save that some had been carted in barrels to quench the thirst of our jaded mules at a point half-way from one station to another. Twice, as I recollect, we sat down to our noonday meal of pork and bread beside springs by courtesy, where water had been found by shallow digging in depressions or "sinks" below the usual surface of the plains; but the warm, sulphurous fluid thence obtained required intense thirst to render it potable. In one place, I recollect several miles of the all-pervading Grease-wood and Sage-brush which had been killed stone-dead, — dried up, apparently, though their power of resisting drouth is unparalleled; yet stunted Bunch Cedar and some Indian Pine thinly covered the brows or the crests of many hills and low mountains; seeming able to resist a drouth even of successive years. The country is so broken and mountainous that I presume Artesian wells have since been, or will easily be, dug in the rockless clay of the valleys, which will supply water, not only for drinking, but for irrigation; and the valleys need but this to render their alkaline clay bounteously productive. I judge that the surface of most of them has been raised twenty to fifty feet by earth washed down, in the course of ages, from the circumjacent mountains, and that, when irrigated, they will be cultivated with facility, and with ample success. The Mormons raise bounteous crops, especially of Wheat, wherever they can coax a stream to meander across and percolate through a portion of one of their valleys; and I presume most of those between the Wahsatch and the Sierra Nevada need but water to prove them equally fertile. Many of the mountains, I doubt not, will prove rich in minerals; but they are rarely or never arable, produce a very little grass in Spring only; and their scanty, fitful covering of wood, once cut off, would not be reproduced in a century.

Bear in mind that the route I travelled rather skirts than pierces the desert of deserts which spreads southwestward of Salt Lake, nearly or quite to the Colorado; covering many thousands of square miles. A friend, now deceased, once found himself "at sea" on this desert, and likely to perish of thirst; but he had a noble horse, to which he gave a free rein; and that horse brought him off alive, — that was all. He crossed miles on miles of pure rock salt, — how deep, he could not say; but he brought away a fragment which had been washed and worn into a nearly round log, as large as a man's thigh, and three or four feet long, which I saw. Another friend, who explored a route from Austin, Nevada, to the Colorado (on the western verge of this desert), rode, for days, down the bed of what had once been a considerable river, but which seemed to have been absolutely dry for years.

There is ample corroborating proof that the Great Basin has been far less parched than it is; and I trust that a more generous rain-fall will again be accorded it. Probably, re-clothing it with timber would renew its rains; but then the rains seem to be needed to start and sustain the timber. Two or three hundred miles north, several streams take rise that make their way northward to the Columbia; as the Humboldt, issuing from the west side of the same mountainous region, runs over three hundred miles W.S.W., to be lost in a sandy, reedy marsh, not a hundred miles from the Sierra Nevada; but, southward of this strange river of desolation, there is rarely a stream large enough to turn a grindstone, till you are very near the banks of the almost equally lonesome Colorado.

I rode more than two hundred miles down the south or left bank of the Humboldt. In that distance, I judge that all the water it receives from tributaries might be passed through a nine-inch ring; and the stream, of course, grew smaller and smaller as it flowed. Possibly, three springs were passed in all that distance, though I cannot remember so many; while I *do* right well remember my scarcely modified thirst. The alkaline water of the Humboldt I could not drink, though others did; in Spring, when its volume is greater, its quality is probably better. Once, we stopped by a small brook tumbling down from high adjacent mountains on the left, and I drank my fill of its warm, sweet water; but for this, I must have remained thirsty throughout. And, in all the two hundred miles, I believe I did not see wood enough to keep a Yankee farmer's fire going through a Winter.

Willow-bushes, skirting the little river, were nearly all. Even the mountain ranges, from one to five miles distant on either side, showed no timber, or next to none. And, when we came at length to that expansion of the stream which is called a lake, no raft, boat, or even canoe, floated on its bosom or was moored to either bank, and a cottage built of stones and clay constituted the mail-station at its foot. Thence, we crossed a waste of sand forty miles wide, which separates the " sink " of the Humboldt from the kindred marsh that drinks up the waters of the Carson, which comes down from the Sierra ; and, following up the latter, by what is now Virginia City, but then was nothing, we stopped to eat at Genoa, — then the only considerable village in what has since become Nevada, — and rested our weary limbs at dark, after a night-and-day ride of four hundred miles (five days and four nights from Shell Creek in Western Utah), in a wooden hotel, at the very foot of the Sierra Nevada.

There was then no Austin, and no real mining in what is now Nevada. The auriferous and argentiferous deposit or vein now known as the Comstock lode had just been discovered, — that was about all. The natural grass of the upper end of Carson Valley had previously attracted a few settlers, who were weary of mining in California, or worn out with travel across the desert and reluctant to scale the Sierra ; and, though the valley must be fully six thousand feet above the sea, and must inevitably be frosty, its beauty and verdure fully justify their partiality. I estimate that three hundred habitations, mainly log, are quite as many as existed in the entire region which is now the State of Nevada, that its civilized population did not exceed five thousand, and that its aggregate product was barely adequate to the subsistence even of this number. To-day, Nevada produces more silver, and little less gold, than any other State or Territory ; and the next census will give her a population of at least two hundred thousand.

XLVI.

THE SIERRA NEVADA. — THE YOSEMITE. — THE BIG TREES.

A CLEAR, warm, golden 1st of August — such a day as the Pacific slope of our continent abounds in — took us across the Sierra Nevada by the double-summit route that follows up one branch of the Carson to its source, then descends rapidly into the valley of Lake Bigler, thence climbs diagonally the mountain west of it by a steep ascent of two miles, crosses its summit, and descends again, following a depression in which springs give birth to rills, which speedily collect into a brook, which goes brawling and leaping down the western declivity of the Sierra, and has become quite a little river (South Fork of the American) at a point twenty or thirty miles down, where we crossed its valley from the northern to the southern bank, and, rising thence to the summit of a ridge or "divide" on the south, ran rapidly down it to the thriving city of Placerville, at the base of the range, in California's great central valley of the Sacramento.

The Sierra Nevada is probably more heavily timbered than any other range of mountains on the continent. On the Nevada side, this timber is of moderate size, and almost wholly of Yellow or Pitch Pine, with a few deciduous trees in the narrow ravines of the streams; while, on the far longer slope that looks toward the Pacific, immense Yellow and Sugar Pines, often eight feet through, thickly cover thousands of square miles, interspersed with White Cedars from four to six feet in diameter, stately Balsam Firs, a considerable variety of White, Red, Live, and Rock Oaks, with a few other trees. Such a wealth of magnificent timber profoundly impresses the traveller, who has seen nothing like it since he left the eastern slope of the Rocky Mountains, and a plentiful lack of trees everywhere else since he bade adieu to the Kansas, now so many hundred miles away. The valleys and lower slopes of California are often quite bare, though wide-branching Oaks are thinly scattered over a portion of the latter; and I saw here — what I never saw elsewhere — living trees (Buck-eye) six to eight inches through, with every leaf killed by drouth on the 1st of August, so that they would exhibit no sign of verdure again till after the heavy rains of the ensuing Winter. The dryness of earth and atmosphere on the Pacific slope in Summer and Autumn can only be realized by those who have experienced it. I saw the Mormon farmers cutting heavy grass by the margin of Salt Lake; but they found no process of hay-making necessary. Though its color was still a bright green, they raked it up unspread, and stacked it without ceremony, knowing that the atmosphere would mean-time have sucked every atom of superfluous moisture out of the greenest of it. I presume this is the case, southward of Oregon, nearly or quite to the Isthmus of Darien.

My visit to the chief wonders of California — the Yosemite and the Big Trees — was necessarily hurried, but otherwise satisfactory. The sky was cloudless, as that of California al-most uniformly is from May till October; the days were warm, but not excessively so; the journey was made on horseback, and in good part under the shade of giant ever-greens. There were hundreds of acres covered almost exclu-sively by the Balsam Fir, sixty to eighty feet high, and one to two feet in diameter, growing at an elevation of fully 5,000 feet above tide, where the snows of Winter are so heavy and so many that the limbs of the Fir are depressed at their ex-tremities, so as to form a series of umbrellas (as it were) rising one above another. Two high, steep mountains — one on either side of the South Merced — are surmounted by what, in 1859, were difficult bridle-paths, ere you strike at "Grizzly Flat," the source of a little runnel which meanders through an upland meadow or grassy morass to the brink of the great chasm, into which it pours itself by a fall of some 2,500 feet,

which dissolves it into a white foam, whence it is afflicted
with the lackadaisical appellati·n of " The Bridal Veil." The
fall is not to blame for this, but some of its early visitors are.

The Yosemite is the grandest marvel of the continent. It
is a rift or cleft in the Sierra Nevada, ten miles long, averaging half a mile wide at the bottom, and perhaps a mile at the
top; its depth ranging from 3,000 to 4,000 feet, though one or
two of the peaks on the north are said to rise 5,000 feet above
the surface of the Merced. There are three points at which
access is had to the valley, — one of them by clambering down
the rocks near its head; the other two by zigzagging down
either brink near its lower end. These are bridle-paths; the
other, a foot-path only. That on the side of Mariposa is two
miles long; and we were two good hours in winding down it
through woods, with the moon's rays obscured to us by the
interposition of the mountain whose north face we were descending. It was midnight when we reached its foot, and
halted in the narrow, grassy valley of the stream, right in
front of a perpendicular wall of gray granite 3,000 feet high,
with a few Yellow Pines rooted in the crevices which at long
intervals creased it, and seeming, with the mountain itself,
about to be precipitated upon us.

Nothing else dwells in my memory that is at all comparable
in awe-inspiring grandeur and sublimity to this wondrous
chasm. I judge that the soft granite frequently found in
streaks or belts by the miners of California — granite in
chemical composition, but of the consistency of a rather solid
boiled pudding — here existed on a much larger scale, until
the little river (in Summer, a large mill-stream only) gradually
dug it out, and bore it away, till the last of it had disappeared.
I was told in the valley that repeated efforts of miners to dig
down to the " bed-rock," in quest of mineral, had proved failures, — the sand and gravel, interspersed with· bowlders, ap-
pearing unfathomable. The little streams from either brink
which, at several points, leap into the valley, have, by the
aid of frost and freshet, hurled millions of tons of rock and
earth into the chasm, forming gigantic deposits of *débris*, over
which the road up the valley carries you, generally through

woods, affording difficult footing for men or animals, especially by night.   Fording brooks, stumbling over rocks, winding among trees, it seemed to me that the six miles from the point where we entered the Valley to the two cottages or huts near its centre would never end; but they *did* end at last, about 2 A. M.; and I dismounted, and lay down to a welcome, though unquiet, slumber.   I was covered with boils (the penalty of drinking the alkaline waters of Colorado, Utah, and Nevada), and had ridden in torture since noon, bearing my weight on my toes, barely stuck into Mexican stirrups far too small for me, whereby my feet had been so lamed that I could scarcely walk; hence, the prospect of soon rising to resume my travels was by no means alluring.   I did rise, however; took breakfast; rode to the head of the Valley; examined with some care the famous fall; dined; and, at 2 P. M., started homeward; reaching Clark's ranche, on the South Merced, at 10 P. M.

Let me explain that the Yosemite fall is not that of the Merced, which enters the valley, at its head, by several successive leaps in a wild, rocky gorge or cañon, and leaves it by one even more impracticable, — giant blocks of granite being piled for hundreds of feet above the surface of the boiling current, and completely hiding it from view.   The Yosemite is a side-stream or tributary, coming from the north or higher mountains, and, having itself worn down its bed to a depth of a thousand feet, leaps thence 2,600 feet into the chasm, making a single plunge of 1,600 feet.   When I saw it, there was barely water in the Yosemite to turn the wheels of an average grist-mill; but in Winter and Spring there is probably twenty to forty times as much.   The spectacle is rather pleasing than sublime, — the Mississippi, when in highest flood, having scarcely sufficient volume to save such a descent from seeming disproportioned and trivial.

Of Big Trees, there are two principal groups in California, — the Calaveras and the Mariposas.   The former is more widely known, because quite accessible; and it boasts two or three of the largest trees; but it has barely 250 in all, while the

Mariposas has 600. They stand in a shallow valley or depression on the mountains, some 5,000 feet above the sea level, and 2,500 above the South Merced at Clark's, five miles distant.

That which was clearly largest fell several years ago, burying itself in the stony earth to a depth of four feet, and exhibiting a length of nearly or quite 400 feet. Formerly, two horses were ridden abreast for some 200 feet through the cavity, which successive fires had enlarged in it. It is still easy thus to ride through it, but the hollow has been burned out, so that it is now much shorter. Several of the trees still standing and alive are said to be over 100 feet in circumference; many are 80 to 90 feet, with a bark at least eighteen inches thick, a very little sap (white) under it, — the residue of the enormous bulk being a light, dry, reddish heart, which burns easily, even while the tree is green, but is scarcely prone to natural decay. Several of these giants rise a full hundred feet before putting forth a limb; none have many branches, but some of these are six feet through. They are a species of Cedar, — identical with the Cedars of Lebanon, our guide asserted; but I presume he only guessed so. Their foliage is scarcely, if at all, larger than that of the Yellow Pines and White Cedars growing among or near them; many of these being six to eight feet in diameter near the earth.

Within the next two years, the Central Pacific Railroad will have been completed, when passengers will leave New York on Monday morning, and dine in San Francisco the sixth evening thereafter. Then the trip, which I found tedious and rugged, will be rapid and easy, with every needed comfort and luxury proffered on arid stretches of desert, where I washed down the Mail Company's ancient pork and hot saleratus bread with more unwholesome and detestable warm alkaline water than (I trust) I shall ever be constrained to swallow hereafter. I hope to be one of the party who make the first excursion through trip to San Francisco, there to rejoice with my countrymen in the completion of the grandest and most beneficent enterprise ever inaugurated and perfected by man.

XLVII.

THE FUTURE OF CALIFORNIA.

I LINGER yet by the shores of the vast Pacific; for I feel
that the general mind is still inadequately impressed with
the majestic promise that impels the resistless tendency of
our Gothic race toward the sands of that mighty sea. I do
grievously err, if the historian of a future century does not
instance the discovery of the Columbia by a Yankee, and the
finding of Gold in Upper California so soon after that country
had fallen into our hands, as among the most memorable and
fortunate incidents in the annals of our continent, and hence
of mankind.

On Gold *per se*, I place no high estimate. If all the science
and labor which have been devoted by our people to the discovery and extraction of the Precious Metals had been as
faithfully applied to the production of Iron, Coal, Copper,
Lead, Tin, Salt, Gypsum, Marble, Slate, &c., I believe our
country would have been richer and our people wiser and
happier. Even if we could regard the abundant possession
of Gold and Silver as a chief good, it is plain that the countries which produce are not those which most amply retain
and enjoy them.

But mines or deposits of Gold and Silver are prominent
among the means whereby attention and population are
drawn to a region previously unpeopled, or thinly peopled by
savages. Men rush madly and in thousands to a district reported auriferous; defying famine, heat, cold, pestilence, and
even death itself. Mining or washing for Gold combines the
fascinations of gambling — the chance of sudden riches —

with the sober incitements of regular and laudable industry : hence, it always did, and always will, allure vast numbers to brave peril and privation in its behoof. In time, the bubble bursts; the glamour is dispelled; but thousands have meantime found new homes and formed new habits; hence, a new civilized community.

I judge that gold-mining in California is nearly " played out." True, there are many good veins there which will continue to be worked at a profit for hundreds of years yet, during which many more and some better will doubtless be discovered and opened ; but this is sober business, requiring capital, science, luck, patience, to insure success ; while the jovial, free-handed heroes of pick and pan have passed away forever, — some to Nevada; some to Arizona; others to Montana, Idaho, &c., &c., — many to the land of shadows, — and the river-beds and "gulches" that knew them shall know them no more. California still exports Gold largely ; but most of it is produced in Nevada, Montana, British Columbia, &c., &c. She for years produced Fifty Millions per annum ; she has fallen off at least half ; she is likely soon to fall still lower. I presume the child is born who will live to see her annual product fall below Ten Millions.

Yet her natural wealth will still be great, being varied, vast, and indestructible. I group it under these heads : —

I. *Soil.* — Of her ninety millions of acres, I should deem not over twenty millions decidedly arable ; but these are, for the most part, exceedingly fertile. I judge that her great valleys were once arms of the sea, since gradually filled up by the continual abrasion and wearing away of the slopes of her omnipresent mountains. Many of them have now from 100 to at least 1,000 feet in depth of warm, mellow soil, — a marine deposit of sand, clay, and vegetable mould, in nearly equal proportions, wherein the plough very rarely disturbs a stone. I never saw land better calculated to produce large crops, year after year, with a moderate outlay of labor. The absence of rain in Summer and early Autumn keeps down weeds ; while the unclouded, fervid sun hastens growth and insures perfection. I am confident that Cotton, and even Cane, might be grown to profit throughout the southern half of the State, in which the Fig, the Olive, and the Apricot grow luxuriantly and ripen unfailingly.

II. *Water.* — Though I saw large fields of heavy Indian Corn which grew and ripened without receiving a drop of rain, I nevertheless realize and admit that water is a desirable facility to vegetable growth and maturity. And, as cultivation is here mostly confined to valleys and the lower slopes of mountains, water is abundantly procurable. Artesian wells are easily dug; their flow is apt to be generous, as well as constant; and a small stream, well managed, amply irrigates a very large field. Trees and vines root deep in that rich, facile mould; the grape needs a very little water for two years, and none thereafter; while its culture requires but half the work needed here or in Europe, because our frequent rains evoke innumerable weeds. I estimate that a ton of Grapes may be produced in California with half the labor required to grow them in Italy; and that Silk, most semi-tropical Fruits, and I trust Tea, also, may be produced with equal facility. Wheat and other small grains yield largely and surely. I saw thousands of acres that had been two months cut and shocked, yet still awaited the coming of the circulating thresher; other fields were yet uncut (September 1), though long so dead-ripe that a large portion of the grain must be shelled out and lost in the field, even under the most careful handling. I saw fifty acres of choice tree-fruits — mainly Peaches and Apples — in a single patch; the Peaches rotting by hundreds of bushels, because they could not be gathered and marketed so fast as they ripened. I saw vast tracts of good Mustard, self-sown and growing wild from year to year, though apparently as good an article as ever ripened. The intense drouth of her long, cloudless, dewless Summer produces cracks and fissures in the earth, into which grains and other seeds drop when dead-ripe; rains come and close the fissures in November and later; the self-sown seed germinates, and produces a " volunteer" crop, — a full one of

Mustard, but a half crop of Wheat, &c. I saw, at the Mission of San José, giant pear-trees, planted some scores of years ago by the Jesuits, and producing largely, but of indifferent fruit, till a Yankee acquired and grafted them, when he sold in San Francisco their product, the next year but one, so as to net him $100 from each tree. I look forward to a day when this country's supply of Raw Silk, as well as of Raisins and other dried fruits, will reach us from our own Pacific coast.

The rains of California are ample, but confined to Winter and Spring. In time, her streams will be largely retained in her mountains by dams and reservoirs, and, instead of descending in floods to overwhelm and devastate, will be gradually drawn away throughout the Summer to irrigate and refresh. For a while, water will be applied too profusely, and injury thus be done; but experience will correct this error; and then California's valleys and lower slopes will produce more food to nourish and fruit to solace the heart of man than any other Twenty Millions of acres on earth.

III. *Timber.* — Most of her highlands are valuable for timber and pasturage only. There are more tons of valuable timber in the Sierra Nevada than in our whole country east of the Rocky Mountains, and southward of the latitude of Chicago. Railroads will yet render much of it commercially available, and incite its diffusion to every country and island washed by the great ocean. Its value will be found to surpass that of all the minerals covered by it, or ever exposed to the avaricious gaze of man.

The Pacific Railroads — for there must soon be three distinct lines, and in time at least three more — will be to California what the Erie Canal is to New York, the Mississippi to the great valley. It is barely possible to over-estimate their importance and value. While they render New York that focus of the world's commerce which London has so long been, they must build up, on our Pacific coast, a traffic with China, Japan, Australia, such as Tyre or Carthage never conceived. California has hitherto seemed, even to her own people, on one side of the earth; they have too generally felt as strangers and sojourners, and talked of "going home," — that is, to the Atlantic slope; but the Pacific Railroads, bringing them within a week's journey of New England, and placing them in daily mail communication with the friends of their childhood, will make thousands contented with their lot, and, after a good visit to the old, familiar firesides, they will return, contented to end their days on the Pacific slope, and will draw their younger brothers and cousins after them. I predict that California will have Three Millions of people in 1900, and Oregon at least One Million.

I close with a mere glance at San Francisco; because her age has nearly doubled since I saw her, and her population, wealth, and business, as well. At the mouth of the only considerable river that enters the Pacific from our continent, — the Columbia and the Youkon excepted, — with a fair entrance, and an ample, safe harbor, I judge that the Pacific Railroad fixes and assures her destiny as the second city of America, — the emporium wherein the farthest East will exchange its products with the remotest West. I dislike her chilly August fogs and winds, her blowing, drifting sands; I might wish her relieved of the giant sand-bank which centuries have piled up between her and the Pacific; but then her Western gales would be fiercer and sharper than now; so it is best to leave her as she is. Since twenty years have raised her from a naked beach to a city of 100,000 souls, who can doubt that eighty more will see these swelled to, at least, One Million? May Intelligence and Virtue keep even step with her material progress! may the great-grandchildren of her adventurous pioneers rejoice in the knowledge that her stormy, irregular youth has given place to a sober, respected, beneficent maturity! may her influence on the side of Freedom, Knowledge, Righteousness, be evermore greatly felt and greatly blest throughout the awaking, wondering, plastic Western world!

XLVIII.

THE PRESIDENTIAL ELECTION OF 1860.

THE events of 1858 – 59, with certain demonstrations against Senator Douglas and his doctrine of "Squatter Sovereignty," by nearly all his Democratic brethren in the Senate, early in the session of 1859 – 60, plainly portended a disruption of the dominant party; creating a strong probability that the Republicans might choose the next President. I had already, for months, contemplated that contingency, and endeavored to fix on the proper candidate for President, in view of its probable occurrence.

My choice was Edward Bates, of St. Louis. He had been sole Representative of Missouri in Congress fully thirty years before, when he had heartily supported the administration of John Quincy Adams. He had since been mainly in retirement, save that he had presided with eminent ability over the River and Harbor Convention held at Chicago in 1847, and had held a local judgeship. Born in Virginia, a life-long slaveholder, in politics a Whig, he was thoroughly conservative, and so held fast to the doctrine of our Revolutionary sages, that Slavery was an evil to be restricted, not a good to be diffused. This conviction made him essentially a Republican; while I believed that he could poll votes in every Slave State, and, if elected, rally all that was left of the Whig party therein to resist Secession and Rebellion. If not the only Republican whose election would not suffice as a pretext for civil war, he seemed to me that one most likely to repress the threatened insurrection, or, at the worst, to crush it. I did not hesitate to avow my preference, though I may have withheld some of my reasons for it.

Many Republicans dissented from it most decidedly; one of them said to me, " Let us have a candidate, *this* time, that represents our most advanced convictions."

" My friend," I inquired, " suppose each Republican voter in our State were to receive, to-morrow, a letter, advising him that he (the said voter) had just lost his brother, for some years settled in the South, who had left him a plantation and half a dozen slaves,— how many of the two hundred and fifty thousand would, in response, declare and set those slaves free ?"   " I don't think I could stand *that* test myself !" was his prompt rejoinder.   " Then," I resumed, " it is not yet time to nominate as you propose."

The Republican National Convention was called to meet at Chicago, May 16, 1860, and I attended it, having been requested by the Republicans of Oregon to act as one of their delegates therein.   Governor Seward was the most prominent candidate for the Presidential nomination, warmly backed by the delegations from New York, Michigan, and several other States, including most of those from Massachusetts.   I was somewhat surprised to meet there quite a number who, in conversations with me and others, had unhesitatingly pronounced his nomination unadvisable, and likely to prove disastrous, now on hand to urge it.   I strongly felt that they had been right before, and were wrong now ; and I did what I could to counteract their efforts ; visiting, to this end, and briefly addressing, the delegations from several States.   I did much less than was popularly supposed ; being kept busy for ten or twelve of the most critical hours just preceding the ballotings in the committee of one delegate from each State represented that framed and reported the platform.   An effort to concentrate, prior to the balloting, all the anti-Seward votes on one candidate, proved unsuccessful ; and the probability of Seward's success seemed thereafter so decided, that one of his leading supporters urged me, just before we began to ballot, to name the man whose nomination for Vice-President would be most effective in reconciling those with whom I acted to the support of Governor Seward.   I advised, through

hjm, the Seward men to make the whole ticket satisfactory to
themselves.   We soon proceeded to vote for a candidate for
President, with the following result : —

	1st ballot.	2d ballot.	3d ballot.
William H. Seward, of New York,	173½	184½	180
Abraham Lincoln, of Illinois,	102	181	231½
Simon Cameron of Pennsylvania,	50½	—	—
Salmon P. Chase, of Ohio,	49	42½	24½
Edward Bates, of Missouri,	48	35	22
William L. Dayton, of New Jersey,	14	10	—
John McLean, of Ohio,	12	8	5
Jacob Collamer, of Vermont,	10	—	—
Scattering,	6	4	2

Mr. Lincoln having very nearly votes enough to nominate
him on the third ballot, others were rapidly transferred to
him, until he had 354 out of 466 in all, and his nomination
was declared.   On motion of William M. Evarts, on the part
of New York, seconded by John A. Andrew on behalf of
Massachusetts, the nomination was then made unanimous.
On the first ballot for Vice-President, Hannibal Hamlin, of
Maine, received 194 votes, which the next ballot swelled to
367 against 99, — when he, too, was unanimously nominated ;
and the Convention adjourned with nine hearty cheers for
the ticket.

The " Constitutional Union " (late " American ") party, met
by delegates three days later in Baltimore, declared its platform to be " the Constitution of the country, the Union of
the States, and the enforcement of the Laws," and nominated
thereon John Bell, of Tennessee, for President, and Edward
Everett, of Massachusetts, for Vice-President.

The Democratic National Convention* had met originally
at Charleston, South Carolina ; had quarrelled over a platform
for a week or more ; and had finally been disrupted by the
withdrawal of a majority of the delegates from Slave States,
because of the adoption (by a vote of 165 to 138) of a platform which was held to favor, ôr at least not explicitly to
condemn, Senator Douglas's " Squatter-Sovereignty " dogma.

* April 23.

After taking 57 ballots for President, whereon Mr. Douglas had a decided majority of all the votes cast on every ballot, and a majority of a full Convention, that body, by a vote of 195 to 55, adjourned* to reassemble at Baltimore, June 18; at which time (the places of most of the seceders having meantime been filled) Mr. Douglas received on the first ballot 173½, and on the second 181½ votes, which was less than two-thirds of a full Convention (303). He was thereupon, on motion of Sanford E. Church, of New York, declared the nominee.

Hon. Benjamin Fitzpatrick, of Alabama, was unanimously nominated for Vice-President; but he declined, and Hon. Herschel V. Johnson, of Georgia, was put up in his stead.

The bolters at Charleston met in Baltimore on the 11th of June, but adjourned to the 25th; at which time, Hon. John C. Breckinridge, of Kentucky (then Vice-President), was unanimously nominated for President, with General Joseph Lane, of Oregon, for Vice-President.

The quadrangular contest thus inaugurated has had no parallel but a very imperfect one in 1824. It seems clear that the bolting Democratic ticket was intended to render the success of the Republicans inevitable; and the probability of that success was openly exulted over in 4th of July toasts at various celebrations in South Carolina, where no other candidate than Breckinridge had even a nominal support. Yet in New York the supporters of Douglas, of Bell, and of Breckinridge united on a common ticket, which was defeated, but only after a most determined canvass. In other States, the "fusion" was incomplete or non-existent, rendering Mr. Lincoln's success a foregone conclusion. Mr. Douglas, alone among the Presidential candidates, took the stump, and spoke with vigor and energy in several States, but to little purpose. The popular vote in the Free States was mainly divided between Lincoln and Douglas; in the Slave States, between Breckinridge and Bell: the totals in either section being, as nearly as they can be apportioned, as follows: —

* May 3.

	Lincoln.	Douglas.	Breckinridge.	Bell.
Free States, ...	1,831,180	1,128,049	279,211	130,151
Slave States, ...	26,430	163,525	570,871	515,973
Total, . . .	1,857,610	1,291,574	850,082	646,124

Mr. Lincoln had 180 electoral votes to 123 for all others; he having the full vote of all the Free States but New Jersey, which gave him 4. Mr. Douglas had barely 3 in New Jersey, with the 9 of Missouri, — 12 in all, — while Breckinridge, with a much smaller popular vote, had 72 electors; barely missing those of Virginia, also Kentucky and Tennessee, making 39 in all.

Mr. Lincoln's popular and electoral vote were each a little larger than those of Mr. Buchanan in 1856; but, practically, the one result had strong points of resemblance to the other. In the former, a united South triumphed over a divided North; in the latter, a United North succeeded over a divided South. But the division affected only the Presidency; the anti-Republicans still held the Supreme Court, with the Senate, and were morally certain of a large majority also in the new House of Representatives, whereof two thirds of the members were chosen with or before the Presidential Electors.

Thus stood the country on the day after that which recorded the popular verdict for Lincoln and Hamlin.

It is true that the moral weight of that verdict was diminished by the consideration that it was pronounced by barely two fifths of the legal voters. Antagonist on other points as the defeated factions were, it was notorious that they were a unit in opposition to the cardinal Republican principle of No Extension of Slavery, which, by acting in concert, they could at any time arrest and defeat. Yet the election of Lincoln, by placing the Executive patronage of the Government in the hands of a Republican, had done much toward the development throughout the South of that latent anti-Slavery sentiment which her aristocracy abhorred and dreaded. In that election, therefore, many slaveholders saw foreshadowed the doom of their cherished "institution."

XLIX.

SECESSION, — HOW CONFRONTED.

THE popular vote * in each State for Presidential Electors having rendered inevitable the success of Lincoln and Hamlin, the result — immediately ascertained and disseminated by means of the telegraph — was nowhere received with more general expressions of satisfaction than in South Carolina, whose ruling caste had, months before, but especially on the preceding 4th of July, indicated their wish and hope that the election would have this issue. Indeed, we Republicans had been fully aware, throughout the canvass, that the division of the Democratic party effected at the Charleston Convention was designed to assure our success, — not as an end, but as a means, — and that those who supported Breckinridge, while they would have regarded his election with complacency, were quite as well satisfied with that of Lincoln. Much as they disliked — nay, detested — the " Black Republicans," they regarded Senator Douglas and his " Squatter Sovereignty " with an intenser aversion, and were bent on their absolute discomfiture at all hazards.

All revolutionary movements derive their momentum from diverse sources, and are impelled by very different agencies. Of the four and a half millions of voters for President in 1860, it is quite safe to say that all who desired Disunion were included within the 850,000 † who voted for Breckin-

---

* November 6, 1860.

† As South Carolina then chose her electors by her Legislature, her people do not count in this aggregate, which they would probably have swelled to about 900,000.

ridge; but even this fraction should, in justice, be divided into classes, as follows : —

I. The Disunionists, pure and simple, who, believing Slavery the only natural and stable basis of social order, and noting the steady advance of the Free States in relative wealth, population, and power, deemed the Secession and Confederation of the Slaveholding States the only course consistent with their interests or their safety. I doubt whether this class numbered half a million of the fifteen hundred thousand legal voters residing in the Slave States, while it could count no open adherents in the Free States.

II. Those who, while they perceived neither safety nor sense in Secession, did not choose to be stigmatized as Abolitionists nor hooted as cowards, but preferred the remote, contingent perils even of civil war to the imminent certainty of persecution and social outlawry, if they should be pointed out as lacking the courage or the will to risk all, dare all, in defence of " Southern rights."

III. Those who, while at heart hostile to Disunion, — deeming it no remedy for existing ills, while it opened a new vista of untold, awful calamities, — yet regarded the *menace* of Secession with complacency, as certain to frighten " the North " into any and every required concession and retraction to avert the threatened disruption.

It was this third class — I judge more numerous than, while superior in wealth and social consideration to, the first and second combined — that I deemed it our first duty to resist and baffle.

I had for forty years been listening, with steadily diminishing patience, to Southern threats of Disunion. Whatever an awakened conscience, or an enlightened apprehension of National interest, commended to a majority of the North as just and politic, was — if not equally acceptable at the South — apt to be met by the bravado, " Do what you propose, and we will dissolve the Union ! " I had become weary of this, and desirous of ending it. In my cherished conception, the Union was no boon conferred on the North by the South, but a voluntary partnership, at least as advantageous to the latter as to the former. I desired that the South should be made to comprehend and respect this truth. I wished her to realize that the North could do without the South quite as well as the South could do without the North.

For the first breath of Disunion from the South fanned into vigorous life the old spirit of compromise and cringing at the North. "What will you do to save the Union?" was asked of us Republicans, as if we had committed some enormity in voting for and electing Lincoln, which we must now atone by proffering concessions and disclaimers to the justly alarmed and irritated South.

At once, the attitude of the North became alarmed, deprecatory, self-abasing. Every local election held during the two months succeeding our National triumph showed great "Conservative" gains. Conspicuous Abolitionists were denied the use of public halls, or hooted down if they attempted to speak. Influential citizens, through meetings and letters, denounced the madness of "fanaticism," and implored the South to stay her avenging arm until the North could have time to purge herself from complicity with "fanatics," and demonstrate her fraternal sympathy with her Southern sister, — that is, attest her unshaken loyalty to the Slave Power. An eminent Southern Conservative (John J. Crittenden) having proposed, as a new Union-saving compromise, the running of the line of 36 degrees 30 minutes North latitude through our new territories to the Pacific, and the positive allotment and guaranty of all South of that line to Slavery forever, the suggestion was widely grasped as an olive-branch, — even the veteran Thurlow Weed commending the proposal to popular favor and acceptance as fair and reasonable. The Republican party — which had been called into existence by the opening of free soil to Slavery — seemed in positive danger of signalizing its advent to power by giving a direct assent to the practical extension of Slavery over a region far larger and more important than that theoretically surrendered by the Kansas-Nebraska bill. In fact, the attitude of the North, during the two last months of 1860, was foreshadowed in four lines of Collins's Ode to the Passions : —

> " First, Fear his hand, its skill to try,
>   Amid the chords bewildered laid ;
> And back recoiled, he knew not why,
>   E'en at the sound himself had made."

And the danger was imminent that, if a popular vote could have been had (as was proposed) on the Crittenden Compromise, it would have prevailed by an overwhelming majority. Very few Republicans would have voted for it ; but very many would have refrained from voting at all ; while their adversaries would have brought their every man to the polls in its support, and carried it by hundreds of thousands.

My own controlling conviction from first to last was, — There must, at all events, be no concession to Slavery. Disunion, should it befall, may be calamity ; but complicity in Slavery extension is guilt, which the Republicans must in no case incur. It had for an age been the study of the slaveholding politicians to make us of the North partners with them in the maintenance, diffusion, and profit or loss of their industrial system. " Slavery is quite as much your affair as ours," they were accustomed to say in substance : " we own and work the negroes ; you buy the cotton and sugar produced by their labor, and sell us in return nearly all we and they eat, drink, and wear. If they run away, you help catch and return them : now set us off a few hundred thousand miles more of territory whereon to work them, and help us to acquire Cuba, Mexico, &c., as we shall say we need them, and we will largely extend our operations, to our mutual benefit." It was this extension that I was resolved at all hazards to defeat.

But how ?

Good and true men met the Disunionists (whether earnest or affected) in this square, manly way : " You must obey the laws. The Union will not be tamely surrendered, and cannot be dissolved by force. Whoever shall attempt thus to dissolve it will have reason to repent of his temerity. Behave yourselves, or you will rue your turbulence !"

To me, as to some others, a different course seemed advisable. We said in substance: "You Disunionists claim to be the Southern people, and rest your case on the vital principle proclaimed in our fathers' immortal Declaration of Independence, — 'Governments derive their just power from the consent of the governed.' We admit the principle, — nay, we affirm, we glory in it; but your case is not within it. You are *not* the Southern people; you are not even a majority of the Southern Whites; you are a violent, unscrupulous, desperate minority, who have conspired to clutch power and wield it for ends which the overawed, gagged, paralyzed majority at heart condemn. Secure us a fair opportunity to state our side of the case, and to argue the points at issue before your people, and we will abide their decision. We disclaim a union of force, — a union held together by bayonets; let us be fairly heard; and, if your people decide that they choose to break away from us, we will interpose no obstacle to their peaceful withdrawal from the Union."

Whether this was, or was not, in the abstract, sound doctrine, it is clear that those who uttered it exposed themselves to ready misapprehension and grave obloquy, which were counterbalanced by no advantage or profit to themselves. Their consolation was that they had done something toward arresting the spring-tide of Northern servility that set strongly in favor of "conciliation" through the adoption of the Crittenden Compromise.

They were right at least in their fundamental assumption of fact. The South was *not* for Secession. Though its partisans had previously made skilful use of the machinery of the Democratic party to secure Governors, Legislatures, &c. in their interest, and the Federal officers — appointed by Pierce and Buchanan while Jefferson Davis, Jacob Thompson, John B. Floyd, Howell Cobb, John Slidell, &c., were their trusted advisers — were nearly all implicated in their conspiracy, the Disunionists, wholly unresisted by President Buchanan, were enabled, by their utmost efforts, to alienate but a minority of the Southern States or People from the

Federal Union. South Carolina, Georgia, Alabama, Mississippi, Louisiana, Florida, and Texas — seven States in all, entitled to but twenty-eight representatives in Congress — were claimed as having seceded, up to the hour wherein War was formally inaugurated by an order from the Confederate War Department to open fire upon the Federal fortress named Sumter, in Charleston harbor. In no one of these States but Texas had the ordinance of Secession been submitted to, and ratified by, a direct popular vote. The eight other Slave States, which had double their free population and double their representation in Congress, had not merely declined to secede, — Virginia, Kentucky, Tennessee, and Missouri, had given such majorities against it as they never gave before ; North Carolina and Arkansas had expressly voted it down ; while Maryland and Delaware refused even to take the matter into consideration. In fact, the people of the South, like those of the North, were as yet unripe for Disunion, and shuddered at the prospect of civil war. The bombardment of Sumter, which summoned the Nation to arms, was impelled by a consciousness that the mushroom Confederacy would otherwise collapse and disappear. Said Jeremiah Clemens, formerly United States Senator from Alabama, at a Union meeting at Huntsville, March 13, 1864 : —

" I wish to state a fact in relation to the commencement of this war. Some time after the ordinance of Secession was passed I was in Montgomery, and called on President Davis, who was in that city. Davis, Memminger, the Secretary of War [Leroy Pope Walker], Gilchrist, the member from Lowndes County, and several others, were present. As I entered, the conversation ceased. They were evidently discussing the propriety of firing on Fort Sumter. Two or three of them withdrew to a corner of the room ; and I heard Gilchrist say to the Secretary of War : ' *It* must *be done. Delay two months, and Alabama stays in the Union. You must sprinkle blood in the faces of the people.*"

So said, so done, — except that the " sprinkle " swelled into a cascade, the cascade into a river, which inundated and reddened the whole breadth of our country.

L.

OUR CIVIL WAR, — ACTUAL AND POSSIBLE.

HOSTILITIES on the part of the Confederacy had been inaugurated weeks before Mr. Lincoln's accession to the Presidency. The Federal forts, arsenals, armories, sub-treasuries, &c., &c., located in the seceding States, had, in good part, thus changed hands, — often with the hearty assent and coöperation of their custodians, — always without serious resistance offered by them or commanded from Washington. Fort Sumter, Key West, and Fort Pickens (at Pensacola) were all that held out for the Union. General Twiggs's surrender* of the greater part of our little Army, then posted along the exposed frontiers of Texas, with all the forts, arms, munitions, stores, &c., occurred two weeks before the close of Mr. Buchanan's term. Still, the fact that war existed, or even that it was inevitable, was not generally realized in the Free States, till the telegraph flashed far and wide the startling news that fire had been opened† on Fort Sumter from the Rebel forts and batteries whereby it was half encircled, — following this, next day, with the tidings that the feebly manned and nearly foodless fort had surrendered. Hereupon, Virginia was promptly plunged by her Convention into the widening vortex of Secession; and was soon followed by Arkansas,‡ North Carolina,§ and ultimately by Tennessee.||

Meantime, President Lincoln, directly on hearing of the fall of Sumter, had summoned the new Congress to meet in

---

* February 18, 1861. ‡ May 6, 1861. || June 8, 1861.
† April 12, 1861. § May 20, 1861.

extraordinary session on the 4th of July ensuing, and had called on the Governors of the presumptively loyal States for their respective quotas of a volunteer force of 75,000 men to defend the capital and public property of the Union. The Governors, not only of Virginia (which was then on the point, if not in the act, of seceding), but of North Carolina, Tennessee, Missouri, Kentucky, and even Delaware, responded only with "railing accusations," implying amazement that any President should ask or expect their help in the nefarious work of "coercion." From the Governors of the Free States (nearly or quite all Republicans) very different responses were received, swiftly followed by the required volunteers. One of the first regiments on foot was from Massachusetts, and was fiercely assailed * on its passage through Baltimore by a vast pro-Slavery mob, whereby three of its men were slain and eight seriously wounded. The residue made their way through the city, and proceeded to Washington; but a Pennsylvania regiment, just behind it, was roughly handled by the mob, and constrained to take the back track to Philadelphia. Baltimore thereupon ranged herself on the side of Secession, stopping the trains and cutting the wires that connected Washington with the still loyal States; the Federal Arsenal at Harper's Ferry, being menaced, was fired and abandoned; the Navy Yard at Norfolk was culpably deserted, leaving two thousand cannon and large supplies of munitions to the exulting Confederates; a Confederate camp was established near St. Louis, under the auspices of Governor Jackson, and men openly enlisted and drilled there for the work in prospect; the South was closed to Northern travel and commerce, and everything portended a formidable, bloody, devastating war.

Yet President Lincoln persisted in what seems to me his second grave mistake, — that of underestimating the spirit and power of the Rebellion. He had called for but 75,000 men when apprised that Fort Sumter had fallen; he called for no more when assured that Virginia and North Carolina had been swept into the vortex of Secession by that open

* April 19, 1861.

defiance of the National authority and assault on the National
integrity; that Arkansas and Tennessee were on the point
of following their bad example; and that even Maryland and
Missouri were, at least for the moment, in the hands of those
who fully shared the *animus* and sympathized with the aims
of the Disunionists. It was now plain that the Slave Power
was the Nation's assailant, and that its motto was, "War to
the knife!" I think the President should have changed his
tactics in view of the added gravity of the public danger. I
think he should have invited the people to assemble on a designated early day in their several wards and townships, then
and there to solemnly swear to uphold the Government and
Union, and to enroll themselves as volunteers for the war,
subject to be called out at his discretion. Each man's age, as
well as name, should have been recorded; and then he should
have called them out in classes as they should be wanted, —
say, first, those of 20 to 25 years old; secondly, those between
25 and 30; and so on. I judge that not less than One Million able-bodied men would have thus enrolled themselves;
that the first two calls would have provided a force of not
less than two hundred thousand men; and that subsequent
calls, though less productive, would have supplied all the men
from time to time required, without cost and without material
delay.

The Confederate Congress had met at Montgomery, Alabama, held a brief session, and adjourned to reconvene at
Richmond on the 4th of July. I hold that it should not
have been allowed so to meet, but that a Union army, One
Hundred Thousand strong, should have occupied that city
early in June, — certainly before the close of that month.
Richmond was not yet fortified; it was accessible by land
and by water; we firmly held Fortress Monroe; the designated capital of the Confederacy should never have received
its Congress, but should have witnessed such a celebration of
the anniversary of American Independence as had never yet
thrilled its heart. The war-cry, "Forward to Richmond!"
did not originate with me; but it is just what should have

been uttered, and the words should have been translated into deeds.

Instead 'of energy, vigor, promptness, daring, decision, we had in our councils weakness, irresolution, hesitation, delay; and, when at last our hastily collected forces, after being demoralized by weeks of idleness and dissipation, were sent forward, they advanced on separate lines, under different commanders; thus enabling the enemy to concentrate all his forces in Virginia against a single corps of ours, defeating and stampeding it at Bull Run, while other Union volunteers, aggregating nearly twice its strength, lay idle and useless near Harper's Ferry, in and about Washington, and at Fortress Monroe. Thus what should have been a short, sharp struggle was expanded into a long, desultory one; while those whose blundering incapacity or lack of purpose was responsible for those ills united in throwing the blame on the faithful few who had counselled justly, but whose urgent remonstrances they had never heeded. "Forward to Richmond!" was execrated as the impulse to disaster, even by some who had lustily echoed it; and weary months of halting, timid, nerveless, yet costly warfare, naturally followed. Men talk reproachfully of the heavy losses incurred by Grant in taking Richmond, forgetting that his predecessors had lost yet more in *not* taking it. In war, energy — prompt and vigorous action — is the true economizer of suffering, of devastation, and of life. Had Napoleon or Jackson been in Scott's place in 1861, the Rebellion would have been stamped out ere the close of that year; but Slavery would have remained to scourge us still. Thus disaster is overruled to subserve the ends of beneficence; thus the evil of the moment contains the germ of good that is enduring; and thus is freshly exemplified the great truth proclaimed by Pope: —

> "In spite of pride, in erring Reason's spite,
> One truth is clear, — WHATEVER IS, IS RIGHT."

LI.

ABRAHAM LINCOLN.

THERE are those who say that Mr. Lincoln was fortunate in his death as in his life: I judge otherwise. I hold him most inapt for the leadership of a people involved in desperate, agonizing war; while I deem few men better fitted to guide a nation's destinies in time of peace. Especially do I deem him eminently fitted to soothe, to heal, and to reunite in bonds of true, fraternal affection a people just lapsing into peace after years of distracting, desolating internal strife. His true career was just opening when an assassin's bullet quenched his light of life.

Mr. Lincoln entered Washington the victim of a grave delusion. A genial, quiet, essentially peaceful man, trained in the ways of the bar and the stump, he fully believed that there would be no civil war, — no serious effort to consummate Disunion. His faith in Reason as a moral force was so implicit that he did not cherish a doubt that his Inaugural Address, whereon he had bestowed much thought and labor, would, when read throughout the South, dissolve the Confederacy as frost is dissipated by a vernal sun. I sat just behind him as he read it, on a bright, warm, still March day, expecting to hear its delivery arrested by the crack of a rifle aimed at his heart; but it pleased God to postpone the deed, though there was forty times the reason for shooting him in 1860 that there was in '65, and at least forty times as many intent on killing or having him killed. No shot was then fired, however; for his hour had not yet come.

Almost every one has personal anecdotes of "Old Abe."

I knew him more than sixteen years, met him often, talked with him familiarly; yet, while multitudes fancy that he was always overflowing with jocular narrations or reminiscences, I cannot remember that I ever heard him tell an anecdote or story. One, however, that he *did* tell while in this city, on his way to assume the Presidency, is so characteristic of the man and his way of regarding portents of trouble, that I here record it.

Almost every one was asking him, with evident apprehension if not perturbation: "What is to be the issue of this Southern effervescence? Are we really to have civil war?" and he once responded in substance as follows: —

"Many years ago, when I was a young lawyer, and Illinois was little settled, except on her southern border, I, with other lawyers, used to ride the circuit; journeying with the judge from county-seat to county-seat in quest of business. Once, after a long spell of pouring rain, which had flooded the whole country, transforming small creeks into rivers, we were often stopped by these swollen streams, which we with difficulty crossed. Still ahead of us was Fox River, larger than all the rest; and we could not help saying to each other, 'If these streams give us so much trouble, how shall we get over Fox River?' Darkness fell before we had reached that stream; and we all stopped at a log tavern, had our horses put out, and resolved to pass the night. Here we were right glad to fall in with the Methodist Presiding Elder of the circuit, who rode it in all weather, knew all its ways, and could tell us all about Fox River. So we all gathered around him, and asked him if he knew about the crossing of Fox River. 'O yes,' he replied, 'I know all about Fox River. I have crossed it often, and understand it well; but I have one fixed rule with regard to Fox River: I never cross it till I reach it.'"

I infer that Mr. Lincoln did not fully realize that we were to have a great civil war till the Bull Run disaster. I cannot otherwise explain what seemed to many of us his amazing tameness when required by the Mayor and by the Young

Christians of Baltimore to promise not to have any more volunteers marched across the State of Maryland on their way
to the defence of Washington. Had he then realized that
bloody strife had become a dire necessity, I think he would
have responded with more spirit.

When we were at length unmistakably launched on the
stormy ocean of civil war, Mr. Lincoln's tenacity of purpose
paralleled his former immobility. I believe he would have
been nearly the last, if not the very last, man in America to
recognize the Southern Confederacy, had its arms been triumphant. He would have much preferred death.

This firmness impelled him to what seemed to me a grave
error. Because he would never consent to give up the Union,
he dreaded to recognize in any manner the existence of the
Confederacy. Yet such recognition, after the capture of several thousands of our soldiers, became inevitable. Had Fortune uniformly smiled on our arms, we might have treated
the Rebellion as a seditious riot ; but our serious loss in prisoners at Bull Run rendered this thenceforth impossible. We
were virtually compelled to recognize the Confederates as
belligerents, by negotiating an exchange of prisoners. Thenceforth (it seems to me) we were precluded from treating them
as felons. And I could see no objection, not merely to receiving with courtesy any overtures for peace they might see fit
to make, but even to making overtures to them, as Great
Britain so publicly did to our Revolutionary fathers in the
Summer of '76.

War has become so fearfully expensive, through the progress of invention and machinery, that to protract it is to
involve all parties in bankruptcy and ruin. Belligerents are,
therefore, prone to protest their anxiety for Peace, — in most
cases, sincerely. Napoleon, though often at war, was always
proclaiming his anxiety for peace. It seemed to me, throughout our great struggle, that a more vigorous prosecution, alike
of War and of Peace, was desirable. Larger armies, in the

average more energetically led, more ably handled, seemed to be the National need, down to a late stage of the contest. And I deemed it a mistake to put aside any overture that looked to the achievement of peace. Instead of repelling such overtures, however unpromising, I would have openly welcomed any and all, and so treated each as to prove that the continuance of war was not the fault of our side. And so, when Henry May, Colonel Jacquess, and others, solicited permission to go to Richmond in quest of Peace, I would have openly granted them every facility, asking them only to state distinctly that I had not sent nor accredited them. And I judge that Mr. Lincoln slowly came to a conclusion not dissimilar to mine, since Mr. F. P. Blair's two visits to Richmond were made with his full knowledge; while his own visit to Fortress Monroe, there to meet Confederate Commissioners and discuss with them terms of pacification, was a formal notice to all concerned of his anxiety to stay the effusion of blood. I believe that this conference did much to precipitate the downfall of the tottering Confederacy. I doubt whether any one of Sherman's nearly simultaneous successes did more. And, while Mr. Lincoln would have been a tenacious champion of the authority and dignity of the Union and the rights and security of all its loyal people, I am sure the vanquished Rebels would have found him a generous conqueror.

Mr. Lincoln died for his country as truly as any soldier who fell fighting in the ranks of her armies. He was not merely killed for her sake, — because of the high responsibilities she had a second time devolved on him, and the fidelity wherewith he fulfilled them, — he was worn out in her service, and would not, I judge, have lived out his official term, had no one sought his immolation. When I last saw him, a few weeks before his death, I was struck by his haggard, care-fraught face, so different from the sunny, gladsome countenance he first brought from Illinois. I felt that his life hung by so slender a thread that any new access of trouble or excess of effort might suddenly close his career. I had ceased to apprehend his assassination, — had ceased even to think of it; yet "the sunset of life" was plainly looking out of his kindly eyes and gleaming from his weather-beaten visage.

I believe I neither enjoy nor deserve the reputation of favoring exorbitant allowances or lavish expenditures; yet I feel that my country has been meanly parsimonious in its dealings with Mr. Lincoln's family. The head of that family was fairly elected and inaugurated President for a second term; and he had scarcely entered upon that term when he was murdered because he was President. I hold that this fact entitled his family to the four years' salary which the people had voted to pay him; that the manner of his death took his case entirely out of the category of mere decease while in office; and that they should have been paid the $100,000 which, but for Booth's bullet, would have been theirs, instead of the one year's salary that was allowed them. I am quite aware that Mrs. Lincoln was and is unpopular, — I need not inquire with what reason, since I am not pleading for generosity, but for naked justice. Buchanan, trembling at the rustle of a leaf, served out his term, and was paid his full salary; dying, seven years later, of natural decay. To withhold Mr. Lincoln's pay because he invoked the hatred of assassins by his fearless fidelity, and was therefore bereft of life when in the zenith of his career, is to discourage fidelity and foster pusillanimity. May not the wrong be redressed even yet?

Mr. Lincoln was emphatically a man of the people. Mr. Clay was called "The Great Commoner" by those who admired and loved him; but Clay was imperious, even haughty, in his moods, with aristocratic tastes and faults, utterly foreign to Lincoln's essentially plebeian nature. There never yet was man so lowly as to feel humbled in the presence of Abraham Lincoln; there was no honest man who feared or dreaded to meet him; there was no virtuous society so rude that, had he casually dropped into it, he would have checked innocent hilarity or been felt as a damper on enjoyment. Had he entered as a stranger a logger's camp in the great woods, a pioneer's bark-covered cabin in some new settlement, he would have soon been recognized and valued as one whose acquaintance was to be prized and cultivated.

Mr. Lincoln was essentially a growing man. Enjoying no advantages in youth, he had observed and reflected much since he attained to manhood, and he was steadily increasing his stock of knowledge to the day of his death. He was a wiser, abler man when he entered upon his second than when he commenced his first Presidential term. His mental processes were slow, but sure; if he did not acquire swiftly, he retained all that he had once learned. Greater men our country has produced; but not another whom, humanly speaking, she could so ill spare, when she lost him, as the victim of Wilkes Booth's murderous aim.

Though I very heartily supported it when made, I did not favor his re-nomination as President; for I wanted the War driven onward with vehemence, and this was not in his nature. Always dreading that the National credit would fail, or the National resolution falter, I feared that his easy ways would allow the Rebellion to obtain European recognition and achieve ultimate success. But that "Divinity that shapes our ends" was quietly working out for us a larger and fuller deliverance than I had dared to hope for, leaving to such short-sighted mortals as I no part but to wonder and adore. We have had chieftains who would have crushed out the Rebellion in six months, and restored "the Union as it was"; but God gave us the one leader whose control secured not only the downfall of the Rebellion, but the eternal overthrow of Human Slavery under the flag of the Great Republic.

LII.

JEFFERSON DAVIS.

THE President of the Southern Confederacy was chosen by a capable, resolute aristocracy, with express reference to the arduous task directly before him. The choice was deliberate, and apparently wise. Mr. Davis was in the mature prime of life; his natural abilities were good; his training varied and thorough. He had been educated at West Point, which, with all its faults, I judge the best school yet established in our country; he had served in our little army in peace, and as a Colonel of volunteers in the Mexican War; returning to civil life, he had been conspicuous in the politics of his State and the Nation; had been elected to the Senate, and there met in courteous but earnest encounter Henry Clay and his compeers; had been four years Secretary of War under President Pierce; and had, immediately on his retiring from that post, been returned to the Senate, whereof his admirers styled him "the Cicero," and whereof he continued a member until — not without manifest reluctance — he resigned and returned to Mississippi to cast his future fortunes into the seething caldron of Secession and Disunion. As compared with the homely country lawyer, Abraham Lincoln, — reared in poverty and obscurity, with none other than a common-school education, and precious little of that; whose familiarity with public affairs was confined to three sessions of the Illinois Legislature and a single term in the House of Representatives, — it would seem that the advantage of chieftains was largely on the side of the Confederacy.

The contrast between them was striking, but imperfect;

for each was thoroughly in earnest, thoroughly persuaded of the justice of the cause whereof he stood forth the foremost champion, and signally gifted with that quality which, in the successful, is termed tenacity, in the luckless, obstinacy. Mr. Lincoln was remarkably devoid of that magnetic quality which thrills the masses with enthusiasm, rendering them heedless of sacrifice and insensible to danger; Mr. Davis was nowise distinguished by its possession. As the preacher of a crusade, either of them had many superiors. But Mr. Davis carefully improved — as Mr. Lincoln did not — every opportunity to proclaim his own undoubting faith in the justice of his cause, and labored to diffuse that conviction as widely as possible. His successive messages and other manifestoes were well calculated to dispel the doubts and inflame the zeal of those who regarded him as their chief; while, apart from his first Inaugural, and his brief speech at the Gettysburg celebration,* Mr. Lincoln made little use of his many opportunities to demonstrate the justice and necessity of the War for the Union.

Mr. Davis, after the fortunes of his Confederacy waned, was loudly accused of favoritism in the allotment of Military trusts. He is said to have distrusted and undervalued Joseph Johnston, which, if so, was a grave error; for Johnston proved himself an able and trustworthy commander, if not a great military genius, — never a blunderer, and never intoxicated by success nor paralyzed by disaster. His displacement in 1864 by Hood, as Commander-in-Chief of the Army of Georgia, was proved a mistake; but it was more defensible than the appointment of Halleck as General-in-Chief of our armies, directly after his failure on the Tennessee. Bragg is named as first of Davis's pets; but Bragg seems to me to have proved himself a good soldier, and to have shown decided capacity at the Battle of Stone River, though he was ultimately obliged to leave the field (and little else) to Rosecrans. Pemberton was accounted another of Davis's overrated favorites; but Pemberton, being of Northern birth, was never fully trusted,

---

* November 19, 1863.

nor fairly judged, by his compatriots. On a full survey of the
ground, I judge that Davis evinced respectable, not brilliant,
capacities, in his stormy and trying Presidential career; and
that his qualifications for the post were equal to, while his
faults were no greater than, Mr. Lincoln's.

This, however, was not the judgment of his compatriots,
who extravagantly exaggerated his merits while their cause
seemed to prosper, and as unjustly magnified his faults and
short-comings from the moment wherein their star first visibly
waned. They were ready to make him Emperor in 1862;
they regarded him as their evil genius in 1865. Having
rushed into war in undoubting confidence that their success
was inevitable, they were astounded at their defeat, and impelled to believe that their resources had been dissipated and
their armies overwhelmed through mismanagement. They
were like the idolater, who adores his god after a victory, but
flogs him when smarting under defeat.

A baleful mischance saved Mr. Davis from the fate of a
scapegoat. After even he had given up the Confederacy as
lost, and realized that he was no longer a President, but a
fugitive and outlaw, he was surprised and assailed, while
making his way through Georgia to the Florida coast with
intent to escape from the country, by two regiments of Union
cavalry, and captured. I am confident that this would not
have occurred had Mr. Lincoln survived, — certainly not, if
our shrewd and kind-hearted President could have prevented
it. But his murder had temporarily maddened the millions
who loved and trusted him; and his successor, sharing and
inflaming the popular frenzy, had put forth a Proclamation
charging Davis, among others, with conspiracy to procure
that murder, and offering large rewards for their arrest as
traitors and assassins. Captured in full view of that Proclamation, he might have been forthwith tried by a drum-head
Court-Martial, " organized to convict," found guilty, sentenced,
and put to death.

This, however, was not done; but he was escorted to Sa-
vannah, thence shipped to Fortress Monroe, and there closely

imprisoned, with aggravations of harsh and (it seems) needless indignity. An indictment for treason was found against him; but he remained a military prisoner in close jail for nearly two years, before even a pretence was made of arraigning him for trial.

Meantime, public sentiment had become more rational and discriminating. Davis was still intensely and widely detested as the visible embodiment, the responsible head, of the Rebellion; but no one now seriously urged that he be tried by Court-Martial and shot off-hand; nor was it certain that a respectable body of officers could be found to subserve such an end. To send him before a civil tribunal, and allow him a fair trial, was morally certain to result in a defeat of the prosecution, through disagreement of the jury, or otherwise; for no opponent of the Republican party, whether North or South, would agree to find him guilty. And there was grave doubt whether he *could* be legally convicted, now that the charge of inciting Wilkes Booth's crime had been tacitly abandoned. Mr. Webster * had only given clearer expression to the general American doctrine, that, after a revolt has levied a regular army, and fought therewith a pitched battle, its champions, even though utterly defeated, cannot be tried and convicted as traitors. This may be an extreme statement; but surely a rebellion which has for years maintained great armies, levied taxes and conscriptions, negotiated loans, fought scores of sanguinary battles with alternate successes and reverses, and exchanged tens of thousands of prisoners of war, can hardly fail to have achieved thereby the position and the rights of a lawful belligerent. Just suppose the case (nowise improbable) of two Commissioners for the exchange of prisoners, — like Mulford and Ould, for example, — who had for years been meeting to settle formalities, and exchange boatloads of prisoners of war, until at length — the power represented by one of them having been utterly vanquished and broken down—that one is arrested by the victors as a traitor, and the other directed to prosecute him to conviction and

* In his first Bunker Hill Oration.

consign him to execution, — how would the case be regarded by impartial observers in this later half of the Nineteenth Century ? And suppose this trial to take place two years after the discomfiture and break-down aforesaid, — what then ?

Mr. Andrew Johnson had seen fit to change his views and his friends since his unexpected accession to the Presidency, and had, from an intemperate denouncer of the beaten Rebels as deserving severe punishment, become their protector and patron. Jefferson Davis, in Fortress Monroe, under his proclamation aforesaid, was an ugly elephant on Johnson's hands; and thousands were anxious that he should remain there. Their view of the matter did not impress me as statesmanlike, nor even sagacious.

The Federal Constitution expressly provides * that,

> " In all criminal prosecutions, the accused shall enjoy the right to a speedy and public trial, by an impartial jury of the State and district wherein the crime shall have been committed," &c.

In times of war and grave public peril, Constitutions cannot always be strictly heeded; but what national interest required that this provision should be persistently, ostentatiously defied?

An Irishman, swearing the peace against his three sons for pertinaciously assaulting and abusing him, made this proper reservation : " And your deponent would ask your honor to deal tenderly with his youngest son, Larry, who never struck him when he was down." I confess to some fellow-feeling with Larry.

———

Mr. George Shea, the attorney of record for the defence in the case of The United States *versus* Jefferson Davis, indicted for treason, is the son of an old friend, and I have known and liked him from infancy. After it had become evident that his client had no immediate prospect of trial, if any prospect at all, Mr. Shea became anxious that said client be liberated on bail. Consulting me as to the feasibility of procuring some names to be proffered as bondsmen of persons who had

* Amendments, Art. VI.

conspicuously opposed the Rebellion and all the grave errors which incited it, I suggested two eminent Unionists, who, I presumed, would cheerfully consent to stand as security that the accused would not run away to avoid the trial he had long but unsuccessfully invoked. I added, after reflection, "If *my* name should be found necessary, you may use that." He thanked me, and said he should proffer it only in case the others abundantly at his command would not answer without it. Months passed before I was apprised, by a telegram from Washington, that my name *was* needed ; when I went down and proffered it. And when, at length, the prisoner was brought before the United States District Court at Richmond,* I was there, by invitation, and signed the bond in due form.

I suppose this would have excited some hubbub at any rate ; but the actual tumult was gravely aggravated by gross misstatements. It was widely asserted that the object of giving bail was to screen the accused from trial, — in other words, to enable him to run away, — when nothing like this was ever imagined by those concerned. The prisoner, through his counsel, had assiduously sought a trial, while the prosecution was not ready, because (as Judge Underwood was obliged to testify before a Committee of Congress) no conviction was possible, except by packing a jury. The words "straw bail" were used in this connection ; when one of the sureties is worth several millions of dollars, and the poorest of them is abundantly good for the sum of $ 5,000, in which he is "held and firmly bound" to produce the body of Jefferson Davis whenever the plaintiff shall be ready to try him. If he only *would* run away, I know that very many people would be much obliged to him ; but he won't.

It was telegraphed all over the North that I had a very affectionate meeting and greeting with the prisoner when he had been bailed ; when in fact I had never before spoken nor written to him any message whatever, and did not know him, even by sight, when he entered the court-room. After the bond was signed, one of his counsel asked me if I had any

* May 13, 1867.

objection to being introduced to Mr. Davis, and I replied that I had none; whereupon we were introduced, and simply greeted each other. I made, at the request of a friend, a brief call on his wife that evening, as they were leaving for Canada; and there our intercourse ended, probably forever.

When the impeachment of President Johnson was fully resolved on, and there was for some weeks a fair prospect that Mr. Wade would soon be President, with a Cabinet of like Radical faith, I suggested to some of the prospective President's next friends that I had Jefferson Davis still on my hands, and that, if he were considered a handy thing to have in the house, I might turn him over to the new Administration for trial at an hour's notice. The suggestion evoked no enthusiasm, and I was not encouraged to press it.

I trust no one will imagine that I have made this statement with any purpose of self-vindication. To all who have civilly accosted me on the subject, I trust I have given civil, if not satisfactory, answers; while most of those who have seen fit to assail me respecting it, I have chosen to treat with silent scorn. I believe no one has yet succeeded in inventing an unworthy motive for my act that could impose on the credulity of a child, or even of my bitterest enemy. I was quite aware that what I did would be so represented as to alienate for a season some valued friends, and set against me the great mass of those who know little and think less; thousands even of those who rejoiced over Davis's release, nevertheless joining, full-voiced, in the howl against me. I knew that I should outlive the hunt, and could afford to smile at the pack, even when its cry was loudest. So I went quietly on my way; and in due time the storm gave place to a calm. And now, if there is a man on earth who wishes Jefferson Davis were back in his cell, awaiting, in the fourth year of his detention, the trial denied him in the three preceding, he is at liberty to denounce me for my course, in the assurance that he can by no means awake a regret or provoke a reply.

LIII.

AUTHORSHIP. — WRITING HISTORY.

ALMOST every one who can write at all is apt, in the course of his life, to write something which he fancies others may read with pleasure or with profit. For my own part, beyond a few boyish letters to relatives and intimate friends, I began my efforts at composition as an apprentice in a newspaper office, by condensing the news, more especially the foreign, which I was directed to put into type from the city journals received at our office ; endeavoring to give in fewer words the gist of the information, in so far, at least, as it would be likely to interest our rural readers. Our Editor, during the latter part of my stay in Poultney, was a Baptist clergyman, ·whose pastoral charge was at some distance, and who was therefore absent from us much of his time, and allowed me a wide discretion in preparing matter for the paper. This I improved, not only in the selection, but in the condensation, of news. The rudimentary knowledge of the art of composition thus acquired was gradually improved during my brief experience as a journeyman in various news-paper establishments, and afterward as a printer of sundry experimental journals in this city ; so that I began my distinctive, avowed editorial career in The New-Yorker with a considerable experience as a writer of articles and paragraphs. I had even written verses, — never fluently nor happily, — but tolerably well measured, and faintly evincing an admiration of Byron, Mrs. Hemans, and other popular writers, — an admiration which I never mistook for inspiration or genius. While true poets are few, those who imagine themselves capable of becoming such are many; but I never advanced even to this grade. I knew that my power of expression in verse was defective, as though I had an impediment in my speech, or spoke with my mouth full of pebbles; and I very soon renounced the fetters of verse, content to utter my thoughts thenceforth in unmistakable prose. It is a comfort to know that not many survive who remember having read any of the few rhymed effusions of my incautious youth.

I had been nearly twenty years a constant writer for the newspaper press ere I ventured (in 1850) to put forth a volume. This was entitled "Hints toward Reforms," and consisted mainly of Lectures and Addresses prepared for delivery before village lyceums and other literary associations from time to time throughout the preceding six or eight years. Most of them regarded Social questions; but their range was very wide, including Political Economy, the Right to Labor, Land for the Landless, Protection to Home Industry, Popular Education, Capital Punishment, Abstinence from Alcoholic potations, &c., &c. My volume was an ordinary duodecimo of 425 pages, compactly filled with the best thoughts I had to offer; all designed to strengthen and diffuse sympathy with misfortune and suffering, and to promote the substantial, permanent well-being of mankind. When I had fully prepared it, I sent the copy to the Harpers; and they agreed to publish it fairly, on condition that I paid the cost of stereotyping (about $400), when they would give me (as I recollect) ten cents per copy on all they sold. I cheerfully accepted the terms, and the work was published accordingly. I believe the sales nearly reimbursed my outlay for stereotyping; so that I attained the dignity of authorship at a very moderate cost. Green authors are apt to suffer from disappointment and chagrin at the failure of their works to achieve them fame and fortune. I was fairly treated by the press and the public, and had no more desire than reason to complain.

I have given these unflattering reminiscences so fully, because I would be useful to young aspirants to authorship,
even at the cost of losing their good-will.   I have been solicited by many — O, so many! — of them to find publishers
for the poems or the novel of each, in the sanguine expectation that a publisher was the only requisite to his achievement of fortune and renown; when, in fact, each had great
need of a public, none (as yet) of a publisher.   You are sure,
O gushing youth! that your poems are such as no other
youth ever wrote, — such as Pindar, or Dante, or Milton
would read with delight, — and I acquiesce in your judgment.
But the great mass of readers have not "the vision and the
faculty divine"; they are prosaic, plodding, heavy-witted
persons, who read and admire what they are told others have
read and admired before them, — if the discovery of new
Homers and Shakespeares were to rest with them, none would
henceforth be distinguished from the common herd.   You,
we will agree, are such a genius as Heaven vouchsafes us once
in two or three centuries; but can you dream that such are
discerned and appreciated by the great mass of their cotemporaries ?   How much, think you, did Homer, or Dante, or
Milton receive from the sale of his works to the general public ?   Nay : how much did Shakespeare's poetry, *as* poetry, contribute to his sustenance ?   Nay, more : do *you*, having acquired the greenback-cost of adding a volume to your library,
buy the span-new verses of Stiggins Dobbs or C. Pugsley
Jagger ?   You know that you do not, — that you buy Shelley,
or Béranger, or Tennyson, instead.   Then how can you expect
the great mass of us, who have not the faintest claim to genius
or special discernment, to recognize *your* untrumpeted merit
and buy your volume ?   You ought to know that we shall
follow your example, and buy — if we ever buy poems at all
— those of some one whose fame has already reached even
our dull ears and fixed our heedless attention.   Hence it is
that no judicious publisher will buy your manuscript, nor
print it, even if you were to make him a present of it.   He
can't afford it.   And your talk of the stupidity, the incom-

petency, the rapacity, or the cruelty of publishers is wholly aside from the case. Not one first work in a hundred ever pays the cost of its publication. True, yours *may* be the rare exception; but the publisher is hardly to blame that he does not see it.

A year or two later, on my return from my first visit to Europe, I was surprised by an offer to publish in a volume the letters I had written thence to The Tribune, and pay me copyright thereon. I knew, right well, that they did not deserve such distinction, — that they were flimsy and superficial, — things of a day; to be read in the morning and forgotten at night. But it seems that some who had read them in The Tribune wished to have them in a more compact, portable shape; while it was highly improbable that any others would be tempted to buy them: so I consented, and revised them; and they duly appeared as "Glances at Europe" in 1851 – 52. I recollect my share of the proceeds was about $500; for which I had taken no pecuniary risk, and done very little labor. Had the work been profounder, and more deserving, I presume it would not have sold so well, — at all events, not so speedily.

Years passed; I made my long-meditated overland journey to California; and the letters I wrote during that trip, printed from week to week in The Tribune, were collected on my return, and printed in a volume nearly equal in size to either of my former. As a photograph of scenes that were then passing away, of a region on the point of rapid and striking transformation, I judge that this "Overland Journey to California in 1859" may be deemed worth looking into by a dozen persons per annum for the next twenty years. Its publishers failed, however, very soon after its appearance; so that my returns from it for copyright were inconsiderable.

And now came the Presidential contest of 1860, closely followed by Secession and Civil War, whereof I had no thougnt of ever becoming the historian. In fact, not till that War was placed on its true basis of a struggle for liberation, and not conquest, by President Lincoln's successive Proclamations of Freedom, would I have consented to write its history. Not till I had confronted the Rebellion as a positive, desolating force, right here in New York, at the doors of earnest Republicans, in the hunting down and killing of defenceless, fleeing Blacks, in the burning of the Colored Orphan Asylum, and in the mobbing and firing of The Tribune office, could I have been moved to delineate its impulses, aims, progress, and impending catastrophe.

A very few days after the national triumph at Gettysburg, with the kindred and almost simultaneous successes of General Grant in the capture of Vicksburg, and General Banks in that of Port Hudson, with the consequent suppression of the (so called) "Riots" in this city, I was visited by two strangers, who introduced themselves as Messrs. Newton and O. D. Case, publishers, from Hartford, and solicited me to write the History of the Rebellion. I hesitated; for my labors and responsibilities were already most arduous and exacting, yet could not, to any considerable extent, be transferred to others. The compensation offered would be liberal, in case the work should attain a very large sale, but otherwise quite moderate. I finally decided to undertake the task, knowing well that it involved severe, protracted effort on my part; and I commenced upon it a few weeks later, after collecting such materials as were then accessible. I hired for my workshop a room on the third floor of the new Bible House, on Eighth Street and Third and Fourth Avenues, procured the requisite furniture, hired a secretary, brought thither my materials, and set to work. Hither I repaired, directly after breakfast each week-day morning, and read and compared the various documents, official reports, newspaper letters, &c., &c., that served as materials for a chapter, while my secretary visited libraries at my direction, and searched out material among my documents and elsewhere. The great public libraries of New York, — Society, Historical, Astor, and Mercantile — all cluster around the Bible House ; the two last-named being within a bowshot. I occasionally visited either of them, in personal quest of material otherwise inaccessible. When I had the substance of my next chapter pretty fairly in mind, I began to compose that chapter ; having often several authorities conveniently disposed around me, with that on which I principally relied lying open before me. I oftener wrote out my first draft, merely indicating extracts where such were to be quoted at some length ; leaving these to be inserted by my secretary when he came to transcribe my text ; but I sometimes dictated to my secretary, who took short-hand notes of what I said, and wrote them out at his leisure. My first chapter was thus composed at one sitting, after some days had been given to the arrangement of materials ; but, usually, two days, or even three, were given to the composition of each of the longer chapters, after I had prepared and digested its material. Our rule was to lock the door on resuming composition, and decline all solicitations to open it till the day's allotted task had been finished ; and this was easy while my " den " was known to very few ; but that knowledge was gradually diffused ; and more and more persons found excuses for dropping in ; until I was at length subject to daily, and even more frequent, though seldom to protracted, interruptions. I think, however, that if I should ever again undertake such a labor, I would allow the location of my " den " to be known to but one person at The Tribune office, who should be privileged to knock at its door in cases of extreme urgency, and I would have that door open to no one beside but my secretary and myself. Even my proof-sheets should await me at The Tribune office, whither I always repaired, to commence a day's work as Editor, after finishing one as Author at the " den."

A chapter having been fairly written out or transcribed by my secretary, while I was " reading up " for another, I carefully revised and sent it to the stereotyper, who sent me his second and third proofs, which were successively corrected before the pages were ready to be cast. Sometimes, the discovery of new material compelled the revision and recast of a chapter which had been passed as complete. And, though the material was very copious, — more so, I presume, than that from which the history of any former war was written, — it was still exceedingly imperfect and contradictory. For instance : when I came to the pioneer Secession of South Carolina, I wished to study it in the proceedings and debates of her Legislature and Convention as reported in at least one of her own journals ; and of these I found but a single file preserved in our city (at the Society Library), though four years had not yet expired since that Secession occurred. A year later, I probably could not have found one at all. Of the score or so of speeches made by Jefferson Davis, often from cars, while on his way from Mississippi to assume at Montgomery the Presidency of the Confederacy, I found but two condensed reports ; and one of these, I apprehend, was apocryphal. In many cases, I found officers reported killed in battles whom I afterward found fighting in subsequent battles ; whence I conclude that they had not been killed so dead as they might have been. Some of the errors into which I was thus led by my authorities were not corrected till after my work was printed ; when the gentlemen thus conclusively disposed of began to write me, insisting that, though desperately wounded at the battle in question, they had decided not to give up the ghost, and so still remained in the land of embodied rather than that of disembodied souls. Their testimony was so direct and pointed that I was constrained to believe it, and to correct page after page accordingly. I presume a few, even yet, remain consigned to the shades in my book, who nevertheless, to this day, consume rations of beef and pork with most unspiritual regularity and self-satisfaction. There doubtless remain some other errors, though I have corrected many ; and, as I have stated many more particulars than my rivals in the same field have usually done, it is probable that my work originally embodied more errors of fact or incident than almost any other.

Yet " The American Conflict " will be consulted, at least by historians, and I shall be judged by it, after most of us now living shall have mingled with the dust. An eminent antagonist of my political views has pronounced it "the fairest one-sided book ever written "; but it is more than that. It is one of the clearest statements yet made of *the long train of causes which led irresistibly to the war for the Union, showing why that war was the natural and righteous consequence of the American people's general and guilty complicity in the crime of upholding and diffusing Human Slavery. I proffer it as my contribution toward a fuller and more vivid realization of the truth that God governs this world by moral laws as active, immutable, and all-pervading as can be operative in any other, and that every collusion or compromise with evil must surely invoke a prompt and signal retribution.

The sale of my history was very large and steady down to the date of the clamor raised touching the bailing of Jefferson Davis, when it almost ceased for a season ; thousands who had subscribed for it refusing to take their copies, to the sore disappointment and loss of the agents, who had supplied themselves with fifty to a hundred copies each, in accordance with their orders ; and who thus found themselves suddenly, and most unexpectedly involved in serious embarrassments. I grieved that they were thus afflicted for what, at the worst, was no fault of theirs ; while their loss by every copy thus refused was twenty times my own. I trust, however, that their undeserved embarrassments were, for the most part, temporary, — that a juster sense of what was due to them ultimately prevailed, — that all of them who did not mistake the character of a fitful gust of popular passion, and thereupon sacrifice their hard earnings, have since been relieved from their embarrassments ; and that the injury and injustice they suffered without deserving have long since been fully repaired. At all events, the public has learned that I act upon my convictions without fear of personal consequences ; hence, any future paroxysm of popular rage against me is likely to be less violent, in view of the fact that this one proved so plainly ineffectual.

LIV.

MY DEAD.

"I DO not wear my heart upon my sleeve," and shrink
from the obtrusion of matters purely personal upon an
indifferent public. I have aimed, in the series herewith
closed, to narrate mainly such facts and incidents as seemed
likely to be of use, either in strengthening the young and
portionless for the battle of life, or in commending to their
acceptance convictions which I deem sound and important.
My life has been one of arduous, rarely intermitted, labor, —
of efforts to achieve other than personal ends, —of efforts
which have absorbed most of the time which others freely
devote to social intercourse and to fireside enjoyments. Of
those I knew and loved in youth, a majority have already
crossed the dark river, and I will not impose even their names
on an unsympathizing world. Among them is my fellow-
apprentice and life-long friend, who, after long illness, died in
this city in 1861; my first partner, already named, who was
drowned while bathing in 1832; and a young poet of promise
who was slowly yielding to consumption when the tidings of
our Bull Run disaster snapped short his thread of life, — as
it would have snapped mine had it been half so frail as his.
The faces of many among the departed whom I have known
and loved come back to me as I gaze adown the vista of my
half-century of active life; but I have no right to lift the
veil which shrouds and shields their long repose. I will
name but those who are a part of myself, and whose loss to
earth has profoundly affected my subsequent career.
Since I began to write these reminiscences, my mother's

last surviving brother, John Woodburn, has deceased, aged seventy-two, leaving the old Woodburn homestead, I understand, to some among his children; so has my father's brother, Isaac, aged eighty, leaving, so far as I know, but one of the nine brothers (John) still living. My father himself died on the 18th of December last, aged eighty-six. He had, for twelve years or more, been a mere wreck, first in body only; but his infirmities ultimately affected his mind; so that, when I last visited him, a year before his death, he did not recognize me till after he had sat by my side for a full half-hour; and he ·had before asked my oldest sister, " Did you ever know Henry Greeley ? " — alluding to one of her sons, then several years dead. He had fitful flashes of mental recovery; but he had been so long a helpless victim of hopeless bodily and mental decay that I did not grieve when I learned that his spirit had at length shaken off the encumbrance of its mortal coil, which had ceased to be an instrument, and remained purely an obstruction. Of his protracted life, forty-two years had been spent in or on the verge of New England, and forty-four in his deliberately chosen, steadily retained, Pennsylvanian home.

My son, Arthur Young ("Pickie"), born in March, 1844, was the third of seven children, whereof a son and daughter, severally born in 1838 and in 1842, scarcely opened their eyes to a world which they entered but to leave. Physically, they were remarkable for their striking resemblance in hair and features to their father and mother respectively.

Arthur had points of similarity to each of us, but with decided superiority, as a whole, to either. I looked in vain through Italian galleries, two years after he was taken from us, for any full parallel to his dazzling beauty, — a beauty not physical merely, but visibly radiating from the soul. His hair was of the finest and richest gold; "the sunshine of picture" never glorified its equal; and the delicacy of his complexion at once fixed the attention of observers like the late N. P. Willis, who had traversed both hemispheres without having his gaze arrested by any child who could bear a com-

parison with this one. Yet he was not one of those paragons
sometimes met with, whose idlest chatter would edify a Sunday school, — who never do or say aught that propriety would
not sanction and piety delight in, — but thoroughly human,
and endued with a love of play and mischief which kept him
busy and happy the livelong day, while rendering him the
delight and admiration of all around him. The arch delicacy
wherewith he inquiringly suggested, when once told a story
that overtaxed his credulity, " I 'pose that aint a lie ? " was
characteristic of his nature. Once, when about three years
old, having chanced to espy my watch lying on a sofa as I
was dressing one Sunday morning, with no third person present, he made a sudden spring of several feet, caught the
watch by the chain, whirled it around his head, and sent it
whizzing against the chimney, shattering its face into frag-
ments. " Pickie," I inquired, rather sadly than angrily, " how
could you do me such injury ? " " 'Cause I was nervous," he
regretfully replied. There were ladies then making part of
our household whose nerves were a source of general as well
as personal discomfort; and this was his attestation of the
fact.

There were wiser and deeper sayings treasured as they fell
from his lips; but I will not repeat them. Several yet live
who remember the graceful gayety wherewith he charmed
admiring circles assembled at our house, and at two or three
larger gatherings of friends of Social Reform in this city, and
at the N. A. Phalanx in New Jersey; and I think some grave
seigniors, who were accustomed to help us enjoy our Saturday
afternoons in our rural suburban residence at Turtle Bay,
were drawn thither as much by their admiration of the son
as by their regard for his parents.

Meantime, another daughter was given to us, and, after six
months, withdrawn; and still another born, who yet survives;
and he had run far into his sixth year without one serious
illness. His mother had devoted herself to him from his
birth, even beyond her intense consecration to the care of her
other children; had never allowed him to partake of animal

food, or to know that an animal was ever killed to be eaten; had watched and tended him with absorbing love, till the perils of infancy seemed fairly vanquished; and we had reason to hope that the light of our eyes would be spared to gladden our remaining years.

It was otherwise decreed. In the Summer of 1849, the Asiatic cholera suddenly reappeared in our city, and the frightened authorities ordered all swine, &c., driven out of town, — that is, above Fortieth Street, — whereas our home was about Forty-eighth Street, though no streets had yet been cut through that quarter. At once, and before we realized our danger, the atmosphere was polluted by the exhalations of the swinish multitude thrust upon us from the densely peopled hives south of us, and the cholera claimed its victims by scores before we were generally aware of its presence.

Our darling was among the first; attacked at 1 A. M. of the 12th of July, when no medical attendance was at hand; and our own prompt, unremitted efforts, reënforced at length by the best medical skill within reach, availed nothing to stay the fury of the epidemic, to which he succumbed about 5 P. M. of that day, — one of the hottest, as well as quite the longest, I have ever known. He was entirely sane and conscious till near the last; insisting that he felt little or no pain and was well, save that we kept him sweltering under clothing that he wanted to throw off, as he did whenever he was permitted. When at length the struggle ended with his last breath, and even his mother was convinced that his eyes would never again open on the scenes of this world, I knew that the Summer of my life was over, that the chill breath of its Autumn was at hand, and that my future course must be along the downhill of life.

Yet another son (Raphael Uhland) was born to us two years afterward; who, though more like his father and less like a poet than Arthur, was quite as deserving of parental love, though not so eminently fitted to evoke and command general admiration. He was with me in France and Switzerland in the Summer of 1855 ; spending, with his mother and sister, the previous Winter in London and that subsequent in Dresden; returning with them in May, '56, to fall a victim to the croup the ensuing February. I was absent on a lecturing tour when apprised of his dangerous illness, and hastened home to find that he had died an hour before my arrival, though he had hoped and striven to await my return. He had fulfilled his sixth year and twelve days over when our home was again made desolate by his death.

Another daughter was born to us four weeks later, who survives; so that we have reason to be grateful for two children left to soothe our decline, as well as for five who, having preceded us on the long journey, await us in the Land of Souls.

My life has been busy and anxious, but not joyless. Whether it shall be prolonged few or more years, I am grateful that it has endured so long, and that it has abounded in opportunities for good not wholly unimproved, and in experiences of the nobler as well as the baser impulses of human nature. I have been spared to see the end of giant wrongs, which I once deemed invincible in this century, and to note the silent upspringing and growth of principles and influences which I hail as destined to root out some of the most flagrant and pervading evils that yet remain. I realize that each generation is destined to confront new and peculiar perils, — to wrestle with temptations and seductions unknown to its predecessors; yet I trust that progress is a general law of our being, and that the ills and woes of the future shall be less crushing than those of the bloody and hateful past. So, looking calmly, yet humbly, for that close of my mortal career which cannot be far distant, I reverently thank God for the blessings vouchsafed me in the past; and, with an awe that is not fear, and a consciousness of demerit which does not exclude hope, await the opening before my steps of the gates of the Eternal World.

APPENDIX.

APPENDIX

---o---

I.

THE "Recollections" as prepared by Mr. Greeley, originally for a newspaper, are, in no full sense of the word, an autobiography. Many incidents of his life he preferred or was obliged to leave unmentioned ; and certain slight memoranda of his life, subsequent to the period at which his own "Recollections" close, may have a value to the reader of this volume.

II.

In 1867, Mr. Greeley was elected a Delegate at Large to the New-York State Convention for the revision of the Constitution. The records of that body show that he was a faithful delegate, constant in his attendance, efficient in the discharge of his official duties, and always upon the right side whenever questions of justice and humanity were before the Convention.

III.

In the year 1860, the name of Mr. Greeley had been presented by his friends, for United States Senator, to the Republican Legislative Caucus at Albany. Before this body, there were three candidates, viz : Mr. Ira Harris, Mr. William M. Evarts, and Mr. Greeley. Mr. Greeley began the canvass with a liberal vote, and as the ballot proceeded, he continued to gain largely upon his opponents, when the supporters of Mr. Evarts went over in a body to Mr. Harris, and of course secured the election of that gentleman. During this canvass, Mr. Greeley was engaged in lecturing at the West, where an intimation reached him that some of his supporters meant " to fight fire with fire;" that is, to meet the doubtful manœuvres of the opposition by like expedients. Against this he at once entered his earnest protest. He did not pretend to undervalue the honor of a seat in the United States Senate, for, honorably won, it would be welcome to him or to any other citizen; but not for that or for any other place of dignity and trust, would he have his friends endeavor to advance his pretensions by any act, the publication of which would be discreditable.

In 1867, many of Mr. Greeley's friends and admirers were again anxious to send him to the Senate. Indeed, before the meeting of the Legislature he seemed to be the favorite candidate of prominent Republicans, and he was supported by the leading journals of the party. But Mr. Greeley, now that the War of the Rebellion had happily closed, had made no secret of his ardent desire for peace, in fact as well as in name. He believed firmly in the efficacy of "universal amnesty " and impartial suffrage, and of these alone, for healing the gaping wounds of· the Civil War. It was not in his nature to conceal his opinions, but, as some thought with an unnecessary candor, he took occasion, just before the meeting of the Legislative Caucus, to make as public as possible his views of pacification, by an elaborate article in the *Tribune* over his own signature. He deliberately, by this act, threw up all his chances for the Senatorship ; he perfectly understood the nature of the sacrifice, and its inevitable result. But rather than say what he did not believe ; rather than leave unsaid that which he felt should be uttered, he cheerfully resigned his pretensions to a preferment which would have been agreeable to him or to any public man.

IV.

Mr. Greeley in 1869 was the Republican candidate for State Controller. There was but little if any chance of his election, and several prominent Republicans had already been nominated and had declined. He was defeated as he expected to be, but it is worthy of record that he ran ahead of the whole Republican State Ticket, with the exception of Gen. Franz Sigel, who received a considerable German vote not cast for the other nominees.

V.

Mr. Greeley in 1870 ran for Congress in the VIth Dictrict in opposition to Hon. S. S. Cox. He was unable, through illness, to make a single speech in his district, but his nomination reduced the Democratic majority then from 2700 two years before, to about 1,000, and he ran 300 ahead of Gen. Woodford, the Republican candidate for Governor.

VI.

We have now come to the closing event of this busy life. The political year of 1872 had not brought with it that fraternal feeling and that real reunion which would have been so encouraging and satisfactory. If the Administration had been beset by difficulties in restoring peace, order and prosperity in the Southern States, it could not be said that it had been candid in recognizing or fortunate in meeting these difficulties. The armies of the Confederacy had been disbanded, but in too many cases the spirit which had collected them remained. Mr. Greeley had shown the amicable idea by which he was already animated, when he had become one of the sureties of Jefferson Davis—a prisoner whom the government seemed afraid to try and equally afraid to keep in durance. Matters had been dragging without mending, every day's report from the South being of wrong and outrage upon one side or the other. In other respects the Administration was deemed by many citizens inefficient. The Civil Service, by the admission of Republicans themselves, was in an inefficient and corrupt condition. There were grave charges of Executive corruption which were not then and have not yet been satisfactorily explained. The President's own family had been, it was thought, too much the recipient of Executive favor. There had been many glaring instances of peculation in the Financial Department of the

Government, which had not received the rigid investigation which they demanded. Thus stood political affairs when, on the 1st of May, the Liberal Convention met in Cincinnati, with a very large delegation from all parts of the United States. The occasion of the Convention could not be better stated than it was by Mr. Carl Schurz, its presiding officer, who alluded to the jobbery and corruption which had been stimulated to unusual audacity by the opportunities of the civil war, invading the public service of the Government, as well as almost all members of the social body. Reference was also made in the same speech to a public opinion most deplorably lenient in its judgment of public and private dishonesty—to a Government indulging in wanton disregard of the law of the land, and resorting to daring assumptions of unconstitutional power—to the people, apparently at least, acquiescing with reckless levity in transgressions threatening the very life of our free institutions. It was upon these general charges, sustained by innumerable particulars, that the action of the Convention was based. It was an honest effort to emancipate the country from the domination of rings. It was an attempt to restore the purity of the Presidential office. It was a movement designed to relieve the public service from partisan and personal influence ; but mainly, important as were then the objects of the Convention, it was thought that the time had come for an appeal to the better instincts and latent patriotism of the Southern people, by restoring to them those rights, the enjoyment of which is indispensable for a successful administration of their local affairs. It is not to be denied that the course and conduct of the President met with a sharp rebuke from the Convention ; but no more can it be denied that the justice of the accusations was partially and reluctantly admitted by the friends of the Administration, and that promises of reform were liberally made while the verdict of the people still remained in abeyance. Mr. Greeley, upon the sixth ballot, was nominated for the Presidency, and B. Gratz Brown, of Missouri, for the Vice Presidency.

It is important and interesting to notice the course taken by Mr. Greeley in accepting the nomination of the Convention.

It may safely be said that he was not called upon to come up to the ground taken by the Delegates, for they had simply come up to his. The new position of the Liberal Party was but the old one which had been steadily occupied by him, through good and evil report, ever since any opinion of such matters had been called for by public events. It was no new thing for the candidate to declare that all the political rights and franchises which had been acquired by the war "should be guaranteed, maintained, enjoyed, respected ever more." It was only saying over what he had often said before, when he declared that all political rights and franchises which had been lost through that convulsion should and must be promptly restored and re-established, so that there should henceforth be no proscribed class and no disfranchised class within the limits of the Union. Again as a candidate, as heretofore as an Editor, he called for Re-union and Fraternity. It was only natural for him to speak, and with the strongest words at his command, in defence of local self-government as contradistinguished from centralization. He had, in fact, changed in no respect. He had always advocated genuine Civil Service Reform. He had always thought the Public Lands should be reserved for actual settlers. He had always been specially sensitive upon the points of the Public Faith and the National Credit. The soldiers and the sailors of the Republic had never had a better friend. Warm partisan as he had ever been, there was never a time in his whole career when he might not have promised, if elected to the office, to be the President "not of a party, but of the whole people."

It was perfectly natural that, holding these views, Mr. Greeley should, in the month of July following, receive the nomination of the Democratic Convention at Baltimore—a body comprised of the most liberal and enlightened members of the old party—of men who were superior to old political traditions, who were willing cheerfully to accept the situation, and who believed that kindness would be more effective than force in onciliating an estranged people. The Democrats who gave Mr. Greeley their support could hardly be charged with a blind adherence to their own party, any more than he could be

charged with a practical desertion of his own. Thus Mr.
Greeley was fairly before the country as the Presidential candidate of the Liberal and Democratic parties.

The canvass which ensued was the last great political struggle in which the veteran warrior was to take a part ; nor did
he ever engage in any work more likely to win for his memory
a pure and honorable fame. He entered into the business of
the election with his usual vigor and enthusiasm. He was
constantly speaking in all parts of the country, and he thus
developed a forensic ability for which he had not before
received credit. He engaged in the discussion of the great
questions involved in the contest, everywhere boldly avowing
his own views, and being everywhere received with enthusiastic
kindness and approbation. Upon accepting the nomination
he had retired from the editorial charge of *The Tribune*, but
he was constantly meeting his old readers, and receiving from
them a cordial reception.

The result of the canvass in no way diminishes the excellent
influence which it exercised upon public affairs. Mr. Greeley
received 2,834,079 votes for the Presidency, and Gen. Grant
3,597,070. Thus, though he carried few States, he was supported by an immense number of citizens. Owing to the
peculiarities of our electoral system, while actually receiving
nearly 3,000,000 of votes for the office, he would have secured
the electoral votes, had he lived, only of the States of Georgia,
Kentucky, Maryland, Missouri, Tennessee and Texas. Thus it
will be seen that Mr. Greeley did not carry many States ; but
his was after all a substantial victory. The Liberal movement
was threatening enough thoroughly to arouse the Republican
party to a sense of the necessity of its own reform and purification. Its organs were not slow in communicating its excellent
intentions to the public, nor in re-affirming the promises of the
campaign. Those who best knew and loved Mr. Greeley did
not consider him to be much in need of sympathy when, having escaped the toils and troubles of the Presidency, he came
cheerfully and willingly back to his newspaper, and announced
to the great constituency of its readers that once more he was
at his old post. But only for a very brief period was he to

occupy the position in which he had won such honorable reputation, and we may even predict such lasting fame. How great had been Mr. Greeley's labors during the Summer was not fully comprehended, certainly not by himself, until the battle had been fought and honorably lost. The intellectual strain, continued through so many years of unceasing industry and enormous toil, received its last fatal tension through those excited months of traveling and of public speaking. The cerebral trouble developed itself in the usual form of sleeplessness, with a fatal result. Mr. Greeley died on the 29th of November, sustained by the approbation of a good conscience, tenderly anxious for those loved ones who were to be left behind him, and hopeful of a re-union with the beloved wife who had just preceded him. The toil was over. The kind heart ever pitiful of others' woe had ceased to beat. Rest had come to the laborer at last.

VII.

New York will long remember the funeral of Mr. Greeley. In accordance with a generally expressed public wish, the remains were conveyed to the City Hall, where, during the day, it is estimated that they were visited and viewed by over 40,000 people. It was in speaking of this, that *The Tribune* of the next morning said, " How many his friends were and who they were, may be seen from the descriptions which we publish this morning of this extraordinary scene. A whole city mourns for him. The poor shed tears over him ; the laboring man stops work that he may pay a last tribute to him who spent forty years in working hard for the benefit of workers. A more spontaneous manifestation of universal sorrow has not been seen by this generation."

The public funeral took place on the 4th of December. The services were held in the Church of the Divine Paternity (Dr. Chapin's), which was filled to overflowing. The interior had been appropriately decorated with flags, with a profusion of flowers, and with floral inscriptions. In the procession which followed the remains from the residence of *The Tribune* publisher to the church, were Mr. Chief Justice Chase, Senators Trumbull and Fenton, and Mr. Thurlow Weed. At the church were President Grant, Vice-President Colfax, Gen. Belknap, Secretary of War; Gov. Hoffman and staff; Mr. Washburne, U.S. Minister to France ; Senators Conkling, Fenton, Wilson and Schurz, and Mayor Hall. In the pulpit were Rev. Dr. Chapin, Rev. Henry Ward Beecher, Dr. Edward Beecher, Rev. J. M. Pullman and Prof. R. D. Hitchcock. An address was pronounced by Rev. H. W. Beecher, and a funeral discourse upon the character of Mr. Greeley by the Rev. Dr. Chapin. After the services in the church, a long procession was formed of a remarkably impressive character. It consisted of about one hundred and twenty-five carriages moving abreast. There was no music and no military guard. No banners were displayed ; no regalia was worn, except by a few of the societies in attendance ; and yet it was universally felt that the procession was extremely imposing. Throngs of citizens crowded to gaze upon the demonstration, with a respectful decorum which has never been surpassed upon such an occasion in New York. All along the line which was followed, most of the places of business, and public and private buildings, were draped with the ensigns of mourning. In the cortége were the President, Vice-President, the Vice-President-elect, the Governor, Mayor, and other public functionaries. The route was down the Fifth Avenue to Fourteenth street, through Fourteenth street to Broadway, and down Broadway to Bowling Green, where the line divided, half going through Whitehall street, and the other half through State street, meeting at the ferry. The bells of St. Paul and Trinity were tolled as the procession passed. This, after crossing the ferry, moved on to Greenwood Cemetery, where the remains, with a short and simple ceremony, were consigned to their last resting-place.

It should be noticed that these testimonials of esteem and regret were not confined to the city of New York, but were so general throughout the country that even a brief description of them would fill a volume. Various public bodies passed resolutions appropriate to the occasion. A movement was at once set on foot for the erection of a suitable monument to the memory of Mr. Greeley, and, up to this time, liberal subscriptions for defraying the expense of it have been received.

VIII.

We have thus briefly noticed those events of Mr. Greeley's life which are not mentioned in this Volume, and have indicated the great public interest which his death awakened. This seemed to be a necessary supplement to the work ; but, in order that its conclusion may be in accordance with the modest simplicity of the greater part of its contents, we have abstained from the language of eulogy. The book is in some respects a sacred one, and we have sought to place nothing here which Mr. Greeley would not himself have approved. The only lesson which we venture to suggest is that of encouragement to all who, whether in a public or private career, may sometimes waver and grow weak in the path of duty. The great man of whom we have been speaking had many disappointments, nor was his life free from failures ; but he won, as no private citizen ever won before, the love and the confidence of his countrymen. This was a reward, the knowledge of which he could only partially enjoy ; but none the less does it remain a bright encouragement to those who are still living and laboring.

AUTOBIOGRAPHICAL REMINISCENCES.

———o———

THE following interesting and valuable Letter was originally published in the *New-York Ledger* shortly after Mr. GREELEY's death. The Editor thus introduces it to his readers :

"Readers of *The Ledger* who followed for many consecutive weeks the Autobiographical Reminiscences of Horace Greeley, which were first given to the public in the columns of this journal, will peruse with renewed interest the following fragment of Mr. Greeley's earlier literary work, never before published. When THE NEW-YORK TRIBUNE was but four years old, and Mr. Greeley himself in his 34th year, he yielded with great reluctance, and after many solicitations, to the request of one of his oldest friends and admirers—a gentleman then living in one of the New-England States—for a sketch of his life and his struggles with adverse fortune. The First Autobiography of Horace Greeley, which we print in full below, was the result of a single afternoon's work. Written in the intimacy of personal friendship, in response to the expressed desire of one to whom Mr. Greeley had been under deep obligation for favors rendered during some of the darkest hours of his early life, the tone of this remarkable production is freer than that of his more elaborate personal history entitled "Recollections of a Busy Life," and in this lies its peculiar charm. It is the frank, full story of Mr. Greeley's life down to the Spring of 1845 — gossipy, cheery, pleasant, marked by characteristic traces of thought, and admirable in every way.

"It is not out of place to add that the copy of this Autobiography which has been furnished for publication in *The Ledger*, was obtained from a gentleman who has had it in his possession for twenty-seven years, having received permission to retain a draft from the original manuscript, on condition that it should not be suffered to appear in print during the lifetime of Mr. Greeley. His death removes the prohibition."

———

NEW YORK, April 14, 1845.

DEAR SIR: I have mislaid your letter, which reached me some days since, but I remember its purport, and have snatched the earliest moment to give you, at your request, an outline of my unromantic life.

I was born February 3, 1811, in the town of Amherst, N. H., five miles northeast of the village or "Plain," in the last house before you pass into Bedford, on the old road to Bedford village and Manchester. I am the oldest living of five children, but a brother and sister preceded me and died, at three and two years of age, a year or two before I came into the world. My father (Zaccheus Greeley), I think, and my mother (originally Mary Woodburn), I know, claim Londonderry for their birth-place. My paternal grandfather (Zaccheus G.) still lives with his son John in Londonderry, aged over ninety, having survived by many years his wife and three of his thirteen children—perhaps more, as they are scattered over the face of the earth. I believe our only notable ancestor was "Capt. Lovewell" of the Paugus fight, both whose names—"Zaccheus" and "Lovewell"—have been perpetuated in the family as Christian names. And yet I may be mistaken as to his being an ancestor. Either of the Nashua Greeleys (cousins of my father) doubtless knew more of the family than I do.

My maternal grandfather, David Woodburn, was descended from one of the original settlers of Londonderry, and his son John still lives on the land which was allotted to our Scotch-Irish progenitor in 1721. At the house of this grandfather I was a guest and a pet in my early childhood ; here I was first sent to school when just three years old ; and if you should ever happen to pass through "the High Range" of Londonderry, near an old, weather-beaten school-house, which was red thirty years ago, you can easily pick up some monstrous exaggerations of my infantile achievements as a scholar. Spelling was my forte, as is natural for a child of tenacious memory and no judgment ; and I recollect that it used to be the custom that the head of the first class and the next should choose sides for a "spelling match" once a week or so. Now, I could spell well enough to be "head" among thirty or forty numskulls, whose incapability of learning to spell is even now a puzzle to me ; but I had not wit enough to choose good spellers. On the contrary, I would choose little children, my playmates, who could not spell at all. After patience and counsel had both been exhausted, it was found necessary to break the old rule, and let the two next choose sides. Some of these spelling matches were held in the evening, and it was difficult to keep such a baby as I awake. When the word came to me I had to be waked up to spell it ; and I have lately found a story quite

current that I could and did spell just as well asleep as awake!
Reading was the only other branch in which I made any
such unseasonable proficiency. I could read very fluently at
four years of age, and quite passably with the book upside
down—an absurd practice, which I was stimulated to persist
in by those who should have known better. This, too, is the
theme of modern fables.

No higher branch of learning has come so easy to me except
Arithmetic, which seemed but play. I cannot remember when
I did not know the Multiplication Table, though I must have
learned it of course. After learning what figures mean, and
what relation they bear to each other, all beyond seemed to
flow naturally from the axiom that two and two are four. But
Grammar came hard to me. I commenced at six years of age,
and having but little schooling, wasted the best part of what I
had for several years before I discovered that our standard
authors on that subject knew nothing about it—Lindley Mur-
ray especially, the intense blockhead, whose gross blunders I
ought to have detected at seven years of age, but did not till
ten or eleven. That obtuseness of perception put me back
sadly, and I had to learn what I know of Grammar after I had
devoted more time to it than it should have required in all.
Ten weeks with the books we now have, are worth ten months
with such as I learned from.

Geography I never studied much at all, for want of books, or
rather maps. I learned my old "Morse's Abridgment" nearly
by heart, but my brother tore the map out soon after I got it,
and I have to this day a most imperfect idea of the relative
position of places, though tolerably acquainted with so much
of geography, or rather of its adjuncts, as is taught through the
medium of letter-press.

My last Summer schooling was at seven years of age, and
then my time was so abstracted to "ride horse to plow" that I
often reached the school-house after ten, and sometimes as late
as eleven o'clock. Our house in Amherst was about two and a
half miles distant from our proper school-house, but we generally attended one in Bedford, about a mile off. But in 1817
my father moved five miles into Bedford, taking a large farm

on shares, in order to let his smaller one to a needy brother. We lived in Bedford two years, and here our school was over a mile distant, and poor at that, being kept but six weeks in Winter and perhaps three months in Summer, the scholars being few and the parents mainly poor. We moved back to our own place in April, 1819, and remained there till the following January, when my father, having become bankrupt, lost all his property, and been sold out by the Sheriff, was glad of a chance to run away to Westhaven, Vermont, with a wife, four children of ten to four years old, about $50 in money, and what household stuff he could carry with us in a hired sleigh with two horses.

My father and mother were both very hard-working people, but bad managers, or rather he was. Beginning with nothing, and meeting with successive misfortunes, he had a proud spirit, and always wished to entertain all friends and relatives as well as they could him, no matter what their circumstances. He bought a little farm of fifty acres in war-time, etc., for over $1,300, and was compelled to sell it at last for $600. He had always much sickness in the family, lost one entire year by it himself, lost heavily (for him) by indorsing to save a brother from jail, and was shamefully defrauded by those whose farm he took in Bedford. They were the immediate cause of his pecuniary ruin. But he always was too fond of great men's smiles and promises, and both he and mother have always used ardent spirits and tobacco—very moderately, they think, but greatly to their injury, I know. But so we were cast out from New Hampshire.

In Vermont we all took hold again and worked hard. We cleared by the job fifty acres of old pine swamp, grown up to ash, alders, etc., and anything but an easy undertaking. On this father and his two sons worked pretty faithfully two years; then he took a saw-mill for a year, and we boys worked a little farm, which turned out badly. The land was a hard clay, utterly exhausted, and overgrown with most invincible Canada thistles. The Summer was intensely dry; so the corn and potatoes died out, while the thistles grew and flourished rankly, in soil where you must strike three spiteful blows to split off a piece of clay as big as a hen's egg. Father's work was more productive; but the place was unhealthy, and we all had the fever and ague severely, either that Fall or next Summer. In the Spring we moved back to our old neighborhood, and for two years worked a large worn-out farm on shares, and cleared twenty acres more upland, losing our labor by the destruction of our wheat crop by Hessian fly. These last years I did not go to school much in Winters, as I had done before; in Summers of course I could not. In the Fall of the last (1825) I re-visited New Hampshire, on foot and alone; and next Spring (being fifteen years of age) I went to East Poultney, Vt., as an apprentice to the printing business in the office of _The Northern Spectator._ I had tried three years before to commend myself to a similar place in Whitehall, N. Y.—eight miles from where I lived—but was rejected as too young and feeble. I narrowly escaped a like fate in Poultney, but an apprentice was much wanted, so I was tried, and made myself acceptable.

Father went West soon after in search of a place to settle, and in September returned and took his family to Erie County, Penn., where he has ever since resided. The parting was a sore trial to me, and I was almost persuaded to go off with them, my place being then hard and disagreeable, but I said good-bye and went back to my cold, strange home with a dry face but a sore heart. Next Fall I went out to see the folks in their new home—over 500 miles by my route—making the journey and back on $12, including three that I ran in debt. I could not do it again. I paid them another visit in the Spring of 1829, and in June, 1830, bade adieu to Poultney, and went West to live, the newspaper stopping at that time.

I spent a part of the following years ('30–'31) at my father's, but worked at my trade when I could find work in Jamestown, Chautauqua County, N. Y.; Lodi, Cattaraugus County, N. Y. and, last and longest, at Erie, Erie Co., Pa. Here I remained five months, and, beginning at a very low estimate, was finally offered a partnership by the editor and printer for whom I worked. The concern was a good one, but it looked as though I should have the work to do against another man's play, and I decined it—rather unwisely, I suspect. Late in

July, 1831, finding no more work in that quarter, I started for this city, reaching here a few months under age, with $10 in my pocket, and not an acquaintance within 200 miles. My clothes were scanty and seedy, my appearance green and unprepossessing, and I had a hard struggle to find work and keep it. (Davy Hale of *The Journal of Commerce* insisted that I was a runaway apprentice, but he was in error.)

I obtained work pretty soon, but it was such as older hands would not do, and I had to work fourteen hours a day to make about $5.50 per week. This lasted eight or nine weeks, after which I walked the streets ten days anxiously looking everywhere for work. I wished to go to Washington to look for work, but could not pay my way, as the purchase of a second-hand suit of clothes (the Hebrew shaved me villainously, for though cheap there was no wear and little warmth in them) had about exhausted all my earnings beyond my board. At the next place I worked a fortnight, but could not get my pay. Soon after, I obtained another job at the old place—hard, but not so bad as the atrocious miniature Testament I first worked on—double columns, twelve ems wide of Agate, full of Greek and superior letters for references, with a center column of Pearl references to other texts. I never found any work so poor as this, at the prices paid for it. So I worried through a year, working from place to place, and witnessing the ravages of the cholera (1832). That Fall I went back to New Hampshire on a visit; saw relatives in Lowell, Londonderry, Manchester, Amherst, Francistown, Alstead, and thence crossed to visit a cousin in Springfield, Vt. Thence went to Newport, N. H., to see an uncle I did not find, and came back to this city just in time to vote against Andrew Jackson's re-election.

I went to work again, and in the course of the Winter joined a fellow-workman (F. V. Story) in buying a few types and undertaking the printing (not publishing) of a two-cent paper. It failed speedily, for the editor and publishers had neither money nor brains, and we were left without our pay, and with the type on our hands. My partner went out to work as a foreman; I kept on our little concern, and soon obtained some business, which proved very good. In July my partner was drowned, and a friend of the family took his interest in the concern. We did well, and next Spring (22d of March, 1834) we issued the first number of my long-projected cheap weekly newspaper, *The New Yorker*. It was tolerably edited and well printed, but never well published, and so anything but profitable. It starved us together for three years, until we dissolved, and my partner took that part of our business which had thus far upheld the paper, leaving the paper alone to me and a most unfit third partner as publisher. He left me in the Fall of 1837, most unhandsomely, and I struggled on in the face of imminent bankruptcy till 1840. I had several partners, one after another, but they proved no helps to me, and soon withdrew. At one time, in 1837, it seemed impossible to stave off bankruptcy another day beyond the next, when a kind friend happened to call upon me, and seeing my evident sadness, learned, on inquiry, that I must have $500 to take up a note next day, and knew not where to look for one cent of it. He offered to lend me the money, and did ; afterward increasing the loan to $1,000.

In 1838, I was engaged to edit a Whig weekly at Albany, entitled *The Jeffersonian*, and was paid $1.000 for a year's service. This was a great help. I regularly went up to Albany Saturday night, made up my paper there by Tuesday night, took the boat down, and got out my *New Yorker* by Friday ; then prepared copy for part of next number, and caught my valise for Albany again. A part of each Winter ('38 and '39) I spent in Albany, doing little for my *New Yorker* but by proxy. In '39 my difficulties were as pressing as ever, though not so hard to bear as in '37, when they were novelties. In 1840 matters gradually brightened with me, in good part owing to my establishment of *The Log Cabin*, a Harrison campaign paper, which acquired an immense circulation—80,000. It was very cheap, and I was obliged to publish it very wastefully, so that the actual gain from it was small: but it supplied me at the outset with a flood of ready money, enabled me to turn myself, and pay off my old debts, so that my credit was better ever after. In 1841, (April 10,) I issued the first number of THE DAILY TRIBUNE, which I should not have done had I not issued a prospectus before General Harrison's death. This enterprise of course required ready money for a time, and a great deal of it, and I was again straitened; but early in the Fall a kind Providence impelled Mr. Thomas McElrath, formerly a bookseller, then a lawyer and Master in Chancery, to call on me and suggest the idea of a partnership. I gladly closed with him on any terms, and from that day to this not another hair has been worn off my head by the aching puzzle of studying out the means of paying to-morrow's note. I have embarrassed myself greatly by indorsing and trying to help others, but the finances of the concern have never cost me an hour's sleep. I have been, as I always wished to be, an editor and a partner in a publishing business, but no burdens but those of editor have fallen on me. Our business is now prosperous, and has been measurably so ever since Mr. McElrath came into the concern. In September, 1841, we discontinued *The New Yorker,* and commenced THE WEEKLY TRIBUNE, which has done well, and now enjoys a large circulation.

I was married in 1836 (before the evil days came) to Mary Y. Cheney—a Connecticut schoolmistress, then teaching in Warrenton, N. C.—a little younger than and just as rich as I was, though I then fancied myself in a way to live comfortably. But *The New Yorker* never yielded me anything. We have had three children, only one of whom survives—Arthur Young Greeley, born 22d March last year, ten years to a day from the date of my first issue of *The New Yorker.*

There, you have my story. I did not mean to write such a yarn, but I never thought of writing on the subject before, and this has run off my fingers unconsciously. I ought to have said that I was offered an education at Exeter Academy, in 1819, (just before our New Hampshire down-fall), by the minister of Bedford and one or two friends. My parents declined it—partly from pride, I believe—but mother said she was not willing to part with me then, nine years of age. Of course, what I have learned has been picked up by the way. I suppose I ought to be sorry, but I am not much.

Yours truly, HORACE GREELEY.

RECEPTION OF MR. GREELEY AT THE LINCOLN CLUB ROOMS,

New York, June 12th, 1871.

———o———

HORACE GREELEY was welcomed at the Lincoln Club-Rooms, in Union Square, by a large number of friends who were assembled under the auspices of the Union Republican General Committee, and who severally congratulated him upon his safe return from his journey to the far South-West, and through the Lower Mississippi Valley. He was received with great applause, and Mr. Enoch L. Fancher, on behalf of the Union Republican General Committee, addressed him as follows :

MR. GREELEY : On behalf of the Union Republican General Committee of the City of New York, and also of many others of your personal and political friends, I have the honor to welcome you home after your journey to a Southern State. We don't come, sir, with any set form of speech or any mere form of words, but we come to tender our heartfelt congratulations, and to express our gratification at seeing you again among us. We feel that your visit to a Southern State will have an influence beyond your own personal gratification and information ; for you, sir, were not only foremost in the support of the Union, in this State, when rebel arms were raised against it, but you were also the foremost champion for peace and pacification in the whole country at large when those rebel arms were laid aside. And now we are glad to listen to your words of wisdom and your counsels of peace. On behalf of the Committee—your personal and political friends—you are tendered this compliment, which you see, in this shape—a spontaneous gathering of the people of this city ; and we welcome you to our circle— the society you have so long adorned—and to the fervent friendship of our hearts.

Mr. Greeley was greeted with renewed applause, and responded as follows:

MR. CHAIRMAN AND GENTLEMEN : It is not your fault, it was not the fault of the Republican party, that the North and South failed to understand each other before they had sacrificed half a million of their best and bravest, burying them in bloody and untimely graves. There never was a time when the representative men of the South were not welcome to express their sentiments and enforce their convictions in any city or in any county of the Free North—in St. Lawrence, in Chautauqua, in Onondaga, or in Washington. There the eminent champions of Southern institutions and Southern principles were always sure to find a patient and respectful hearing. And I firmly believe that if our leading Northern men had been equally free to traverse the South and there advocate boldly and fearlessly the doctrines which the North cherished, our terrible Civil War might have been averted. But such was not our privilege. There was no time while Slavery was dominant in the South that any representative Northern man could have traversed the South, and there boldly and openly asserted the convictions of the North. Never! I recollect distinctly that, in that eventful winter of 1860–61, the correspondents of *The Tribune*, whom we were obliged to keep traversing the South, were uniformly compelled to conceal their business and to deny their views. Brave and true men they were ; but they would have been torn to pieces as if by wolves if they had been known as *Tribune* correspondents. They dared not address their letters to *The Tribune* office ; they had to address them to private individuals in different parts of the City, in order that we might receive them. So, during that momentous winter, I was, for the first time, invited to deliver a lecture in the border city of St. Louis, where there was already a rising Republican party. When I had arrived say within 100 miles of St. Louis—when I was at Springfield, Ill.—I was met by a telegram from leading Republicans in St. Louis, advising me not to come ; my invitation was virtually withdrawn, and I was compelled to return to the North. I was not expected to say one word in St. Louis concerning politics. I was journeying there at the invitation of a literary society to deliver a literary lecture ; yet, since now it is said that at that time *The Tribune* was aiding and inciting the Southern Secession, it may well be remembered that its editor was turned back from a border city of the South, simply because it was proposed to have him deliver a literary lecture before a literary society. I wish it had been otherwise, and that we could have saved the half million of true and brave men whose lives have since been sacrificed, because the North and South failed to understand each other.

Fellow-citizens, two months ago, I, for the first time, received a formal and commanding invitation to visit the extreme South-Western State of our common country. I at first declined peremptorily, believing it impossible for me to spare time to make the journey required. But friends gathered around me ; invitation upon invitation poured in ; and finally leading men of our City—capitalists who were wisely and nobly investing their money in large sums to open up Texas to the world and bring her into free and untrammeled intercourse with the North—these, too, insisted that I should go. They said, " By all means go down to Texas, for in so doing you may render the whole country a great service." There were so many of these urgent appeals to me to go there, that finally I reconsidered my determination and consented to go.

Now, fellow-citizens, I hear it suggested that I went to Texas with too much parade and circumstance ; that I too often was found making speeches from the platforms of cars and from the balconies of hotels, when it would have been much more dignified if I had simply delivered my Address at Houston and returned to you. Well, gentlemen, I fully concur in the justice of that criticism, and should have gladly deferred to it. Though all I did say was said in the hope of promoting a clearer and better understanding between the North and the South, I would have preferred to speak more deliberately and less frequently. But invitations to speak, poured in upon me by rail and by telegraph, were not less pressing than numerous. I could not find time even to acknowledge, much less accept those invitations: so that a New Orleans editor was excusable—

though I trust not justified—in suggesting that my farming, however indifferent, must be rather better than my *breeding*. I answered when I could ; I consented when I could ; and for the rest I kept silence.

And here, fellow-citizens, allow me to make some reply to a kindred criticism from like friendly sources. It is urged, in several journals, that my name has too often been before my countrymen in connection with office ; and I fully concur in that suggestion. If my own choice had been consulted, you know very well that it would not have been so. But I am, to some extent, a public man ; I am identified with party contests and party principles ; and I am known to have reproved and reproached better men than myself that they shrink from public life, leaving important offices to be filled by second-rate men, because first-rate men will not accept them. I have said this too often and too publicly to be able now to shrink entirely out of sight and refuse to do the very thing which I have required of others. So, then, during the last twenty years, if I recollect rightly, my name has been four times before you as a candidate ; once for the Constitutional Convention, in which I for some time earned $6 per day and paid $4 for my board, and twice as a candidate for Congress ; first in the lower district of this City, where I was perfectly certain to be beaten several thousand votes honestly and twice as many dishonestly. Our friends in 1866 saw fit to use my name for Congress in that district where I have worked for the last forty years, where I know a great many people, and where whatever I may have of property or business is located. They put up my name and ran me for Congress, giving me all the Republican votes and some more. So, again last Fall, our friends in the Sixth District saw fit—when I was prostrated by sickness and unable to fulfill engagements to speak made for me by the State Committee—to unite on me as their candidate for Congress ; and they supported me in the face of twenty-eight hundred Democratic majority in the previous contest. I could not speak to them. I could not even visit them ; but I stood in my lot, and shared the fate of my party and its other candidates. Well, gentlemen, there was one other time. In the Fall of 1869, your

State Convention met, nominated a most respectable and acceptable State Ticket and adjourned. My name was not even thought of. But a few days later, consternation was spread by the news that three leading candidates on that ticket had peremptorily declined ; so your State Committee was hastily assembled, and saw fit—being obliged to make a second nomination in order not to let the election go by default and give up the Legislature without a struggle—to fill one of these places on the ticket with my name. I was not consulted. I knew nothing of their purpose. I was absent from the City, and only returned after all had been done, to be told, "Don't say a word; you must stand; that is the end of it;" and I stood.

Now, fellow-citizens, I am not at all grateful to the Republican party for these several nominations. I accepted them, as I accept any public duty that seems to be fairly incumbent upon me; and I did what I could to secure the success of the ticket on which my name was printed. I am very grateful to those generous and gallant Republicans who, in the face of certain defeat, rallied around me and gave me a hearty support, running my name in each case a little ahead of the average of my ticket. For that support, I am grateful; for the several nominations, not at all.

But, gentlemen, the past is past. "Let the dead bury their dead." I am perfectly willing to pass receipts with the Republican party and say that our accounts are now settled and closed. They owe me nothing for being a Republican; I could not have helped being one if I had tried; and, being a Republican, it was in my nature to do all I could for the success of that party which embodied and enforced my personal convictions. I was just as grateful to you as you were to me. I was just as much obliged by your co-operation as you were by mine; and there the matter ends. But for the future, I can say, gentlemen, fully and heartily, that I need no office, I desire no office, and, though I never shall decline any nomination that has not been offered me, I certainly shall seek no office whatever. I am with you and of you; willing to do my part; willing to bear my share of our responsibilities; but I have work enough, reasonable pay for it, sufficient consideration, with too much notoriety; and the more quiet and peaceful my remaining days may be, the better I shall be satisfied.

Now, then, I went to Texas to deliver an Agricultural Address at Houston, and I delivered it. That was my work, and it was done. But, on my way down, a Club of Union soldiers now living in New Orleans pressed me to make a speech to them in their club-room, and I did so. I attempted in that speech to vindicate the right of this nation, this republic, to that vast Louisiana territory purchased by her money, and defended by the blood of her sons; organized into States by her Congress, and so made an integral portion of this American Union. I argued that the southern part of the Mississippi Valley could not possibly wish to be separated from the northern part by two menacing lines of frowning fortresses and hostile custom-houses. I urged—as I always have believed—that never did the people living on the lower Mississippi, in their sober senses, seek to be divorced and alienated from the people of the upper Mississippi; and I affirmed the right of the American people to navigate that great river, from the Rocky Mountains to the Gulf, unembarrassed and unimpeded by any boom across its channel or by any gunboats stationed on it to cause vessels to heave-to for custom-house scrutiny and examination. So I talked, because I so believed.

Then, again, visiting the little city of Columbus, Texas—the only place I did visit on the western side of the Colorado river —I was, about this time of night, while sitting in my hotel, waited upon by a German deputation, who asked me to come over to their club-room and talk to them a little while, they being all loyal Union men. Well, I went over. They had a hastily assembled crowd, and I spoke for half an hour, perhaps, in vindication and explanation of the late great struggles for unity in this country and for unity in Germany; for the defense and protection of these two great nations in their rights of territory and of nationality. I argued, as well as I could, that, though some men honestly believe that our struggle and the triumph therein of the National cause will tend to despotism on this continent, and that some so hold with regard to the German triumph in *their* great struggle, I, on the contrary, believe that the ultimate tendency and result of these two great consummations will be the promotion and advancement of liberal ideas and institutions alike in the Old World and the New.

Well, gentlemen, as I was leaving Texas, a pressing invitation was given me by the Republicans of Galveston to make a speech to them on the last night I spent in their State; and I acceded to their request. I tried before them to vindicate the North against the charges made against her in the South, and to prove that the North did not make war on the South (as too many Southern people still believe she did). I tried to show them that the war was commenced in the South, *by* the South—nay, in Texas itself—by capturing, through treachery, the United States Army, and turning its arms and munitions against the flag and against the integrity of our country; and that, all the way through, we stood virtually on the defensive, against what seemed to me a most indefensible and wanton aggression. I said what I could to vindicate the North from the reproach of malignity—of wishing to oppress or plunder or cripple the South; and tried to make my Southern countrymen believe that we were all Americans, and all together interested in and striving for the prosperity and the growth of our whole widely-extended country. Such was my theme at Galveston.

Well, gentlemen, I have heard it objected that, in my speech at New-Orleans, I asserted that, if there had been Universal Amnesty four years ago, there would have been no Ku-Klux in 1871. I do not think I said exactly that; but I *did* say that I regarded the policy of excluding from office the leading men of the South as a very great mistake, and a very great injury to the National cause and to the Republican party. I said no more than Gen. Sickles had said in substance four years earlier, when he was Military Governor of South Carolina, and declared that he was crippled and enfeebled in his efforts to govern that State well by the fact that her best men, her most intelligent men, her most considerate and conservative men, were not available to him as magistrates, because of an exclusion whereof Andrew Johnson was the author. He said, "I cannot govern South Carolina as well as I could if I were able to choose her best men to help me, instead of her second-best." I am entirely of that conviction. I believe it was a mistake, when you allowed a million Confederates to vote for Members of Congress, to deny them the right to vote for just such men as they preferred. I believe their first-rate men would be safer and more useful in Congress than their second-rate men—better for us and better for their Country. So I argued, because I so believed; and still I say that, if the men were allowed to represent the South who express the sentiment of the South—if the Toombses, Wises, and Wade Hamptons had been allowed to go to Congress, and had been sent there four years ago—the Republican party would have been a great deal stronger and Reconstruction very much further advanced and more certain than it is to-day. Why, gentlemen, whenever one of these extreme men say anything, you see it caught up and carried all over the Union in the very journals that insist on keeping those men out of Congress and in positions where their words carry with them the least possible weight. If their words are so beneficial and pregnant to us, why not let them speak where the whole country will hear them?

But I have been asked, "Are there any Ku-Klux down South?" Yes, gentlemen, there are. They didn't come up to me and tell me they were Ku-Klux very often. They didn't undertake to perform their delicate operations upon me. I should have had very much more respect for them if they had.

I am moved with profound disgust when I think of these men, covering themselves with second-hand calico, masking their faces, arming themselves to the teeth, and riding around to the cabins of poor, harmless negroes, dragging them from their beds, and whipping and maiming them until they are compelled to swear they will never again vote the Republican ticket. I hold that to be a very cowardly procedure as well as a very base one; and I hold it to be the duty of the Government of the Union to oppose with all its power and all its force every such execrable outrage as this. Do you tell me that those men are liable to State laws for the assaults and batteries they have committed? I don't doubt it; but I say they are also in substance and purpose traitors to the Government, rebels against its authority, and the most cowardly, skulking rebels ever known to this or any other country.

I hold our Government bound, by its duty of protecting our

citizens in their fundamental rights, to pass and enforce laws for the extirpation of the execrable Ku-Klux conspiracy; and, if it has not power to do it, then I say our Government is no Government, but a sham. I, therefore, on every proper occasion, advocated and justified the Ku-Klux act. I hold it especially desirable for the South; and, if it does not prove strong enough to effect its purpose, I hope it will be made stronger and stronger.

Why, fellow-citizens, these very men that asked me if I saw any Ku-Klux have themselves read the returns of the last Presidential election in Louisiana, when that State, with 30,000 Black majority on its registers, was made to vote for Seymour and Blair by more than 30,000 majority; counties which had 3,000 negro voters alone giving three, two, one, and in several instances _no_ vote at all, for Grant and Colfax. Now, friends, you and they know perfectly well that this result was secured by terror and by violence; by telling those Black men, " You shall vote for Seymour and Blair, the enemies of your fundamental rights, or you shall not vote at all, or you shall be killed." That was the way Louisiana was made Democratic in 1868; and that is the way that I trust she will never be made so to vote again. Therefore I uphold and justify the Ku-Klux law.

Fellow-citizens, the Ku-Klux are no myth, although they shroud themselves in darkness. They are no flitting ghosts; they are a baneful reality. They have paralyzed the Right of Suffrage in many counties throughout the South, and have carried States that they ought not to have carried; but they are not the only enemies to Republican ascendancy in the South.

There is another influence equally pernicious with theirs, and a great deal more detrimental to the fame and character of the Republican party. I allude to what are known as the "thieving carpet-baggers." Fellow-citizens, do not mistake me. _All_ the Northern men in the South are not thieves. The larger part of them are honest and good men, some of whom stay there at the peril of their lives, because they believe it their duty. Next to the noble and true women who have gone down South to teach Black children how to read—nobler there are not on the earth than these, whom a stupid, malignant, dilapidated aristocracy often sees fit to crowd into negro hovels to live, not allowing them to enter any White society because they are teaching negro children—next to these, who rank as the noblest women in the South, are the honest and worthy Northern men, who, in the face of social proscription and general obloquy and scorn, stand firmly by the Republican cause.

There was a most urgent and special necessity for rigid economy in the reconstructed States of the South, even aside from their impoverishment by war and the disruption of their industry by peace. For despotic government has this advantage over free, that its agencies are apt to be simple and cheap. The old Slave governments of the South were thoroughly aristocratic, and they were very rarely corrupt or prodigal. The planters paid most of the taxes; they decided who should be legislators; and they did not abide jobbers. Legislative stealing was almost an unknown art among them. Then they had no public support of the poor; each subsisted, after a fashion, his own used-up slaves. The Poor Whites lived or died as they might; and, except for the Whites of two or three great cities, there were no public schools: and this made government cheap and taxes light.

With Emancipation, came a great change. There was an urgent demand for free schools, and the school-houses had to be built, to begin with; for the public support of paupers, White and Black, and there were no alms-houses; and so with many public institutions. Just when the people were poorest, they were required to bear the heaviest public expense, though only accustomed to the lightest. Dissatisfaction and complaint were inevitable; but every effort should have been made, every nerve strained, to mitigate them by vigorous economy. I regret to say that the reverse was the course pursued in some States by men who rode into power on the artillery wagons of the Union, under the flag of Emancipation.

The public is often heedlessly unjust. Let a Government have 10,000 official subordinates in power, of whom 9,900 are honest and true men who do their duty faithfully, while barely 100 are robbers and swindlers, the public will hear a great deal more about the 100 robbers than about the 9,900 true men. The 100 stand out in the public eye—they are always doing something which exposes them to the scornful gaze of the multitude- while the honest and true men pass along silent and unobserved, and nothing is said, very little is *thought*, of them. All attention is concentrated upon the 100, who are defaulting, and stealing, and forging, and running away.

Well, gentlemen, the thieving carpet-baggers are a mournful fact; they do exist there, and I have seen them. They are fellows who crawled down South in the track of our armies, generally at a very safe distance in the rear; some of them on sutlers' wagons; some bearing cotton permits; some of them looking sharply to see what might turn up; and they remain there. They at once ingratiated themselves with the Blacks, simple, credulous, ignorant men, very glad to welcome and to follow any Whites who professed to be the champions of their rights. Some of them got elected Senators, others Representatives, some Sheriffs, some Judges, and so on. And there they stand, right in the public eye, stealing and plundering, many of them with both arms around negroes, and their hands in their rear pockets, seeing if they cannot pick a paltry dollar out of them; and the public looks at them, does not regard the honest Northern men, but calls every "carpet-bagger" a thief, which is not the truth by a good deal. But these fellows—many of them long-faced, and with eyes rolled up, are greatly concerned for the education of the Blacks, and for the salvation of their souls. "Let us pray," they say; but they spell pray with an "e," and, thus spelled, they obey the apostolic injunction to "pray without ceasing."

Fellow-citizens, the time has been, and still is, when it was perilous to be known as a Republican or an Abolitionist in the South; but it never called the blush of shame to any man's cheek to be so called, until these thieving carpet-baggers went there —never! They got into the Legislatures; they went to issuing State-bonds; they pretended to use them in aid of railroads and other improvements. But the improvements were not made, and the bonds stuck in the issuers' pockets. That is the pity of it.

"Well," some say, "you have just such thieves at the North." Yes, we have—too many of them! But the South was already impoverished—was bankrupt—without money, without thrift, almost without food; and these fellows went there robbing and swindling when there was very little to steal, and taking the last ten-cent shin-plaster off of dead men's eyes. They were recognized by the late aristocracy not merely as thieves but as enemies. Says Byron's Greek minstrel,

> " A tyrant—but our masters then
> Were still at least our countrymen."

Thus we regard the men who annually rob us at Albany, at Trenton, and at Harrisburg. They do not carry their plunder out of the State when they get any. These fellows do ! The South was not merely beaten in the late contest; she was profoundly astonished by the result. Her people have not fairly got over their amazement at their defeat; and what they see of us are these thieves, who represent the North to their jaundiced vision, and, representing it, they disgrace it. They are the greatest obstacle to the triumph and permanent ascendancy of Republican principles at the South, and as such I denounce them.

" Well, then, do you justify the Ku-Klux ?" I am asked. Justify them *in what ?* If they should choose to catch a hundred or two of these thieves, place them tenderly astride of rails, and bear them quietly and peaceably across the Ohio, I should of course condemn the act, as I condemn all violence; but the tears live in a very small onion that would water all my sorrow for them. But they do nothing like that; they don't go for the thieving carpet-baggers; but they skulk around wretched cabins, and drag out inoffensive negroes, to lash and torture them, merely for standing up for their rights as men. For this, I do execrate the Ku-Klux. I say they are a disgrace to Southern Chivalry; and they would be drummed out of the South if there were any true Chivalry there.

But it has been reported very widely that at Vicksburg, addressing a mainly Southern audience, and trying to awaken in them something of the sentiment of nationality and patriotism which burns in a true American bosom, I said that I trusted the time would come when we of the North would honor Lee and Stonewall Jackson. I did not say that. What I did say was that I hoped the time would come when Americans North, as well as Americans South, would feel a just pride in the soldierly achievements and military character of Lee and Stonewall Jack-son, just as I trusted the late Confederates would learn to feel a patriotic pride in the achievements of Grant and Sherman, and Thomas and Sheridan. I said that, or something very like it. Possibly, you are not willing to go so far as that. Very well, there is no hurry. Take your time; I can wait. Yes, I can wait.

THE NEW DEPARTURE.

But, gentlemen, my voice fails, yet I want to say a few words about the New Departure. When men are in a bad fix, I reckon they had better depart from it; and I fully justify those Demo-crats who have determined to depart from the foolish old busi-ness of running their heads against a stone wall. If I were there, I should depart; and I think it well for them to do it; and, since they do it, I am not inclined to criticise the manner too severely, nor to judge them too harshly. I have made a rule for some time never to conjure up a bad motive for a good action. They are where they ought not to be; they propose to depart; and I think they should.

Our Ohio friends do not take quite so charitable a view of the New Departure as I do. They say there was a particularly rough character once, who was noted for violating the Sabbath, among other bad deeds. But finally he became converted, "got reli-gion," and joined the church. All right. One day, a gentleman came along and asked a neighbor of his, "Do you see any great change in Nokes since he joined the church?" "O yes, very great; he used to go out chopping Sunday mornings with his ax swung over his shoulder; now he carries it under his coat." Gentlemen, I am very glad that the Democratic party has taken off its shoulder the ax which it has wielded so many years in deadly hostility to the rights of the Colored race. I am glad even if it has put it under its coat; but I hope it will think better of it and put it back into the wood-house, and meet the Blacks with open hands, saying, "We are going to treat each of you just as you shall deserve to be treated, no matter what is the color of your skin." I do believe they mean hereafter to wear their Democracy somewhat more than skin-deep. At any rate, I shall urge and encourage them to do so.

Fellow-citizens: I would not make too much of this New Departure. I do not understand these gentlemen even to profess any penitence for their past warfare against the Equal Rights of Men. I don't understand them even to promise that they will never renew that warfare. I only understand them as pledged to this extent: They admit that the three Republican amendments to the Federal Constitution are now a part of that Constitution, and, while they shall remain there, they must be obeyed. That I understand to be the extent of the New Departure; and I deem it worth a great deal. So long as they admit that these Amendments are in, I shall feel pretty sure that they are not likely to get them out. I shall rest content that the rights of all men, being citizens of the United States, are safe under the guaranties of the Federal Constitution.

Twenty-five years ago, I stood at the polls of the XIXth Ward of this city all one rainy, chill November day, peddling ballots for Equal Suffrage. I got many Whigs to take them, but not one Democrat. Again in 1860—not eleven years ago—I again stood at my poll all day, and handed out the same kind of vote; and I do not remember that a single Democrat took one. Some Republicans, even, would not take them; but no Democrat would.

I believe in human progress. I believe that men are rather wiser and better to-day than they were twelve years ago; and here is proof of it. It is not two years since our Democratic State Legislature withdrew the consent given by its Republican predecessors to the XVth Amendment, and, by a party vote, so far as New York could do it, they tried to defeat that amendment. Now, we have a New Departure. Was it not high time? I think it was.

Fellow-citizens: I am weary, weary, of this sterile strife concerning the fundamental principles of republican institutions. I am tired of trying to teach Democrats the A, B, C's of Democracy. I rejoice to know that they have taken a New Departure; and I tell you that, when they have once taken it, it will be a great deal harder to get back to the old ground than to go on. Some one says, "Isn't it going to put the Republicans out of power?" I cannot tell. Immediately, I think not. Mr. Burke well says: "Confidence is a plant of slow growth;" and I think it will take some time for the people to realize that the Democrats mean to uphold Equal Rights—some time for their own folks to realize it—a great deal longer to make any Black man believe that they mean it.

I don't anticipate any sudden change in the relative strength of parties, because of the New Departure. Ultimately, I think, it will strengthen the Democrats. "Then," one says, "*you* will go out of power" Yes, we shall some time, no doubt. If it were to be my fate to go out this moment, and every year of my life thereafter to be in the minority, prostrate and powerless, I should still thank God, most humbly and heartily, that He allowed me to live in an age, and to be a part of the generation, that witnessed the downfall and extinction of American Slavery.

Fellow-citizens: I trust the day is not distant wherein, putting behind us the things that concern the Past, we shall defer to that grand old injunction of the Bible: "Speak to the children of Israel that they go forward." I am weary of fighting over issues that ought to be dead—that logically *were* dead years ago. When Slavery died, I thought that we ought speedily to have ended all that grew out of it by Universal Amnesty and Impartial Suffrage. I think so still; and that if the Democratic party shall concede Impartial Suffrage, the Republican party will concede Universal Amnesty; if not, it will have a *very* short lease of power. So, then, friends, I summon you all, Republicans and Democrats, to prepare for the new issues and new struggles that visibly open before us. In the times not far distant, I trust we shall consider questions mainly of industrial policy—questions of national advancement—questions concerning the best means whereby our different parties may, through co-operation, or through rivalry, strive to promote the prosperity, the happiness, and the true glory of the American people. To that contest I invite you. For that contest I would prepare you. And so, trusting that the bloodshed in the past will be a sufficient atonement for the sins of the past, and that we are entering upon a grand New Departure, not for one party only, but for the whole country—a departure from strife to harmony, from devastation to construction, from famine and desolation to peace and plenty—I bid you, friends and fellow-citizens, an affectionate good-night.

LETTERS OF ACCEPTANCE.

—o—

LETTER OF ACCEPTANCE OF THE LIBERAL REPUBLICAN NOMINATION FOR PRESIDENT.

NEW YORK, May 20, 1872.

GENTLEMEN : I have chosen not to acknowledge your letter of the 3d inst. until I could learn how the work of your Convention was received in all parts of our great country, and judge whether that work was approved and ratified by the mass of our fellow-citizens. Their response has from day to day reached me through telegrams, letters, and the comments of journalists independent of official patronage and indifferent to the smiles and frowns of power. The number and character of these unconstrained, unpurchased, unsolicited utterances satisfy me that the movement which found expression at Cincinnati has received the stamp of public approval, and been hailed by a majority of our countrymen as the harbinger of a better day for the Republic.

I do not misinterpret this approval as especially complimentary to myself, nor even to the chivalrous and justly-esteemed gentleman with whose name I thank your Convention for associating mine. I receive and welcome it as a spontaneous and deserved tribute to that admirable Platform of principles, wherein your Convention so tersely, so lucidly, so forcibly, set forth the convictions which impelled and the purposes which guided its course — a Platform which, casting behind it the wreck and rubbish of worn-out contentions and by-gone feuds, embodies in fit and few words the needs and aspirations of To-Day. Though thousands stand ready to condemn your every act, hardly a syllable of criticism or cavil has been aimed at your Platform, of which the substance may be fairly epitomized as follows :

I. All the political rights and franchises which have been

acquired through our late bloody convulsion must and shall be guaranteed, maintained, enjoyed, respected, evermore.

II.   All the political rights and franchises which have been lost through that convulsion should and must be promptly restored and re-established, so that there shall be henceforth no proscribed class and no disfranchised caste within the limits of our Union, whose long estranged people shall re-unite and fraternize upon the broad basis of Universal Amnesty and Impartial Suffrage.

III.   That, subject to our solemn Constitutional obligation to maintain the equal rights of all citizens, our policy should aim at local self-government, and not at centralization ; that the civil authority should be supreme over the military ; that the writ of habeas corpus should be jealously upheld as the safeguard of personal freedom ; that the individual citizen should enjoy the largest liberty consistent with public order ; and that there shall be no Federal subversion of the internal polity of the several States and Municipalities, but that each shall be left free to enforce the rights and promote the well-being of its inhabitants by such means as the judgment of its own people shall prescribe.

IV.   There shall be a real and not merely a simulated Reform in the Civil Service of the Republic ; to which end it is indispensable that the chief dispenser of its vast official patronage shall be shielded from the main temptation to use his power selfishly by a rule inexorably forbidding and precluding his reelection.

V.   That the raising of Revenue, whether by Tariff or otherwise, shall be recognized and treated as the People's immediate business, to be shaped and directed by them through their Representatives in Congress, whose action thereon the President must neither overrule by his veto, attempt to dictate, or presume to punish, by bestowing office only on those who agree with him or withdrawing it from those who do not.

VI.   That the Public Lands must be sacredly reserved for occupation and acquisition by cultivators, and not recklessly squandered on the projectors of Railroads for which our people have no present need, and the premature construction of which is annually plunging us into deeper and deeper abysses of foreign indebtedness.

VII. That the achievement of these grand purposes of universal beneficence is expected and sought at the hands of all who approve them, irrespective of past affiliations.

VIII. That the public faith must at all hazards be maintained, and the National credit preserved.

IX. That the patriotic devotedness and inestimable services of our fellow-citizens who, as soldiers or sailors, upheld the flag and maintained the unity of the Republic shall ever be gratefully remembered and honorably requited.

These propositions, so ably and forcibly presented in the Platform of your Convention, have already fixed the attention and commanded the assent of a large majority of our countrymen, who joyfully adopt them, as I do, as the bases of a true, beneficent National Re-construction—of a New Departure from jealousies, strifes, and hates, which have no longer adequate motive or even plausible pretext, into an atmosphere of Peace, Fraternity, and Mutual Good Will. In vain do the drill-sergeants of decaying organizations flourish menacingly their truncheons and angrily insist that the files shall be closed and straightened; in vain do the whippers-in of parties once vital because rooted in the vital needs of the hour protest against straying and bolting, denounce men nowise their inferiors as traitors and renegades, and threaten them with infamy and ruin. I am confident that the American People have already made your cause their own, fully resolved that their brave hearts and strong arms shall bear it on to triumph. In this faith, and with the distinct understanding that, if elected, I shall be the President not of a party, but of the whole People, I accept your nomination, in the confident trust that the masses of our countrymen, North and South, are eager to clasp hands across the bloody chasm which has too long divided them—forgetting that they have been enemies in the joyful consciousness that they are and must henceforth remain brethren.

Yours, gratefully,   HORACE GREELEY.

To Hon. CARL SCHURZ, President; Hon. GEORGE W. JULIAN, Vice-President; and Messrs. Wm. E. McLean, John G. Davidson, J. H. Rhodes, Secretaries of the National Convention of the Liberal Republicans of the United States.

LETTER OF ACCEPTANCE OF THE DEMOCRATIC NOMINATION FOR THE PRESIDENCY.

NEW YORK, July 18, 1872.

GENTLEMEN: Upon mature deliberation, it seems fit that I should give to your letter of the 10th inst. some further and fuller response than the hasty, unpremeditated words in which I acknowledged and accepted your nomination at our meeting on the 12th.

That your Convention saw fit to accord its highest honor to one who had been prominently and pointedly opposed to your party in the earnest and sometimes angry controversies of the last forty years, is essentially noteworthy. That many of you originally preferred that the Liberal Republicans should present another candidate for President, and would more readily have united with us in the support of Adams or Trumbull, Davis or Brown, is well known. I owe my adoption at Baltimore wholly to the fact that I had already been nominated at Cincinnati, and that a concentration of forces upon any new ticket had been proved impracticable. Gratified as I am at your concurrence in the Cincinnati nominations, certain as I am that you would not have thus concurred had you not deemed me upright and capable, I find nothing in the circumstance calculated to inflame vanity or nourish self-conceit.

But that your Convention saw fit, in adopting the Cincinnati ticket, to re-affirm the Cincinnati Platform, is to me a source of the profoundest satisfaction. That body was constrained to take this important step by no party necessity, real or supposed. It might have accepted the candidates of the Liberal Republicans upon grounds entirely its own, or it might have presented them (as the first Whig National Convention did Harrison and Tyler) without adopting any platform whatever. That it chose to plant itself deliberately, by a vote nearly unanimous, upon the fullest and clearest enunciation of principles which are at once incontestably Republican and emphatically

Democratic, gives trustworthy assurance that a new and more auspicious era is dawning upon our long-distracted country.

Some of the best years and best efforts of my life were devoted to a struggle against Chattel Slavery—a struggle none the less earnest or arduous because respect for constitutional obligations constrained me to act for the most part on the defense—in resistance to the diffusion rather than in direct efforts for the extinction of Human Bondage. Throughout most of those years my vision was uncheered, my exertions were rarely animated, by even so much as a hope that I should live to see my country peopled by freemen alone. The affirmance by your Convention of the Cincinnati Platform is a most conclusive proof that not merely is Slavery abolished but that its spirit is extinct—that, despite the protests of a respectable but isolated few, there remains among us no party and no formidable interest which regrets the overthrow or desires the re-establishment of Human Bondage, whether in letter or in spirit. I am thereby justified in my hope and trust that the first century of American Independence will not close before the grand elemental truths on which its righfulness was based by Jefferson and the Continental Congress of '76 will no longer be regarded as "glittering generalities," but will have become the universally accepted and honored foundations of our political fabric.

I demand the prompt application of those principles to our existing condition. Having done what I could for the complete emancipation of Blacks, I now insist on the full enfranchisement of all my White countrymen. Let none say that the ban has just been removed from all but a few hundred elderly gentlemen, to whom eligibility to office can be of little consequence. My view contemplates not the hundreds proscribed but the millions who are denied the right to be ruled and represented by the men of their unfettered choice. Proscription were absurd if these did not wish to elect the very men whom they are forbidden to choose.

I have a profound regard for the people of that New-England wherein I was born, in whose common schools I was taught. I rank no other people above them in intelligence, capacity, and moral worth. But while they do many things well, and some admirably, there is one thing which I am sure they cannot wisely or safely undertake, and that is the selection, for States remote from and unlike their own, of the persons by whom those States shall be represented in Congress. If they *could* do this to good purpose, then republican institutions were unfit, and aristocracy the only true political system.

Yet what have we recently witnessed? Zebulon B. Vance, the unquestioned choice of a large majority of the present Legislature of North Carolina—a majority backed by a majority of the people who voted at its election—refused the seat in the Federal Senate to which he was fairly chosen, and the Legislature thus constrained to choose another in his stead or leave the State unrepresented for years. The votes of New-England thus deprived North Carolina of the Senator of her choice, and compelled her to send another in his stead—another who, in our late contest, was, like Vance, a rebel, and a fighting rebel, but who had not served in Congress before the war as Vance had, though the latter remained faithful to the Union till after the close of his term. I protest against the disfranchisement of a State — presumptively, of a number of States — on grounds so narrow and technical as this. The fact that the same Senate which refused Vance his seat proceeded to remove his disabilities after that seat had been filled by another only serves to place in stronger light the indignity to North Carolina, and the arbitrary, capricious tyranny which dictated it. I thank you, gentlemen, that my name is to be conspicuously associated with yours in a determined effort to render Amnesty complete and universal, in spirit as well as in letter. Even defeat in such a cause would leave no sting, while triumph would rank with those victories which no blood reddens and which evoke no tears but those of gratitude and joy.

Gentlemen, your platform, which is also mine, assures me that Democracy is not henceforth to stand for one thing and Republicanism for another, but that those terms are to mean in politics, as they always have meant in the dictionary, substantially one and the same thing—namely, Equal Rights, regardless of creed, or clime, or color. I hail this as a genuine New Departure from outworn feuds and meaningless contentions in the direction of

Progress and Reform. Whether I shall be found worthy to bear the standard of the great Liberal movement which the American People have inaugurated is to be determined not by words but by deeds. With me if I steadily advance, over me if I falter, its grand array moves on to achieve for our country her glorious, beneficent destiny.

I remain, gentlemen, yours,

HORACE GREELEY.

To the Hon. JAMES R. DOOLITTLE, Chairman of the Convention, and F. W. Sykes, John C. Macabe, and others, Committee.

---o---

CAMPAIGN SPEECHES.

—

AT PORTLAND, MAINE, AUGUST 14TH, 1872.

LADIES AND GENTLEMEN: It is certainly true that, throughout the course of my life, so far as I have been connected with public affairs, I have struggled, with such capacity as God has given me, for, first, impartial and universal liberty; second, for the unity and greatness of our common country; third, and by no means least, when the former ends were attained, for early and hearty reconciliation and peace among our countrymen. For these ends I have struggled, and I hope the issue of the third is not doubtful.

I thoroughly comprehend that no personal consideration has drawn together this vast assembly. Other, higher, and grander considerations have collected you around me to-day. Mr. Chairman, it is a part of the unwritten law of our country that a candidate for President may not make speeches in vindication and commendation of the principles whereon he is supported, the measures which his election is intended to promote, though a candidate for Vice-President is under no such inhibition. I not merely acquiesce in the restriction; I recognize and affirm its propriety. the temptation to misreport and misrepresent a candidate for the higher post is so great, the means of circulating such perversions among people who will never see a word of their refutation are so vast, that a candidate has no moral right to subject his friends to the perils he must brave, if not invite, by taking a part in the canvass. Yet there is a truth to be uttered in behalf of those who have placed me before the American people in my present attitude, which does them such honor that I claim the privilege of stating it here and now.

NO OFFICES PROMISED TO ANY ONE.

This is the truth : No person has ever made the fact that he proposed to support, or actually did support, my nomination, whether at Cincinnati, at Baltimore, or in the action which resulted in sending delegates to either Convention, the basis of a claim to office at my hands. No one who favored my nomination before either convention has sought office at my hands, either for himself or any one else, ; nor has any one suggested to me that I might strengthen myself as a candidate by promising to appoint any one to any important office whatever. In a very few instances,—less than a dozen, I am sure—certain of the smaller fry of politicians have, since my double nomination, hinted to me by letter that I might increase my chance of election by promising a Post-Office or some other place to my volunteer correspondents respectively. I have not usually responded to these overtures, but I now give a general notice that, should I be elected, I will consider the claims of these untimely aspirants after those of the more modest and reticent shall have been fully satisfied.

In two or three instances, I have been asked to say whether I would or would not, if elected, confine my appointments to Republicans. I answer these by pointing to that plank of the Cincinnati platform wherein all who concur in the principles therein set forth are cordially invited to participate in their establishment and vindication. I never yet heard of a man who invited his neighbors to help him raise a house, and proceeded to kick them out of it so soon as the roof was fairly over his head. For my own part, I recognize every honest man who approves and adheres to the Cincinnati platform as my political brother, and as such fully entitled to my confidence and friendly regard.

NO PLEDGE TO THE SOUTH SAVE HIS RECORD ON AMNESTY.

One other point demands a word. Those adverse to me ask what pledges I have given to those lately hostile to the Union to secure their favor and support. I answer: No man or woman in all the South ever asked of me, either directly or through another, any other pledge than is given in all my acts and words from the hour of Lee's surrender down to this moment. No Southern man has ever hinted to me an expectation, hope, or wish, that the Rebel debt, whether Confederate or State, should be assumed or paid by the Union; and no Southern man who could be elected to a legislature or made colonel of a militia regiment ever suggested the pensioning of Rebel soldiers, or any of them, even as a remote possibility. All who nominated me were perfectly aware that I had upheld and justified Federal legislation to suppress the Ku-Klux conspiracy and outrages, though I had long ago insisted, as strenuously as I now do, that complete amnesty and general oblivion of the bloody, hateful past would do more for the suppression and utter extinction of such outrages than all the force bills and suspensions of habeas corpus ever devised by man. Wrong and crime must be suppressed and punished, but far wiser and nobler is the legislation, the policy, by which they are prevented.

From those who support me in the South I have heard but one demand—Justice; one desire—Reconciliation. They wish to be heartily reunited and at peace with the North, on any terms which do not involve a surrender of their manhood. They ask that they shall be regarded and treated by the Federal authorities as citizens, not culprits, so long as they obey and uphold every law consistent with equity and right. They desire a rule which, alike for White or Black, shall encourage industry and thrift, and discourage rapacity and villainy. They cherish a joyful hope, in which I fully concur, that, between the 5th of November and the 4th of March next, quite a number of the

Governors and other dignitaries who, in the abused names of republicanism and loyalty, have for years been piling debts and taxes upon their war-wasted States will follow the wholesome example of Bullock of Georgia, and seek the shades of private life—the darker and denser those shades the better for themselves and for mankind. And the hope that my election may hasten this much desired hegira of the thieving carpet-baggers has reconciled to the necessity of supporting me many who would otherwise have hesitated, and probably refused.

THE NATIONAL VERDICT FOR REFORM.

Fellow-citizens: The deposed and partially exiled Tammany Ring has stolen about $30,000,000 from the City of New-York. That was a most gigantic robbery, and hurled its contrivers and abettors from power and splendor to impotence and infamy; but the thieving carpet-baggers have stolen at least thrice this amount—stolen it from the already impoverished and needy; and they still flaunt their prosperous villainy in the high places of the land, and are addressed as Honorable and Excellency. I think I hear a voice from the honest people of all the States declaring that this iniquity shall be gainful and insolent no longer, at farthest, than to the 4th of March next. By that time these criminals will have heard a national verdict pronounced that will cause them to "fold their tents like the Arabs, and silently steal away;" and that, I trust, will be the end of their stealing at the cost of the good name of the country and the well being of her people.

AT PITTSBURGH, PENN., SEPT. 19TH, 1872.

FELLOW-CITIZENS: The wise king says, There is a time for war and a time for peace. The city of Pittsburgh has recently witnessed a rehearsal of the pomp and pageantry, the blazonry and circumstance, of civil war. A very large number of men were collected here at a vast expense with the single purpose of rekindling the bitterness and hatred, the animosities and antipathies, the fears and exultations, of civil war for the advantage of a political party. I take you to witness that the greater portion of the journals of Pittsburgh, as well as the orators on that occasion, have been trying their best to make our people hate each other for the sake of a partisan advantage. A stranger who was reading the journals of Pittsburgh for the last few days would imagine that we were at war, and their purpose was to revive and to exasperate the hatred and animosity of civil war in order to intensify and invigorate their side of the conflict. They talk about Rebels and traitors. Fellow-citizens, are we never to be done with this? We demanded of our adversaries in the great civil war that they surrender their arms and go to their homes. They surrendered them. We demanded that they abandon Slavery, and they abandoned Slavery. We demanded that they enfranchise the Blacks, and the Blacks were enfranchised. None but White men now stand disfranchised on the soil of our country. We demanded that they stipulate that the emancipated slaves shall not be paid for, and that the Rebel debt shall never be paid, whether by the Union, or by the States, and they assented to that. So far as I can see, every single demand made on the part of the loyal States and the loyal people has been fully complied with on the part of those lately in rebellion. Every thing has been done that we asked; everything has been conceded; and still they tell us, " Why, we want them to repent." Have they not brought forth works meet for repentance?

Coming together in a solemn Convention, the representatives of that Southern people have given their assent to the platform of the Cincinnati Convention, which was the most intense, the most complete Republican platform that had ever been presented by any National Convention whatever. All this being done, we are told by the gentlemen who met here: " All this is mockery, all this is fraud, you don't mean anything by it;" and the cry goes on, " Rebels and traitors, rebels and traitors," with denunciation and proscription, the same as ever. Four years ago, in the Republican National Convention, it was declared that this proscription shall speedily cease. Four years have passed, and still it is maintained. There are this day thousands of people in Arkansas alone—the most intelligent, the most responsible people of that State—forbidden to exercise the right of suffrage—forbidden exclusively by the party that meets here and shouts for Grant and Wilson. Nobody else asks for proscription. No other party asks that any human being should stand proscribed on our soil for a rebellion that ceased seven and a half years ago—no party, no men of any party but this, that held a great military parade here this week in order to further and further alienate the hearts of the American people from each other. They hold it essential to their triumph that hatred should continue, that distrust, suspicion, and alienation, should continue. Do what you will, do what you may, they are determined not to be satisfied. Now, fellow-citizens, it is not enough that those who fought against the Union should be proscribed; those of us who stood for it are equally denounced, if we do not happen to agree with them in our present politics. Here stands one who is charged by them with being a Secessionist. Could that be true, fellow-citizens? Look the facts in the face:

When Lincoln had been elected, and this conspiracy for secession began to develop, we Republicans were told by some of our own men, and still more by those out of our circle, " You must back out of your Republicanism; you must surrender your opposition to the extension of Slavery, or consent to a great civil war." This they said was the only alternative—bloodshed and devastation over the whole country, or you shall surrender the principles on which you have just carried the election. I was one of those who said, " No, there is no such alternative." I denied that the great majority of the Southern people were against the Union. I demanded that there should be an open, free discussion, that the Southern people might have an honest, unterrified, unconstrained vote, and, if they approved, if the people of the South said they wanted disunion, I would consent to it. I knew they would not. I knew that the great majority of the Southern people would have voted, as they actually did vote that Winter—not for Secession, but for clinging to the Union. And now, to-day, if the nation were thus imperiled, and there were just two modes of saving it, to trust to the chances of civil war or to the result of a free vote by the Southern people, I would very greatly prefer to risk the latter chance rather than the former. For, fellow-citizens, they do greatly misunderstand and malign this American people, when they assume that, in cold blood, before there had been any clash of arms, the people in the South, any more than the people in the North, desired disunion.

In its inception, in its origin, the great masses of those who consented to this Secession movement meant nothing by it but to make us consent to the extension of Slavery. That was their purpose; and that purpose I did my best to resist and defeat. Well, the war is ended. I think it ought to be ended. We had a great, a terrible, a bloody, a destructive civil war. Our success was perfect. The defeat of our adversaries was more complete than any other recorded in history. They have suffered much; they have conceded all. Cannot we afford to be magnanimous at last? But, fellow-citizens, they say that the Southern people may vote. Some of them may; but the instant they do vote the cry is raised: "See how those fellows vote! You must vote the other way." Is that an election? Or is it only the spirit of war in another aspect?

Fellow-citizens, you belong to one of the great hives of American industry. I plead here for peace and reconciliation as the interest especially of this busy, prosperous, energetic people. I have always sympathized with Pittsburgh. I have rejoiced in her prosperity. I have wondered at and admired her magnificent growth. You surely know that no place on this continent has been dearer to me than Pittsburgh. There has been no spot in whose prosperity I have more heartily rejoiced than this, because I believed her prosperity was firmly linked and bound up with the prosperity and growth of our whole country. Now I appeal to her business men, I appeal to her merchants, I appeal to her manufacturers, to stop this war. It has gone on long enough. You cannot afford to teach a part of your countrymen to hate you, to feel that your success, your greatness, is identical with their humiliation. People of Pittsburgh, I ask you to take a generous part in this work of reconciling your countrymen to each other. I ask you to take the hand held out to you by your Southern brethren in their adoption of the Cincinnati platform, by those who were our enemies, but are again our countrymen. I ask you to grasp that hand and say, " Brothers, we differed; we fought. The war is ended. Let us again be fellow-countrymen, and forget that we have been enemies." Friends and fellow-citizens, I bid you good-night.

---o---

AT CINCINNATI, OHIO, SEPTEMBER 20TH, 1872.

ADDRESS BEFORE THE EXPOSITION.

A SOLITARY soldier, equipped and plumed for war, is not an imposing spectacle. Surrounded by the agencies and incidents of Peace, he seems incongruous and fantastic—a relic of some by-gone age—a representative of a social order long since fallen into decay. But mass one hundred thousand such as he into an army, carefully ranked, thoroughly disciplined, and supplied with all the requisite enginery of defacement and destruction, and its majestic power, its terrible significance, are plain even to the awed, admiring gaze of childhood.

So the work of the lonely pioneer, buried deep in the primitive forest, wherein his rude log cabin has just been thrown up, around which he is slowly beating back the empire of shade and savageism by dint of ax and fire, seems petty and casual when regarded by itself ; but could we, from some commanding hight, some ship of the air, look down at once upon the whole body of pioneers at their daily labor, we should recognize in their desultory array the skirmish line of advancing civilization, the harbinger of intelligence, comfort, thrift, humanity, religion. The wolf, the bear, the serpent, perishing or vanishing as the pioneer host slowly, irregularly, yet inexorably, moves on, are now seen to be types of a moral order, which civilized society is destined to supplant and replace.

I take this to be one chief end of Industrial Expositions, to make the workman realize the essential value and true dignity of his work. The infinite division and subdivision of labor exacted by modern invention and machinery are calculated to obscure these inspiring considerations. The artisan or artificer devotes his days to making, not a whole watch, but a wheel or pinion—at most, a spring. He may give his life to watch-making, yet never see one watch perfected, as the most skillful and valued worker in a factory may spend his years in setting up looms or compounding dyes and never make one yard of cloth. The Exposition is needed to inspirit each with a thorough, cheering consciousness of what has been effected by the combined labors and efforts of all.

I gazed with interest on the opening of the first World's Exposition in London, twenty-one years ago. Apparently, superficially, the procession of Queen and Princes, of Dukes and Garter-Knights, in honor of the efforts and products of smiths and weavers, smacked of grimace and affectation. How could they truly honor manual industry who had all their lives shunned it as degradation? And yet that parade of feudal trappings and gewgaws *did* honor productive labor, however blindly and even insincerely. No prophecy of the auspicious day when swords shall be beaten into ploughshares and spears into pruning-hooks was ever clearer than that procession of royalty and aristocracy, of plenipotentiaries and gold-sticks-in waiting, to usher in the display of all nations' products in the domain of Art and Industry at the Crystal Palace in Hyde Park, April 30, 1851.

Our work too generally compels us to look down—to fix our gaze on something petty and minute—to shut out the view of stars and mountains, and concentrate our thoughts on bits of metal or a few pounds of Wool or Cotton. We work with bowed heads and bent frames; we need occasionally to straighten up, to expand our chests with full inspirations of the free air of heaven. We need to realize that Work has other and nobler ends than the highly needful replenishment of basket and store —that its best result is the skillful, modest, upright, faithful large-souled workman. Such is the lesson which this Exhibition is teaching to tens of thousands. The material recompense of labor is indispensable; but the honor paid to the achievement of the highly deserving workman is beyond and above this as the sky is above the earth.

Nor is this all. I see in every great Exposition an incitement to that Industrial Co-operation which seems to me, even though distant and difficult, nevertheless inevitable. Strikes for high wages, strikes for shorter days, lock-outs, trades unions, all suggest to me the radical vice of our mode of determining the workman's compensation. He should manifestly be paid in proportion to the value or excellence of his product; he is oftener paid in proportion to the time he manages to consume in creating or fashioning it. Hence eye-service, dawdling, and the production of fabrics or wares that look well, but fail to wear or serve well. This cannot always endure.

You need not tell me that any essential change is difficult; for I know already that all genuine reforms are exceedingly so—that they are only achieved through suffering, and sacrifice, and after repeated failures. You do not frighten me by asserting that Co-operative Industry involves complicated, troublesome account-keeping; for I know that Despotism is the simplest form of government, and Slavery requires much less reckoning, and bargaining, and book keeping, than any system of Free Labor. Do not ask me to say just how Co-operation is to be reduced to practice, for I cannot tell. That there will be experiments, and mistakes, and failures, in the earlier, tentative stages of the reform, I foresee; that rogues and charlatans will seize upon it in the hope of thereby promoting their own selfish ends; I clearly see all this; but I think I discern a brighter vista stretching away beyond it. Now that the Republican theory has been fully applied to government, and proved a success, after making all due allowance for drawbacks, I believe its application to Industry is only a question of time—that the workers who make clothes, or shoes, or whatever else may minister to human sustenance and comfort, will learn how to do this as partners rather than hirelings, dividing equitably and wholly the proceeds, instead of accepting a share of them as wages. Years, if not ages, may yet be required to perfect the safeguards whereby the co-operation of workers alone may be rendered practicable, beneficent and secure; and yet I feel assured that the day will come in which he who wants a house built in Cincinnati will apply to a corporation of practical builders, organized like any bank or railroad company, bargain with the agent of that corporation as he now does with a master-builder or firm, and have his work done at least as well and as reasonably as now, while the stipulated price will be wholly and fairly apportioned among those who have earned it. If you ask, "Where is the capital to be had?" I point to the hundreds of millions now deposited in Savings Banks, whereof at least two-thirds belong to working men and women, and say "There it is!" The depositors are careful, saving, thrifty persons, who will not risk their scanty hoards in rash experiments—(as, indeed, they should not)—but whenever it shall have been demonstrated that they may as safely invest in co-operative undertakings as lend to those by whom the Laboring Class are now hired and paid, there will be no lack of capital for such investment, even though the rich should supply none of it.

Ours is pre-eminently an age of Invention—of Industrial Progress. I can remember a time when the steamboat was still a novelty and a fireside marvel—when no mile of iron track had yet been laid on the surface of our planet—when American canals were merely contrivances for circumventing cataracts, and of small account anyhow—when no steam-propelled vessel had ever crossed a sea—and when the Electric Telegraph was as inconceivable as a broad, firm highway to the moon. To mow grass, cut grain, or sew garments by machinery, was then unimagined; we exported no grain but that grown near the shores of the Atlantic, its bays and inlets; and our mails were wholly drawn by horses at an average speed of less than fifty miles per day. Looking back at the immense strides of Invention and Machinery, of Steam and Electricity, during the present century, and mainly in my day, who can rationally doubt that Industrial Progress is yet on the threshold of its career—that the inventions of the next half-century must far surpass in scope and utility those of the preceding? Happy the generation just entering upon this stage of being, if its leaders and teachers shall realize that the noblest achievement toward which its exertions should be directed, the highest attainment within its reach, is a more generous, more enlightened, more courageous, more devoted generation to follow it, qualified and incited to take up the work which its predecessor has laid down, and bear it on to still grander, more beneficent triumphs.

———

AT THE BURNET HOUSE, IN THE EVENING.

CITIZENS OF OHIO : I am here a guest on the invitation of the Common Council of Cincinnati. It is their desire, as it is my wish, that I should, while their guest, abstain from any remarks which seem to savor of a partisan purpose, and I should have chosen so to speak that no one of any party could possibly have taken objection. But an attack has been made upon me since I came here, which I will trust to the hospitality and the generosity of my entertainers to permit me to repel here and now. Last evening, at Pittsburgh, in the course of some off-hand remarks to a vast assemblage like this, I took pains to explain the circumstances—the extraordinary, unprecedented circumstances—under which I was impelled, in the Winter of 1860, to offer in good faith to submit the whole question of Union or disunion to a free, unconstrained vote of the Southern people, after due deliberation and discussion. I said that it was my belief then, as it is still my belief, that, if that people had been allowed such free, fair opportunity, they would have decided, as you would have decided—that the Union should be maintained. Those remarks which I made last evening have been misrepresented, have been, I think, perverted, into the expression of a *present* belief, a *present* conviction, that any State has a right to dissolve this Union at its own good pleasure. Fellow citizens, I utterly repudiate and condemn that sentiment. I do not believe that one State, nor that ten States, nor that even a majority of all the States, have a moral, legal, or constitutional right to dissolve our Union.

That Union is founded on a constitution which is a charter of government, not a mere alliance. It does not create a league merely, nor a confederacy, but a nation, under a government of limited and defined powers, but of unlimited duration. I believe that the Union is not only destined to be, but was intended to be, perpetual ; and I believe our great civil war, if there ever was any reasonable doubt as to the nature of that Union, has settled that doubt forever. That Slavery is dead, and that the Nation abides forever, is the sum and substance of the verdict pronounced through the issues of our great contest. There is no longer a question, there can never again arise a question as to the perpetuity of the Union. The apple of discord, the only thing that ever made an American hostile to his own country and Constitution, has utterly perished. Henceforth the American Union abides forever, grounded in the affections, the necessities, and in the fervent devotion, of the whole American people. If there shall ever again arise a cloud of disunion, it will not arise in the Southern section of this country. But no such question will or can arise. As perpetual as the hills, as solid as the everlasting rocks, the union of these States abides, and must abide forever. One sentiment, one purpose, animates the American heart, and that is that the Union of the States must and shall be preserved.

THE DUTY OF CINCINNATI.

Now, fellow-citizens, let me add a few words in regard to your position, your duties, and your prospects. Cincinnati may be regarded as nearly the industrial and commercial centre of our present population. What the future may bring forth we cannot tell, but to-day this city is nearly in the middle of the great commercial movement, of the industrial activity, of the American people. These hills, smiling in their Autumn abundance, look lovingly on each other from the north and from the south.

This mighty river, which laves your city with its gentle current, should persuade to Union and to reconciliation. We are to be evermore one people. Let us be a harmonious people, united in heart and hope as well as in geography and in political association. Let us resolve to cultivate the graces and the charities of fellow-citizenship. Let us resolve that from this city shall go forth an influence to the North and to the South which shall bind the people together in a bond of sweeter and stronger affection than they have ever yet known.

Fellow-citizens, I rejoice to stand here in this, the city which has been honored by holding within its limits the Cincinnati Convention, wherefrom emanated the noblest platform of principles ever presented to the American people. Those principles commend themselves to my judgment. They are dear to my heart. If I could do anything to give ascendency, perpetual and complete, to those principles, I would gladly do it. If my success or defeat can promote their advancement and commend them to the hearts of this people, I shall rejoice alike in that success or in that defeat. I believe they represent the best thought, the best purpose, the best aspirations, of the American people. As such, I accept them, as such I am proud to be in any capacity identified with their presentation. It was not my expectation to be presented as a candidate by that Convention. That honor was conferred upon me, and I gratefully and readily accepted it. And I thank you, my fellow-citizens, for the cordiality, the unanimity, the majestic strength, in which you have responded to it. As one of your number, I take the place in your ranks which has been assigned me, and will endeavor to bear your banner with honor, truth and justice, wherever fortune may lead, and wherever the good providence of God may enable me to carry it. And so, fellow-citizens, unable to make myself heard, I will relieve you from further attention."

BEFORE THE CHAMBER OF COMMERCE.

MR. PRESIDENT AND GENTLEMEN OF THE CHAMBER OF COMMERCE : You will do me the justice to believe that I would not have chosen to appear before you as an instructor, (for so it will seem to you), with regard to matters which you must understand better, perhaps, than I. I am here because I am asked to be here ; and, being here, I propose to make to you a few suggestions, which I trust will have a practical hearing. I fully comprehend that you are business men, that this is a business hour, and that whatever is said by me must, at any rate, be very brief.

To plunge at once, then, into the middle of the subject, I am one of those who do not feel entirely satisfied with the financial and commercial condition and prospects of our country. I realize that we have just secured very abundant harvests, and that these are important elements in our commercial prosperity. I realize that we have a currency quite abundant in its volume and acceptable at par over the larger portion of our country. We have many elements of strength, and yet there seems to be also elements or portents of weakness, which ought not to be passed over in silence.

CONCERNING CORNERS.

You will bear me witness that, for the last two or three years, we have heard more, felt more, suffered more, of commercial collapse—I might say commercial difficulty—from the operations of what are popularly called " rings," than ever before in the history of this, or, I think, in the history of any country. Corners in wheat, corners in oats, corners in pork, corners in gold, corners in stocks, and so on, and so on. Now, gentlemen, I am not here to say that this particular clique, which tried to force up prices, or that opposite clique which tried to force them down, was right or wrong in any instance ; I am not sufficiently familiar with the facts to judge. What I say, and think you must believe with me, is that these exhibitions, these ebullitions, are symptoms of financial weakness, if not of financial disease.

They are incidents which are not likely to occur in a perfectly sound and healthy condition of the business and the currency of the country.

Well, we get on with them as well as we can, or, rather, we chase one away and another soon presents itself, and every now and then, in the great commercial center where my work has been carried on, there comes a superior corner, a kind of "Black Friday," or something that threatens a general disaster ; and then appears the Secretary of the Treasury with his horn of plenty, and he lets loose something or other ; he either buys stocks, or he sells gold, or he does both, and he puts us at ease for a little time again. Now, I am not here to decide that that is not the best he can do ; I don't know about that ; but I do insist that the business of the country ought not to be in a condition to require this continual application of something artificial, something let down from above ; that there should be a state of things wherein business men and business interests should take care of themselves, and not require the continual interposition of some public authority in such a dictatorial form. Some men are swamped when the Secretary appears ; other men are relieved ; perhaps the greatest good to the greatest number is accomplished, for aught I know ; but I want to see a state of things where the Government is not continually called upon to help us out. It reminds me of the state of things that existed in my earlier days, when every once in a while Mr. Nicholas Biddle was called to Wall Street in about the same capacity as the Secretary of the Treasury is now, to put his shoulder to the wheel and lift us out of some mire, or ward off some catastrophe.

RESUMING SPECIE PAYMENT.

I think we ought to be able—that you, gentlemen, ought to be able—to devise the ways and means, not only of getting us out of one particular corner, but of preventing corners in the future ; rendering them impossible, or, at all events, disastrous to their contrivers. Now, I am supposed to be a man of isms— or, what is the word?—a man of hobbies on this subject. Some men imagine that I am a very furious demander of the immediate resumption of specie payments. My opinion was, years ago, and I have seen no reason to change it, that when we had one-hundred and twenty-five millions of money in the Treasury, mainly gold, and when we had a revenue exceeding the necessary outlays of the Treasury by more than one hundred millions per annum, we were then in a condition to resume specie payments; that if the Government had chosen to say, "We will resume ; we will redeem our greenbacks, and will receive them as gold," there would have been no difficulty in making that resumption. Under that state of affairs I have seen the Bank of England resume ; I have known the banks of our country to resume with a very much smaller proportion of immediately available assets to their liabilities than the Treasury of the United States had at that time ; so that it seems to me to be a perfectly feasible thing ; but we did not resume, mainly because the people—I mean the business people—did not want to resume ; and that, in my judgment, is a reason that will operate just as forcibly next year, two years, five years hence, as it operated then. It is my judgment that we are not likely to resume in any near period of time.   Then, I say, if we want to resume, we need all the resources we had then, and we ought to have husbanded them carefully ; but if we were not, as you and I know we were not, to resume for a long time to come, then it seems to me a different policy was required of the Government—that is, to pay out all its gold, all its money, beyond a fair working balance, reduce the debt by so much, stop the interest, and leave the gold and currency in the hands of business men, instead of hoarding it up in the Treasury to make one of these periodical —[the conclusion of the sentence was drowned by the applause.] But I am not a dogmatist.   I do not pretend to present this as a matured and settled conclusion.

THE DUTY OF BUSINESS MEN.

What I do suggest—what I ask this Chamber to originate— is an inquiry and investigation by men of business and capital as to where the proper remedy for these disorders of which I speak is to be found.   Let us be calm about it.   Let us take time ; let us investigate slowly, carefully, and let the business men of the country come to a conclusion as to the proper remedy, not for a particular disorder for to-day, but against the periodical recurrence of these disorders. This is what I would have the business men of this country do. Look at the matter as a disease, not at one particular symptom, and determine just what and where is the remedy. I venture to say if the men who compose Chambers like this will agree upon what that remedy is, they can have behind them the press of the country with scarcely an exception, and the public sentiment of the country ; and whatever shall seem to them, after mature deliberation, after careful discussion, the true cure for our financial disorders and dangers will be accepted by the general judgment of the country, and carried into effect. This is all, gentlemen, and I thank you for your patient attention.

-----o-----

AT LOUISVILLE, KENTUCKY, SEPTEMBER 22, 1872.

Citizens of Louisville : Standing on this soil of Kentucky, I ask you, who are my associates in the great Liberal movement of the day, to bear testimony with me to certain truths. First, is it not true that we desire a government of just and equal laws, which shall extend equal favor and equal protection to every American citizen? Is it not true, that while we demand a repeal of all disfranchisements, of all proscriptions of Americans because of the part they bore in our late strugggle, that we desire that no man shall be disfranchised, that no man shall be proscribed, but that every man shall stand on an equal platform with ourselves? Is not that the fact? Is it not true that we have no expectation, no purpose, no understanding, that the rebel debt shall be paid, or the rebel soldiers pensioned, or the slaves emancipated by the result of the war paid for? Is it not true that we have no purpose, or expectation, or understanding, that any of these things shall be done?

THE UNJUST PREJUDICES OF THE COLORED MEN.

Now, fellow-citizens, I wish to call your attention to an aspect of this struggle which has not yet been presented. There is no class of our citizens, no part of the American people, who have so real and great an interest in the success of our movement as the colored people of this country. They know we all admit that their rights are perfectly secured by the constitution, and that no one can go back of that. But it is their interest that their rights should not only be accorded, but that they should be cheerfully accorded ; that there should be no opposition, no objection, to their enjoying just the same political and civil rights that we do. It is their interest, even more than yours and mine, that all contention concerning Black men or White men shall absolutely cease ; that every individual shall be judged and estimated according to his works, with no respect whatever to his color or condition. If our movement succeeds, there is no party, there is no considerable faction, there is really nobody left in the field opposing or objecting to their standing on a common platform of American nationality. I say, then, it is their clear interest that our movement shall be welcomed and ratified by the entire American people ; and yet it is a very discouraging fact that there is no other class so generally and so bitterly opposing us as they are.

There is no other class, as a class, which insists so thoroughly on misapprehending and misrepresenting us. I say not this to excite prejudice against them. They are ignorant, and their ignorance is not their own fault, though it is their and our misfortune. They are misled and we are calumniated in their ears. Why, I have been repeatedly asked to contradict assertions that I have been a negro-trader. Even on my way to this place, one Quadroon girl, on hearing me speak, said : "I would like to stick a knife into his heart ; he sold my mother in Richmond, Virginia." I can imagine a reason why lies like that should be told. I can imagine no reason why good men and women should not everywhere discountenance and refute them. It is, I say, a misfortune of the colored people, as well as of our people, that they, as a class, are steeled against us. They will not hear us.

They do not believe us. They are told that this movement is a contrivance to get them enslaved again virtually, if not absolutely, and that all the professions of the Cincinnati platform and Baltimore indorsement in favor of equal rights, are frauds and lies. "If this party succeeds," Mr. Wendell Phillips tells them, "you must conceal your property and take care of your arms."

LIBERAL GOOD-WILL TOWARD THE NEGROES.

Now, fellow-citizens, I state these facts here, not that I would have you think any worse of these misguided people, but because I want you Kentuckians to realize that ignorance is a public peril ; that you cannot well afford to have a part of your population growing up in such dense unacquaintance with public men and public affairs that they can be deceived and misled as this people are. You must take care that they shall be educated, so that they shall be too wise, too well-informed, to be thus deceived and misguided. Fellow-citizens, if our movement should prevail, as I trust it will prevail, we will sweep away all this refuge of lies in three months. We will say to the colored man : "We proffer you nothing except the protection of the laws, the same for you as for us. You have your living to earn as well as we. You will have to use all your abilities, all your energies, all your faculties, and make the most of them you can. The laws do not favor you, but they will thoroughly protect you." In three months, if we succeed, the colored people will be so disabused that the same men can never deceive them again.

But suppose we fail, and we may fail? If the colored men did not believe that power was against us, that money was against us—if they did not realize that the Treasury, the Army, the one hundred thousand office-holders, were all banded against us in a force which they believe we cannot overcome,—they certainly would not be so universally hostile to us. But they think we cannot succeed, and they want to be upon the winning side. That is a part of it, but they are also deluded in regard to our purposes. We say to them : "We are not your enemies. We will not be your oppressors. We will not be unjust, though you have done us injustice. We will try as well as we can to have your children educated and enlightened, so that the mistake you have made cannot be made over and over again." That is where we stand.

THE EVILS OF DISFRANCHISEMENT.

Now, fellow-citizens, why do we condemn proscription? They mistake who say that there are only two or three hundred left, now forbidden to exercise the common rights of American citizens. It is not so; there are many thousands disfranchised in the State of Arkansas alone—and the men who hold them disfranchised expect to carry that State against us by virtue of that disfranchisement. But it is not merely the number of the proscribed. Men who are not under this ban feel themselves proscribed because others are for an offense which was their offense as well. So long as you have a proscribed class in the country, men all around them—honorable, generous men—will feel, "*I* ought, too, to be proscribed the same as that man. The difference was only an accident; he happened to take an oath or fill an office before the struggle that I did not; but his guilt was no more than mine; accident, only, makes him proscribed and leaves me free." So that, as long as there shall be a proscribed class in this country, the proscription will rankle in the hearts of millions of Americans, who feel that they themselves are condemned and banned in the act which dooms their leaders. It is not for the sake of the proscribed alone that I speak; every community has the right to the best services of all its citizens. Men say to me, "Why, you don't want to elect Toombs, or Wise, or somebody else, do you?" No, I don't want to elect any of those men; but suppose other people do? Who are you, or who am I, to say whether they shall or not? It is not a question for me, but whether American citizens, who, you say, have the same right to vote and hold office as you, shall be at liberty to vote for the men they prefer, or shall be compelled to vote for the men you prefer. These questions reach not several hundreds but several millions of our people. "Well," they say, "what do the people care about this? The banks are making money, the people are prospering, the manufacturers are thrifty. Who cares that a few hundred or thousand men are disfran-

chised?" *I* care.   I say a war which ended nearly eight years
ago ought to have had nearly all its bloody traces wiped out
before this time.

THE WISDOM OF AMNESTY.

I say that, while we have often been amused with promises of
general amnesty, the Government of the country has practically
been controlled by men like Senators Morton and Chandler, and
General Butler, one of whom says : " God may forgive the rebels if He will, but I never can." Now that spirit is not one
which should rule a Republican country.   A republic should be
generous and trustful—especially generous to an error whereof
the very last evil consequences have long since faded away.
Grant that secession was wrong—indefensibly wrong ; the
attempt has been nobly resisted and defeated.   Grant that the
whole Confederate movement was as heinous as you please, still,
it was utterly defeated ; it became a lost cause; and there is no
more probability, and I may say, no more possibility, of another
serious attempt to divide the American Union, than there is of
an attempt to disrupt and destroy the Solar System.   Never
before did the Union stand so strong as to-day, and never did
any movement result in a more complete and utter discomfiture
than the Confederate movement.   Then, I say, with seven and
a half years passed after the last shot was fired in behalf of that
movement, it is time for Amnesty, complete and perfect. It is
time for oblivion of offenses that so long since passed away.

ADMINISTRATION MISREPRESENTATION.

Fellow-citizens, we stand on the principles embodied in our
platform.   Those principles our adversaries do not assail ; they
confess judgment ; but they insinuate that a purpose is therein
indicated which is not our real intention, and that we mean
something utterly different ; and thereupon they proceed to
attribute to us designs which we never cherished, which we
positively disavow, and which they ought to know are utterly
absurd.   The most important of them are utterly forbidden by
the Constitution, and they know it.   No man can go to Congress or be chosen President without taking a solemn oath to

sustain the Constitution, which absolutely forbids the payment of rebel debts or payment for emancipated slaves.

AN APPEAL TO AMERICANS.

I commend our cause to the sober judgment of the American people. I ask them to judge us without prejudice, without passion, and with spirits uninfluenced by wrath and vengeance. I ask them to judge us as citizens who are sincerely trying to do what we believe best for our country; and I do trust that passion and prejudice will not prevail—that we shall be judged as we are, and not as we are represented, and that the beneficent triumph which will increase the value of every acre of land in the Southern States, which will increase the products of those States, make the people harmonious, Black and White, and make them live in a more trustful, peaceful and fraternal relation than they have hitherto held toward each other, will be secured. I trust that this result will be attained, and that generations to come shall rejoice over the inception, the progress, and the triumph of the Liberal cause. Friends, I bid you good night.

———o———

AT JEFFERSONVILLE, IND., SEPTEMBER 23, 1872.

Mr. Mayor and Citizens of Jeffersonville : I should be very inconsistent and ungrateful if my life had not been devoted, according to my best understanding, to the interest and welfare of the great laboring class, from which I sprang, and with which I have always been connected. Beginning life as a laborer on a farm, going thence into a mechanic's shop, and learning my trade as a printer, I have devoted the rest of my life first to my employment as printer and editor, and afterward to some extent to the calling of a moderate farmer. I feel that my sympathies could not have been otherwise than with the immense majority of mankind, who in all ages are required to subsist by their own manual industry. I have meant to be, in my politics as in my business, the friend of labor. I may have made mistakes (who has not?) in the policy which I thought best adapted to promote the interests of the workingman. I may just as well have been mistaken as equally honest, equally earnest men who have advocated a different policy; but I know what my purpose was.

VIEWS CONCERNING SLAVERY.

I was, in the days of Slavery, an enemy to Slavery, because I thought Slavery inconsistent with the rights, dignity and highest well-being of Free Labor. That might have been a mistake, but it was at any rate an earnest conviction. So when our great trouble came on, I was anxious first of all for labor—that the laboring class should be everywhere free men. I was anxious next that our country's unity might be preserved, without bloodshed if that were possible—by means of bloodshed, if that dire alternative should be fastened upon us. For, friends and neighbors, bloodshed is always a sad necessity—always a woeful necessity—and he who loves his fellow-man must desire to make it as short as possible, and, so soon as peace can be restored, to efface as speedily as may be every trace not merely of blood on the earth, but of vengeful feelings from the hearts of his fellows. Such has been the impulse of the course I have pursued throughout the last few eventful years.

My life has been an open book; all could read it. My thoughts have been given to the public warm and fresh, sometimes before an opportunity had been afforded for due consideration and correction—very often mingled with thoughts of others which were not my own, but which it was very easy to attribute to me. So I have come on to this time. No one who heard my utterances or listened to them in any way directly after the close of the war, when I pleaded for magnanimity, for forbearance, for the speediest possible effacement of all sores and sorrows from the public mind—no one who heeded me then can doubt where I must stand now—no one!

LAWLESSNESS MUST BE SUPPRESSED.

My course has been plain and simple. Down with all manner of lawlessness and violence! If there are Ku-Klux or other disturbers, put them down with a strong hand ; for mercy to them is quite a different thing from mercy to the quiet, peaceable men of the country. Violence and lawlessness must be suppressed, speedily, energetically and earnestly ; but when they are suppressed, then forget wrath and remember mercy. I pleaded for Universal Amnesty. "What," says some, "were there no men who committed crime during the war? I say, if there were, punish their crimes ; Amnesty won't forbid that. If men committed crimes during the civil war, whether on one side or on the other—if they committed acts contrary to humane war—then I would punish them sternly for those acts, and I would have done it long ago, for every such act and outrage against the laws of war in war is as black a crime as though it were done in time of peace. Punish those men always. ·But for all those men who were simply our antagonists in that great struggle, I have no vengeful wrath after they have laid down their arms and complied with all reasonable requirements of the Government and of public safety. Such has been the feeling, such the convictions that I cherished through the war and since the war.

THE TIME FOR AMNESTY.

Now I say the time has come for Universal Amnesty, so that no human being shall feel that, because he was on what you and I regard as the wrong side in our great struggle, he is proscribed, disfranchised, or subjected to any penalty. The time has come when we should proclaim that Amnesty, and, having secured the rights of every Black man in the country, so that he is just as good as you or I, we should give the White man a chance. So let us say to those who were mistaken, who fought against us and against themselves—for it was as much against themselves as against us—let us say : "Fellow-countrymen, you were wrong ; you undertook to divide a country that ought not to be divided. You were mistaken ; but that is all over, and the country is re-united. We are all free now. Let us make you free also ; let us all together, every one of us, be citizens of this country, with equal liberties and privileges so far as men can give them. If God has imposed disabilities, we cannot remedy those ; we can only say the law is just as good for the ignorant —for the colored people—as for you and me. Their standing in courts is the same as yours ; their oath is the same. Let every one tell his story ; and let the jury, giving each story due weight, determine which is correct, and let not Color entitle to favor."

WHAT MR. GREELEY HAS FOUGHT FOR.

This is the ground for which I have fought—not to have a subject class ; a proscribed class ; an alien class ; an outlaw class in the country ; but to have men stand on the equal and lawful platform of our common nationality—citizens, free to exercise such faculties as God has given them for their own sustenance and for the upbuilding of their own families and fortunes. That seems to me statesmanship. I know that it is humanity, and I feel that it is patriotism that we should all alike remember no more harshly and bitterly the conflicts of the past. We are henceforth to be one American people, and each should have every chance so far as the Constitution and laws give him opportunity. They say that few are proscribed ; but in truth many are proscribed—not few. Whenever it is said that my captain shall be punished for what he and I did, I am punished with him ; I feel the blows inflicted on him. The ring that holds him to his dungeon eats into my heart as well as his. No part of that great people who struggled against us in the South now feel that they are entirely pardoned and restored to citizenship so long as their leaders and chiefs in the struggle are punished for a common sin or error, whatever it is. So here I stand before you an advocate of the right and the principles of Universal Amnesty. So long as there was any quarrel about Impartial Suffrage, I fought for it. Now there are none to be enfranchised but some thousands whom we disfranchised. Four years ago, the Republican National Convention resolved that their disabilities should speedily cease. I have waited in patience four years, and they do not cease. I now demand that the people shall say : "Let all liabilities be abolished. Let disfranchisement pass away. Let us be united. Let amnesty and good feeling be restored, so that we all stand on one common ground."

AN APPEAL TO INDIANA.

This is all I would say to you. I have little time to be among you ; but I do appeal to Indiana, standing now, as she does, the leader of the vanguard of the old Free States—I appeal to her to let her voice be heard in her coming election on the side of National Reconciliation and Universal Amnesty. Other States will heed her, if that is her judgment. Let no false pride, let no party attachment, let no devotion to leaders, however able, however good—let nothing stifle that voice. Let it echo across the land, a herald of peace and gladness. Let the disfranchised hear it as a token of good cheer and good will. Let the people everywhere read and learn that Indiana has declared for the restoration of the last American to the common privileges of American citizenship, and the country will rejoice that the reign of proscription is over, and that the people have declared that all our countrymen shall be free.

——o——

AT INDIANAPOLIS, SEPTEMBER 23, 1872.

AFTER a few words of introduction from Hon. D. W. VOORHEES Mr. Greeley said :

PEOPLE OF INDIANA : The distinguished gentleman who just addressed you has pronounced the two watchwords of the present canvass. The first is Reconciliation, the second is Purification. I have spoken heretofore on Reconciliation, I propose to speak to-night in the interest of Purification. Our country has recently encountered and vanquished the peril of disunion. She is to-day confronted with the deadlier peril of corruption. The cancer is eating into her vitals, whereof the essence is purchased legislation, bribed public servants, and heinous betrayals of the highest trusts. I will endeavor to illustrate her present peril by simply recounting to you undeniable facts which illustrate the history of legislation by Congress with reference to the Union Pacific Railway. I would fix your attention on this, as a sample of the means whereby scheming, selfish, avaricious men contrive to glut their own greed while they talk of public beneficence.

HISTORY OF THE CREDIT MOBILIER.

Ten years ago, Congress passed an act chartering the Union Pacific Railway. That act was calculated and intended to secure a connection, by railway, of our Pacific with our Atlantic States —a noble purpose, and one which cannot be too strongly commended. As it was certain that private capital would not build a road through 2,000 miles of uninhabited mountain and desert, Congress resolved to aid that enterprise generously. In the first place the right of way was granted with the right also to take materials free, from any part of the public domain. Next, a large land grant was made in aid of the work. Third, bonds of the Government to the extent of at least $25,000 per mile were lent to the Company in aid of this project, and a first mortgage on the railroad taken therefor. It was thus provided that the railroad should be built with public money for public use by a chartered Company. After a few years, this project having passed into the hands of capable, grasping men, some of whom were members of Congress, a new step was taken. Congress was induced to authorize a new loan in aid of this project, of an equal amount with the Government aid—that is to say, to the extent of at least $25,000 per mile—and this new loan was authorized to take precedence of the Government loan. In other words, Congress relinquished our first mortgage on the railroad, and took a second mortgage, authorizing the Company to place a first mortgage of equal amount ahead of ours. Thus our security was destroyed. In a little while, a private company was somewhere chartered, entitled "The Crédit Mobilier of America," and that private company or ring was composed of a lot of active members of the Union Pacific Railroad Company, some of them members of Congress.

A NOVEL BUSINESS TRANSACTION.

No list of the stockholders of the Credit Mobilier was ever published or can be obtained ; but these gentlemen proceeded to make contracts virtually with themselves ; that is to say, the same gentlemen, officiating as officers of the Union Pacific Railroad, contracted with themselves as officers of the Credit Mobilier of America to construct the Union Pacific Railroad at enormous prices, which absorbed both the bonds lent by Government and the private loan of the Company of equal amount, which was now the first mortgage on all the property of the road. In other words, these gentlemen contracted with themselves to pay themselves twice the fair cost of entirely building and equipping the road ; and, building the road with the proceeds of the money lent by the Government, they proceeded to divide among themselves the other bonds, equal to the amount for which Congress had made a mortgage on the entire road. By these means, $20,000,000 or $30,000,000 were divided among the parties ; and all that money so divided we are called upon to pay. They divided the Company bonds, and built the road with the Government bonds, which were a second mortgage on their road.

STILL ANOTHER ADVANTAGE.

Now, you see, these same gentlemen who engineered through Congress this project of making the road cost double what it should cost, and making half that cost a private dividend among themselves—these gentlemen now appear before Congress for still further advantages. Congress had thus far reserved to the country such sums as this railroad earned by carrying the mails and provisions, etc., for the Army of the United States ; but the Company said "No! We want to reserve half of the money. You can pay over half of the money to us." Consequently, in March, 1871, by an amendment fastened on the Army Appropriation bill, the Secretary of the Treasury was instructed to pay over to these companies half the money they earned by carrying the mails and army supplies, and only reserve half of those earnings toward the payment of the interest semi-monthly accruing on the bonds loaned them by the United States. So that already the people of this country are paying some millions per annum out of their hard earnings for interest on these bonds lent to the Pacific Road; paying this money as interest to meet the vast sums divided by these gentlemen among themselves, as profits of the Credit Mobilier of America.

PROOFS OF CORRUPTION—NEED OF PURIFICATION.

Now, gentlemen, I do not say what individuals have received this money, but I do say that by corrupt legislation $30,000,000 or $40,000,000 have been saddled on this country—an unjust and unrighteous debt. We are called upon to pay the interest now every six months, and after thirty years must pay the principal; and all this because the men who were at the same time legislators and corporators corruptly used their legislative power to fasten this unjust debt upon the people of the United States. Now, then, I stand here, fellow-citizens, to insist that the legislation of your country, National and State, needs purification, and that the leading men in our Government who are Speakers, and members of the Committees on the Pacific and other railways, should be called to justice. We need reconciliation. We need also purification, and this not less than the other. The letters of Oakes Ames, the undenied and undeniable letters of a member of Congress and a corporator and large stockholder in the Union Pacific Railroad, whereof he was lately President, these letters incontestably prove corruption, and corruption in high places. Such legislation as I have briefly exposed to you could not have been accomplished, could not have been effected, without the connivance and support of men high in authority; and these facts assure you that purification is urgently needed.

A PLEA FOR RECONCILIATION.

Fellow-citizens, let me say one word for Reconciliation. For years I have pleaded, for years I have implored, that strife and contention should cease; for years I have said: "Let us have Universal Amnesty and Impartial Suffrage." We have achieved Impartial Suffrage. No man contests it. No man disputes it. Now give us universal Amnesty. We ought to have it. It is time that alienation should cease. It is time that the hatreds engendered by the late contests should cease. It is time that the American people, the whole of them, should be asked to resume their rights as citizens under our common nationality—no outcast, no aliens, none proscribed, and then, united once more, take the vows of allegiance, and support the honor, and unity, and the prosperity henceforth of this great Republic. I plead for Reconciliation, perfect and complete. I stand for Amnesty so thorough that no man shall stand outside of its circle. I desire to see every American recalled to loyalty by being asked to stand equally with us on a common platform of American nationality. Fellow-citizens, we were promised this four years ago in the Republican National Platform. It has not been conceded to us. We must take it. We have asked for it long enough ; now let the people say " We will have it." In several States—in Virginia, in Missouri, in West Virginia—the people have been asked, " Will you have every man enfranchised; no man proscribed?" and they h..ve uniformly answered, " Yes, yes ! No proscription! Universal Amnesty !" The whole people will so answer if the question can be fairly presented. I have put the question. I represent the affirmative of that question ; and I call on the people so to vote that no man shall doubt that the American people demand Universal Amnesty, and the restoration of every withheld right to every American born or naturalized on our soil.

People of Indiana, I know your generous hearts are with me. I believe that your votes will testify that your hearts are sound and true. I believe that you cannot be bought. I know that you cannot be bullied ; and I feel that when your verdict shall be pronounced it will thrill the hearts of the friends of Reconciliation from one end of the country to the other. I know you and trust you. Your hearts beat responsive to mine. Make it sure that there shall be no ambiguity in your verdict, and nothing to mar its completeness.

HORACE GREELEY IN 1872.

—

MR. GREELEY'S POLITICAL POSITION AND MOTIVES IN THE LATE PRESIDENTIAL CONTEST.

To the Editor of the Tribune:

SIR : In the numerous notices and "recollections" of Mr. Greeley by partisan hands, since the death of that distinguished man, the intimation is often made that he not only lost caste as a Republican, but lost character by becoming the candidate of the opposition at the late election ; and this chapter of his life is patronizingly passed over as one which might better be treated with silence and left to oblivion.

In the first place, no such thing is possible in a life as eminent and as conspicuous as that of Mr. Greeley. In the next, it is an impertinent imputation which every friend of his desires promptly to repel. No such forbearance is asked or desired. His friends challenge the closest scrutiny on this as on every other chapter of his eventful life. Mr. Greeley threw himself into the canvass as the determined opponent of a sordid corruption that he believed was disgracing the Republican party and destroying the public morals. · The late numerous and painful disclosures of Credit Mobilier, Senatorial, and other corruptions, that have simultaneously burst upon and astounded the country, demonstrate to the world how well founded his convictions were.

These developments throw a flood of light upon the late canvass by making plain to all what was previously known to but comparatively few ; namely, that our national politics had long been becoming thoroughly corrupt. They have also widened the basis of the knowledge possessed by those few, and more than confirmed all their worst suspicions. There is no longer any doubt that widespread rottenness prevails in our public affairs and among our public men. The question now is getting to be, how much have we left that is sound ? How many States and how many Congress districts exist that are not under the control of corrupt agencies and influences?

THE BEGINNING OF PUBLIC CORRUPTION.

The fruitage season of corruption, now running to seed in Washington, and all over the country, was preceded by its budding and blossoming time at the Capitol. It began in the period of war contracts in the time of Mr. Lincoln ; it continued under the hybrid administration of Andrew Johnson ; and flowered vigorously at the close of the war, when Gen. Grant's military and personal friends took possession of our civil affairs. Its growth was at that period viewed with the deepest concern by every observer cognizant of public affairs. The inauguration of Gen. Grant became an epoch in its progress. The instant raid made upon the offices by a rough shod and eager crew, who knew what they became Republicans for, was one of the most significant events in our political history. The old Republicans were everywhere displaced by the new crowd.

It was not long before there came reports of numerous accomplished and attempted thefts, robberies, defalcations, and swindling transactions in the various Departments, in addition to the usual supply in Congress. The most conspicuous of these, and the one which first excited wide attention, arose in the Post-Office Department, and subsequently became notorious as the " Chorpenning Claim." Mr. Postmaster-General Creswell had deliberately sanctioned an attempt to take from the Treasury the sum of $440,000, on a claim urged by his former law-partner, which the House of Representatives, by a nearly unanimous vote, declared fraudulent and void. This was deemed a proper occasion for some of the best Republicans in Congress to break ground, and make a resolute stand against an evidently still rising tide of corruption, which, if not checked by some concerted and authoritative measures, it was seen would soon debauch the new Executive Government, further demoralize Congress and the country, and result finally in endangering the ascendency of the Republican party. In the event of Gen. Grant's failing to invite Mr. Cresswell to resign, it was suggested that Congress should give a significant hint to that gentleman to retire. But while Congress was prompt to stamp Mr. Cresswell's action as infamous, it exhibited an incredible reluctance to do anything which looked like personally antagonizing members against him. The reasons for this reluctance were not then understood, and until lately have only been but partially disclosed. They become surprisingly clear in the light of recent developments.

MR. GREELEY ENTERS THE LISTS AGAINST CORRUPTION.

It was at this period that Mr. Greeley was approached and solicited to make open proclamation against the Creswell transaction and throw the whole weight of THE TRIBUNE into a resolute demand for his removal. Mr. Greeley was at that time a warm friend and supporter of Gen. Grant and the Administration. It was urged upon him that the good name and honorable character of the Republican party demanded that Creswell should go overboard ; that in no other way could so much be done to check the bold march of venality and corruption ; that it was the duty of the Republican press to call upon the President to set his face like a flint against this first open and flagrant attempt at public robbery ; that it might be early understood that the new Administration would not for one moment tolerate transactions like this. It was the first actual and threatening crevasse that had opened, and it must be promptly stopped if an inundation was to be averted. These views were enforced by suggesting the inquiry as to what would probably be Mr. Creswell's fate if, instead of Gen. Grant, Mr. Chase, or Mr. Fessenden, or Mr. Charles Francis Adams, were at the head of the Administration. There was no one to contest the conclusion that in either case Mr. Creswell's place would not be worth an hour's purchase. Mr. Greeley recognized the force of the considerations alleged, and offered to print anything in aid of the object in view, and did publish some strictures on the transaction ; but, as it was thought that Gen. Grant's pertinacity and pride of opinion, in the selection of his Cabinet officers, was not likely to be overcome by any mere newspaper solicitations, Mr. Greeley did not see his way clear to make such a pronounced effort as was desired. It proved subsequently that this view of the case was correct, so far as any action of Gen. Grant in the premises was concerned. For the President was afterward approached on the same subject by eminent Republicans in Congress, who were his supporters then, and who are his supporters now, and a reconstruction of his Cabinet urged on the ground of this and other scandals, of which it was argued the Republican party ought not to bear the weight; but the attempt to secure such reconstruction signally failed, though backed by high Senatorial names. The President thought that Creswell and Robeson were as good as any of the rest of his Cabinet.

HOW MR. GREELEY AIMED TO CORRECT ABUSES.

But it is not Presidential obtuseness that I wish to illustrate, but the character of Mr. Greeley. Always a warm partisan and ardent supporter of the Republican party, seeking the forefront of the battle, he was not anxious to find flaws in the Administration, but sought to excuse rather than condemn. He was unwilling to make sharp issues with Gen. Grant's Administration, even while condemning its tone and many of its acts. He thought there was a better way, and that friendly solicitation would serve better than indignant comment. It is known to all readers of THE TRIBUNE that he pursued that course through all the Cabinet scandals, and all the carpet-bag rascalities and robberies, the irregularities and swindling operations of the vast crowd of revenue officers in New York and elsewhere, the defalcations and speculations of what was known as the "Military Ring," and the general gorging of the new tribe who had gained possession of the Government places, till at length he could stand it no longer. Mr. Greeley steadily aimed at the friendly correction of these abuses, by, as might almost be said, supporting Gen. Grant against Gen. Grant's Administration. Fully recognizing the necessity of Reform, he aimed to secure it by continuing his support of the regular organization of the Republican party. Party divisions in the State of New York greatly embarrassed this line of action, and Mr. Greeley was often made to feel, by the action of party managers, how unavailing were his efforts.

I mark the epoch of the Creswell transaction because it was

about that time that Mr. Greeley's mind began to be more impressed with the magnitude and wide-spread character of the corruptions that had seized hold of the country, and which neither the precept nor the example of the national administration was calculated to check. Revolving the subject in his mind, he finally came to the conclusion that things ought not to go on in the old ruts any longer, and that a change was necessary. He accordingly avowed his opposition to Gen. Grant's re-nomination. He used to speak privately of affairs in Washington as being "rotten, through and through" in Congress and the Departments, but especially in the Post-Office Department; and that he could see no remedy except in a complete change from top to bottom. A particular point of discouragement was, that Gen. Cox's efforts to begin a civil service reform at Washington, while a member of the Cabinet, was hooted at, and cost that able and honest man his place. A man high in the long exercise of his Senatorial office at Washington used at the time to regale the willing ears of the President with his views of the absurdity of attempting any such reform, and by volunteering his judgment that Mr. Cox was only fit to be Secretary of the Interior in the "Kingdom of Heaven." But this question afterward took on such a threatening aspect that the President felt compelled, at a late day, to declare himself a convert to the doctrine to which Cox had been sacrificed.

PARTY CONSIDERATIONS REJECTED.

But at length Mr. Greeley saw, what became apparent to everybody, that Gen. Grant's renomination was a foreordained event. That his re-election would only perpetuate and intensify a state of things which he was firmly persuaded had gone on already quite too long for the public good, Mr. Greeley felt that he knew. The question with him at this juncture was, whether he would bow to this coming decision of the Republican party, and support its nominee, or whether he would resist and contest the issue. Mr. Greeley's position at this time was viewed by Republicans with great interest and concern, and many doubts were expressed as to whether he would "stick." It was generally believed that his active Republican sentiments and his old strong partisan feelings would finally prevail to shape his action, and that he would, in obedience to them, do as he did in the canvass of 1848, when he determinedly opposed Gen. Taylor's nomination. At that time, after finding his opposition fruitless, he reluctantly wheeled into line and supported the ticket. It was thought he would do so now.

But the event proved this expectation groundless. Mr. Greeley gave abundant notice from time to time, in his journal, that the period had arrived when he would no longer be swayed by partisan considerations, but that he would renounce the position of party organ, and, following the dictates of his own judgment and conscience, throw himself and his paper exclusively upon the general public intelligence for support. He claimed that he could not conscientiously support the continuation of the existing state of things, and would not countenance by his voice or his vote the men who were corruptly, as he believed, controlling public affairs. He demanded that these be given over to purer custodians. He was not tired of Republicans or Republicanism. His faith was unchanged. But he hated corruption, and he longed for honesty and purity and moral perception in administration. He was ready to make every sacrifice and fight the battle on a forlorn hope rather than yield his convictions of what the public good demanded.

This was the position of Mr. Greeley at a period anterior to the call of a body of independent Reformers who were in motion for a convention in the interests of Civil Service and Revenue Reform.

MR. GREELEY STILL A REPUBLICAN.

It is easy to say from a partisan point of view that, in taking this position, Mr. Greeley left the Republican party. He did no such thing. He dissented from the action of a majority of its representatives, in their nomination of a candidate for President. He did this from high motives of public policy, as well as in the interest of Republicanism itself. He did not wish to overthrow it or defeat it, but to purify and vitalize it. He did not wish to undo one of its great achievements. He did not wish to modify one of its great results. He was still for emancipation, for enfranchisement, for the equal rights of all men, in behalf of which a great war had been successfully waged. He aimed at the education and elevation of the benighted children of the African race on this continent, and to see that not one right of theirs was abridged by any measure of public policy. More than this, he aimed to advance the Republican standard still further forward in the direction it had been steadily moving since the rebellion began, and to gain in the future even greater triumphs by harmonizing the antagonisms between the two races at the South, and by softening and removing the asperities between the North and South which those triumphs had created. He patriotically aimed at these lofty purposes in the future, thus to secure more completely the Republican achievements of the past. These were his plain, transparent, well defined, often explained motives and purposes in the position he assumed, after dissenting from the nomination of Gen. Grant.

Was this to cease to be a Republican, or was it to be more of a Republican than ever? How absurd and preposterous then to charge or to intimate that Mr. Greeley deserted his Republicanism, or changed his ground, or lowered his tone upon one single point embraced in the original creed, or any of its accretions, of the Republican party, from the beginning to the end of his luminous career.

He declined to support the Republican nomination of Gen. Grant. He did it, as we have seen, from high moral and patriotic considerations. He aimed to defeat his election, still holding to every political principle and dogma he had espoused since the foundation of the Republican party. And this is all. To condemn Mr. Greeley for this, or in a review of his character to hold this conduct up for animadversion as reflecting upon his honesty or his truth, or his consistency even, is to measure him by a standard and weigh him in a scale which have no recognition among the eternities. It is only by applying a high moral standard that we can determine whether a man has acted unworthily. To refuse to go with the majority of one's party may be the hight of virtue. It depends on the motive, and it depends on the object. If these be pure, the act is commendable ; and it may happen that such an act is the most resplendent of a political life. Without caring to claim so much as this for

Mr. Greeley, I do hold that it is only a short-sighted partisanship that can see in Mr. Greeley's course, up to this point, anything to censure or condemn. And where such censure or such condemnation is expressed, it must be deemed rather the measure of the critic himself than of the object criticised. For those who say they cannot reconcile Mr. Greeley's position with his previous career, his friends have only to say that such a remark is tantamount to admitting an inability to understand how a high motive can prevail against a low one.

THE CANDIDATE OF THE DEMOCRACY.

But it is the complaint of Mr. Greeley's critics, not only that he declined to support the nomination of the Republican party, but that he became the candidate of their great adversary, the Democratic party, of whom Mr. Greeley himself had been the lifelong and persistent opponent. The implication from this fact is that he deserted his own and went over to the Democratic party.

While the facts alleged are notorious, the implication is wholly without foundation. A simple narrative of events as they occurred dispels the charge. His being a candidate was purely a secondary and accidental circumstance. His position, as I have endeavored to elucidate it, was taken wholly independent of this circumstance. It was assumed when he was scarcely thought of as a Presidential candidate, and when any betting man would have offered a thousand to one against his chances for such a nomination. Mr. Greeley himself was not thinking of it, but only of leading the way at the head of his great and influential journal, in protesting, in behalf of thousands and tens of thousands of thinking and earnest Republicans, against the corruptions of the men who are influential leaders of the Republican party. He was polishing his weapons for a contest in which he knew he should delight, and into which he proposed to enter with his whole heart and soul. He felt his power, and he knew it was greatest in an aggressive war against corruption and incompetency, against criminality and falsehood in the guise of political virtue. He looked for a great defection in the Republican ranks under this protesting banner. In this

he differed from many of his personal friends, who believed that
the public confidence in Gen. Grant remained in the main unshaken, and that when his name came again before the people all secondary considerations would be overlooked and overborne, and that he would be triumphantly elected. But Mr.
Greeley would fight his battles all the same, regardless of consequences, and regardless of all temporary sacrifices, pecuniary
and otherwise, that he knew his course would inevitably entail.
He undoubtedly believed he was laying the foundation for a
broad and successful Reform movement in the future, and that
the losses now would be more than compensated by the gains
hereafter. It was Mr. Greeley's intellectual habit to be always
preparing the way for a better future. He was a man ever im-
patient for progress. He was never content to rest on accomplished results. He was always on the alert for new positions
and new issues. It was a favorite theory of his that frequent
political changes were useful to the public. He held that every
party became corrupt by being long in power, and that this corruption was never fully probed and never destroyed except by
such changes. He cared nothing for the preservation of party,
except as an agency to promote high principles and useful
measures. He did care everything for principles ; but if they
were ignored or disregarded, he cared not what became of the
party that only emptily professed them.

HIS POSITION CONCERNING THE TARIFF.

There is really no reason whatever to believe Mr. Greeley anticipated any other result than that we have indicated in the
opposition he had now avowed. With the people who originally
proposed to meet at Cincinnati for Civil Service and Revenue
Reform, Mr. Greeley had no sympathy. Their cardinal object
was to make head against that protective policy which he had
long warmly supported. But as a body favorable to reform in
general, Mr. Greeley aimed to utilize it in the direction of such
reforms as he himself favored. He thought the two classes of
reformers might act harmoniously in pursuance of a common
object, by agreeing each to remit the chief subject of disagreement between them, namely, the Tariff question, to the popular

constituencies of the Congress Districts. It is hard to see anything blamable in this, but only a wise precaution; since practically it did not alter the position of the question in the present or the future by a hair's breadth. But it has been made a matter of reproach to Mr. Greeley, in the allegation that he thereby abandoned his own previous position on the subject. The reproach is unmerited, since the allegation is wholly untrue. He did not abandon any position he ever occupied on the subject, and did not propose to forego its discussion or even the advocacy he had so long practiced. But Mr. Greeley was endeavoring to harmonize the elements of the opposition for the common advantage, and without reference to himself. He wanted that Convention to agree on a Presidential candidate he could support, and he did not conceal his preferences that that candidate should be Lyman Trumbull. But he did not go to the Convention, and did not seek in the least, either by solicitation or combination, to influence its action.

But in due time, to the utter surprise of everybody, and especially of Mr. Greeley himself, it did nominate him as its candidate for the Presidency. As much of the reproach heaped upon Mr. Greeley is because he became the candidate of the opposition, we should like to ask just here, what was Mr. Greeley to do under the circumstances? He certainly was not to blame for his nomination. He had not contrived it; he had not anticipated it. The result was a spontaneous judgment at Cincinnati that he was the most fit man to nominate. Was he to repel this judgment? Was he to withdraw, and say he would not run? It is none too much to say that he could with propriety do neither. Of all men in the movement, it was not for him to balk at the first step of the Convention, and thus interpose an obstacle to its success by discrediting its judgment. Mr. Greeley, then, was in no sense responsible for his own nomination, and thus deserves no reproach for it. He had it thrust upon him, and he could not escape its consequences. No conditions were attached to it, and no promises exacted. He was taken on a position he had long before marked out for himself, when he originally resolved on fighting the battle in the ranks, in behalf of whoever might lead.

HIS POSITION CONSISTENT THROUGHOUT.

Neither because the Democrâts subsequently thought it for their interest to confirm the nomination, and to accept Mr. Greeley for their candidate, is it to be imputed to him for a crime. He was but the passive recipient of unexpected honors from his old adversaries. Their action did not change his own self-chosen position, or swerve him a hair from his principles. He did not become a Democrat or a representative of Democracy by accepting the nomination. He was the same Horace Greeley and the same Republican as before, and would have so remained had the fates been propitious and placed him in the Presidential chair. It was his own lofty and independent position, his daring declarations of determined freedom from party shackles when they would bind him to support what he abhorred and execrated, that extorted the admiration of his old foes and won the support of such of them as could be moved by sentiments of magnanimity toward so noble and fearless a leader. Unhappily these did not comprise the whole of the Democratic party. There were numerous Democrats in every State, who, in the zeal of their partisanship, opposed him to the end, and threw State after State into the hands of Gen. Grant's friends. They at least believed Gen. Grant to be a better Democrat than Mr. Greeley. They knew that Mr. Greeley had never belonged to the Democratic party, had never joined it, had never qualified his hostility to its views in every issue it ever raised with the Republican party in the past, and for these reasons refused their support to his nomination. It was these Democrats, who would not go over to Mr. Greeley's position and yield him their support, who compassed his defeat. They declined being parties to the sacrifice that the Baltimore Convention of the representatives of the party were willing to make, and did make, as the declaration of principles they adopted amply attest. Mr. Greeley himself stood firm in his own place, that of a consistent, pronounced, distinctive, but liberal and non-partisan Republican. This is not left to conjecture or assertion. His writings and his speeches, from first to last, at once luminous and copious, all show it, and are an everlasting testimony to his truth, his consistency, and his unswerving fidelity to his principles and his convictions.

No friend of his is perplexed as to his motives, or in doubt as to his inspirations, or questions the perfect integrity of his acts. His pathway needs no hedge to conceal devious and labyrinthine ways. His road was clear and open and plain to all who do not choose to be blinded by the fogs of a shallow partisanship. It is at once an insult to his memory and an insult to the personal friends who supported him through the Presidential contest, either to charge or to intimate that his reputation and his honor are best conserved by throwing a vail over the most prominent facts and circumstances of his whole political life. His friends say, No! Uncover everything. Let all be told. Conceal nothing. We challenge the sharpest scrutiny. But why say even this? There is nothing to scrutinize that the broad light of open day does not already shine upon and reveal, and the impartial biographer and historian of the future, when he shall review Mr. Greeley's life and character, will find no flaw therein, and will be compelled to pronounce the inevitable verdict : "Well done, good and faithful servant."

Yours,   JAMES S. PIKE.

CHARLESTON, S. C., FEB. 24, 1873.

MISCELLANIES.

LITERATURE AS A VOCATION.

THE world is a seminary; Man is our class-book; and the chief business of life is Education. We are here to learn and to teach, — some of us for both of these purposes, — all at least for the former. Happy he, and greatly blest, who comes divinely qualified for a Teacher, —fitted by nature and training to wrestle with giant Ignorance and primal Chaos, to dispel unfounded Prejudice, and banish enshrouding Night. To govern men, in the rude, palpable sense, is a small achievement; a grovelling, purblind soul, well provided with horsemen and artillery, and thickly hedged with bayonets and spears, may do this. Nero ruled the Roman world at the height of its power and glory, and ruled it so sternly that no man dared speak of him, while he lived, save in the language of abject flattery. Caligula did it likewise; and so, in an uncouth, second-hand, deputizing way, did (or might have done) Caligula's horse; but which of these, think you, could have *instructed* the millions he so sternly swayed? Alaric had no difficulty in cutting off ten-score thousand heads; but he leaves to our own Everett the writing of the poem wherein the nature of his exploits is duly celebrated. Had he been obliged to slice off as many more heads, or write such a poem, he would have chosen the former task without hesitation or self-distrust.

The true king, then, — the man who *can,* — from which root I would derive also *ken* and *cunning,* — is he who sways the mighty realm of Thought; whose achievements mimic those of the Infinite Father by building out into void space, and peopling Chaos with living and beneficent, though bodiless, creations. Who knows or cares what was the name of Homer's temporal sovereign? The world could not spare Cicero's Orations, but what recks it of his consulate? George III. ruled respectably a mighty realm through the most memorable half-century in the history of man; yet his age will be known to remote posterity, not as his by any means, nor even as that of Napoleon or Wellington, but as that of Goethe, Wordsworth, and Byron. Bonaparte himself was a reality and no sham; yet he missed his best chance of earthly immortality when he allowed Fulton to leave France with the steamboat still in his brain. The burning of Moscow was unlucky for the conqueror of Austerlitz; but this non-comprehension of our great countryman was a betrayal of incapacity, — a downright discomfiture, of which no Grouchy can be made the scapegoat.

Inevitable, then, is it, and by no means to be lamented, that, in an age so eventful and stirring as ours, an innumerable multitude should aspire to Write, — that is, to Teach. Nay, it is greatly to be desired, and every way to be encouraged, that the largest possible number should aspire to sing and shine as enlighteners and monitors of their fellow-beings. Brother in the tow frock and ragged unthinkables! have you an idea humming in your brain, that seems to you fitted to cure even the lightest of human maladies? Out with it, I pray you, in mercy to a benighted, heart-sick, and blindly suffering race! Sister in linsey-woolsey, and wearing a red-cotton handkerchief by way of diadem, have you aught to say, that, if uttered, would cheer and bless the weary steps whereby we are all measuring off the little span which divides us from the grave? For sweet Charity's sake, do not withhold it, but let your light shine, even though the darkness be sure *not* to comprehend it, — a by no means novel nor uncommon case. Heed not the croaker's warning that the world overflows with books and authors, — so it did in Solomon's time; yet how many very good ones, that mankind could hardly spare, have been written since! Truly, the universe is full of light, and has been these thousands of years; yet, for all that, we could not dispense with the sunshine of to-morrow, whether as a realization or as an assuring prediction. Never believe those who tell you that our Race are surfeited with teachers, — that their present needs are material only, not spiritual, — and that your humble lay will be drowned by the crashing volume of the world's great choral harmonies, — for if you have something to say, and do really *say* it, never doubt that it will find or make its way to the eyes and hearts of those fitted to appreciate and enjoy it.

But the real perplexity, the one great source of disappointment and mortification in the premises, is this, — Of the legions who aspire to teach and sing, only a very small proportion do so from any hearty, intrinsic, essential love of the work, while the great multitude seek primarily and mainly their own glory or aggrandizement, rather than the good of their kind. They aspire to be teachers, not because the world needs to be taught, but because they must somehow be fed. Minim's "lays" are inspired by his laziness, and not by any of the Muses, who would be tortured by his invocations if they paid any sort of heed to his twanging. Crotchet's treatise on Hydraulics and Dynamics was impelled by the vacuum in his own stomach, rather than by any painful sense of deficiency or error in popular conceptions of natural science. Van Roamer's "Travels" were constrained by the stern alternative of quitting his native soil or cultivating it; he is enabled to tell us how the Camanches grow corn, or the Mohaves harvest beans, through his own invincible repugnance to assisting in either process at home. And thus the domain of letters is continually infested, is wellnigh overrun, by a swarm of adventurers who are only intellectual in their pursuits and tendencies because they dread being, and so have not fitted themselves to be, material, — as Talleyrand accounted all men Military who were not Civil. Hence, the patient earth groans beneath the weight of books written from as grovelling a motive as ever sent a truant whimpering to school, and the moon and stars are persecuted with flatulent apostrophes and impertinent staring by bards whose main incitement to thus tormenting the night is a constitutional abhorrence of getting up and swinging an axe in the morning.

It is high time the current cant affirming the misfortunes of authorship, "calamities of genius," the miserable recompense of intellectual effort, &c., were scouted from the earth. Its groundwork is a total misconception of the relations of things intellectual to things physical, — of Mind to Matter, Time to Eternity. Milton, they say, sold Paradise Lost for ten pounds to its original publisher, Mr. Simmons. Begging your pardon, gentlemen, he did no such thing; if he had done, the mighty epic would have henceforth been *Simmons's* Paradise Lost, no longer Milton's. No such poem was ever written for pounds, few or many, nor ever can be. The author sold only the privilege of multiplying copies for the few years wherein his right of property in his work was protected by law; but the poem was still Milton's, and so must remain while Time shall endure. Trade and Law are mighty in their several spheres; but both together are powerless to vest the proper ownership of Paradise Lost in anybody else than John Milton.

I am not palliating the injustice done to authors by our laws of Copyright; they are indeed gross and indefensible. Their original sin inheres in their attempt to draw a distinction where the laws of the Universe make none, — between Property in the creations of the Brain and in those of the Hands. The distinction is at best imperfect. A poem, as given by the author to the press, is the joint production of intellect and muscles, — so is a plough or a boot-jack. The difference is one of proportion only, — in the poem, the labor of Production is mainly brain-work; the reverse is the case with the plough. The poet's work, *as* poet, is one of creation purely, so far as finite beings can create; while the mechanic's achievement is one of accommodation or shaping merely. No man ever made, no man *can* make, a flour-barrel so thoroughly his as Childe Harold was and is Byron's. On what principle, then, do human laws say that the flour-barrel belongs to the maker, his heirs or assigns, so long as it shall exist, and wherever it may be found, but that Childe Harold was Byron's property only within a narrow territorial radius and for a brief term of years ? Clearly, on no principle at all. The law plunders the author while pretending to protect him. It ought to know nothing of Copyright save to require the author to give fair notice that he regards his production as a property, and forbids the multiplication of copies by any other than a publisher expressly authorized by him. Then, if it were deemed expedient to confiscate the author's right of property, at the expiration of fifty or a hundred years from the date of his work's first appearance, he ought to be fairly compensated for his book, if the demand for it were still active, so as to justify a claim to indemnity on the part of his heirs.

The Law of Copyright is pernicious in all its restrictions on the natural right of property, — wrong in denying that right in one country to the citizen of another, and thereby bribing the author to pander to local and provincial prejudices, instead of speaking to all Humanity. A book which finds readers in all or many lands is presumptively worth far more than one which finds admirers only in the country which produced it. This law is doubly wrong in virtually saying to the author, " Cater to the prejudices, the follies, the passions of the hour ; for the approval of future generations may indeed pile marble above your unconscious dust, but will give no bread to your famishing offspring !" It is very true that the pecuniary recompense is not the main impulse to the production of works which the world does not willingly let die ; but the State has no moral right to rob a man merely because he leaves his doors unlocked. It is bound to render to each his due ; and it sets an evil example in divesting any of what is rightfully his own.

But, to ninety-nine of every hundred literary aspirants, it makes no difference practically whether the copyright accorded to their works is or is not limited both in time and space. Out of every hundred books published, not ten are ever read out of the country which produced them; hardly one will be heard of by the author's own grandchildren. "Come like shadows, so depart," is the motto that would fitliest illustrate the title-page of our booksellers' annual catalogues of their new issues. Like an April snow-shower, they are poured upon us till they threaten to cover, if not transform, the earth; but soon the sun shines out, and, the next hour, they have vanished forever.

Now, while it is quite true that Milton did not write Paradise Lost for Mr. Simmons's ten pounds, nor for any number of anybody's pounds, it is none the less certain that the State has no moral right to bribe its authors to strive for momentary popularity rather than enduring regard. It has no moral right to say to them, "Write skilfully on a level with the passions and prejudices of the day, and you shall have wealth and present fame; but, if you write what the vicinage may condemn, yet what the Ages and the Race must approve and embalm, you shall be punished with poverty for yourself and beggary for your children." That "ye cannot serve God and Mammon" was true enough in the nature of things, before the State undertook to aggravate, as against Mammon's despisers, the severity of the sentence and the intensity of the punishment.

The World of Thought! how vast its extent! how majestic its triumphs! I am not surprised that literary fame is the object of such general aspiration; I should be surprised indeed if it were otherwise. Just consider how potent, how vast, is the sway to-day exercised by Plato, and Virgil, and Tacitus, now so many centuries in their graves, and compare it with the narrow, transient, imperfect dominion of Alexander or Augustus, so omnipotent in his own age and sphere, so impotent elsewhere, and ever after. Xenophon the leader has long been undistinguishable dust, while Xenophon the narrator is still in the zenith of his power and renown. Julius Cæsar holds his place in the world's regard far more by means of his Commentaries than of his victories, and Bonaparte's first campaign electrified Europe not more by his battles than his bulletins. We cannot wonder, then, that men have sacrificed ease and pleasure, youth and strength, grace of motion and power of vision, to win a name among those who worthily wielded that "weapon mightier than the sword"; for, indeed, there is no other field of effort, no other arena for ambition, so inviting, so dazzling, as this. Wolfe on the Heights of Abraham admiringly recited Gray's Elegy, and declared that he would rather be its author than the conqueror of Montcalm and Canada. "All for love and the world well lost," is the surrender of the grandest possibilities to a fleeting delirium of the senses; but well might the conqueror of an empire, the heir of a dynasty, exchange his circumscribed and vanishing dominion for a seat among the Kings of Mind, — the rulers of that World of Ideas, whose sway each year expands and strengthens, though their bones have enriched, centuries ago, the soil with which they wrestled for a meagre subsistence as Homer the mendicant or Æsop the slave.

But have the true Kings of Thought in fact realized their own might, and actually aspired to and struggled for the pre-eminence which Mankind has so cordially assigned them? Did Shakespeare, for instance, know himself the intellectual prodigy he truly was, and apprehend that the lines he dashed off with such facile rapidity would be read in delighted awe and wonder on isles of the Southern main, far beyond the African cape, which in his day bounded in that direction the known world? I find in his writings the presence of amazing power, but not the consciousness of it. Nay: I cannot help suspecting that, had he really known how great a man he was and is, he would have refrained from acting and talking so often like a little one. The world has known men who profoundly esteemed themselves great, and justified that consciousness by every act of their lives. I could not have dared to ask Michael Angelo to build me a tavern-stable out of the crumbling walls of a deserted monastery or fortress; I should have cowered before the glance of his eye as he turned upon me with the question, "Do you think I was sent into the

world to build stables?" Yet I would not have hesitated —
would you? — to ask Shakespeare to write me, for a consideration, an epithalamium, a monody, a pasquinade, an epigram;
and should not have feared rebuke or refusal, if the price named
were sufficient. For I see the man working and delving from
day to day like any journeyman among us, — with immense
courage, certainly, and capacity, and consciousness of power,
— but still working up the ordinary play-house rubbish into
his grand, airy new structure, as any skilful mason might fill
up the centre of his wall with the commonest brickbats, until
the difference between him and other playwrights seems one
of degree purely, and not of kind. But, reading him thoughtfully, I am arrested by passage after passage evincing an
almost Divine faculty, — a faculty in which I discern nothing
of the playwright, but rather the inspiration of the soul-rapt
prophet, who looks straight through all things; for to him the
universe is without opacity, and past, present, and future are
mere lines of demarcation across the great plain lying lucid
and level before him. This man's nature is a riddle which I,
very palpably, cannot read; so I turn away, perplexed and
overmastered, to resume the thread of my discussion. If he
were *always* unapproachable, I could comprehend, though I
might not accurately measure him; if he were only a clever
play-house poet, I could more easily and surely estimate him;
but his starry flights and his paltry jokes — his celestial pene-
tration and his contemptible puns — form together a riddle
entirely too hard for me. I read him; I admire him; but I
do not know him; and all the commentators and critics serve
only to render darkness more visible, — *my* darkness, I freely
admit; but is it not also in some part their own?

The great soul like Milton's, finding utterance through
Authorship because utterance is a necessity of its being, and
because it feels impelled benignly to assure its weaker, more
opaque brethren, that evil is phenomenal and transitory, — the
murky exhalation of a chill night, which heaven's sunshine
will in due time dissipate, — for this I take to be the burden

of all true Literature, as of true Prophecy, — this is, to my eye, the grandest, noblest spectacle beheld on earth. But the literary hack also, — whereof I hold Shakespeare to be the highest type yet revealed to us, — perhaps the highest ever *to* be seen, — he who, finding authorship to be the work directly in his way, takes hold of it and *does* it, heartily, manfully, capitally, with all his might, as he would do anything else that thus planted itself across his path; always evincing talent, energy, resolution; sometimes irradiating these with the celestial fire of genius — he, too, is at least a respectable personage; and contemplating him shall give us added strength and vivacity for the discharge of our own duties, whatsoever they be. But the literary mendicant, — the aspirant to live by literature, while literature begs to be excused from his obsequious and superserviceable attentions, — of him and his works be the heavens mercifully oblivious, be the earth compassionately delivered! He is just the sorriest sight the sun looks down upon, and fills us with the dismalest conceptions of the lower possibilities of human infirmity.

Do but contemplate him, at twenty, thirty, forty, fifty years of age, — a hale, stout, broad-shouldered man, with thews that might chop cord-wood or do some other creditable service to his kind, — at all events, with fingers terminating either fore-arm that would answer for gathering apples or picking up potatoes, — to see him, thus generously furnished, insisting on Authorship as his vocation, when nobody wants to hear or read him, — wandering from publisher to publisher to petition for the printing of his poem or novel, or besieging editor after editor for employment on his journal, — this is a spectacle of human degradation which angels may well weep over. And then to hear *him* talk of the Calamities of Genius! — he whose chief calamity is, manifestly, a total lack of genius, and not of genius merely, but of self-respect, energy, or manhood. Had he but one spark of true genius, it would develop in him a healthful, proper pride, whereof the first dictate would be a revolt against such hawking and auctioneering of his Diviner faculties. "No," he would say, "I need bread, and am not ashamed to solicit the privilege of earning it by such means as naturally bring bread, — by hireling labor in the corn-field, the meadow, the ditch, or the mine; for that is the natural resort of all those who have no estate of their own. I can proudly ask my neighbor to let me saw his wood for a dinner, since such is the obvious way of earning dinners, and sawed wood ministers to a physical necessity akin to my urgent need of victual; but to ask any man to give me a dinner or a dollar for a poem or essay which he never asked me to write, — to beg of him an exchange of his bread for my thoughts, my ideas, — this I cannot stoop to do. If my book be printed, either with my own means or those of a publisher who believes it will do, let any man buy it and pay for it who will; but, if I urgently want bread, let me produce something which is bread's natural equivalent, or let me beg it, if reduced to that dire extremity, in the direct, honest way; but to degrade my faculty of uttering thoughts, such as they are, into a means of indirect beggary, that lowest deep of humiliation, I cannot, dare not, descend to."

Perhaps there is not in all Literature any monument of human perversity and self-exposure more emphatic than the grand chorus of complaint and remonstrance which every year forces its way through some muddy channel or other to the public ear, of which the burden is the stolidity, incapacity and niggardliness of publishers, in not discerning unrecognized merit in the works of young or unknown authors, buying their manuscripts at a generous price, and introducing them, with appropriate ceremonies, to the reading public. There are never less than thousands of these unprinted authors, whose fame is yet in the egg, but who fancy that they need only a spirited and appreciating publisher to cause it to chip the shell and soar away on eagles' wings to immortality. Every year, some hundreds of fresh aspirants to literary distinction contrive to overleap the hated barrier and rush into print; when perhaps the books of ten of them repay the cost of the adventure; two or three are encouraged to try again; and possibly one proves a man of mark, wins popular approbation, and is ever after solicited by publishers, instead of needing to solicit their partiality and favor. But it was not by this one, nor yet by the two or three, that the howl was prolonged as to the obtuseness and rapacity of publishers, — their drinking rare wines out of the skulls of their plundered, starving authors, &c., &c. No : it is from the ranks of the great unpublished, or, if published, unread, that this hideous dissonance goes up, — men who, far from being victims of publishers, have victimized *them*, and will do it again whenever they shall induce one to bring out another of their dreary inanities. All the wine that will ever be made by publishers out of these plaintive gentlemen's productions might be drank out of *their own* skulls, while they are yet living, and leave abundant room therein for all the brains they have to fulfil their ordinary functions undisturbed and unstimulated.

Authors of this stamp rarely consider that not creditable writing only, but true publishing also, is an intellectual vocation, — that as much ability is often evinced in bringing out and selling a book as in writing it. Publishing is a pursuit requiring various talents, ripe scholarship, large capital, and rare sagacity. Of original publications, but a small portion prove profitable, while the great majority involve positive loss. The instances of undeserved or inordinate success in publishing are quite as rare as in authorship.

And you, my unfledged bard ! who croak over the stupidity of publishers, and the indifference of the reading class to unlaurelled merit, out of your own mouth shall you be condemned ! You complain that others are deaf and blind to such merit ; yet *you* are not one whit less so yourself ! *You*, Mr. Epaphroditus Sheepshanks, who grumble that Thackeray or Tennyson is read, yet your novel or poem untouched, — is tacitly condemned by thousands who cannot *know* that it is not excellent, — do *you* buy or read the novels of Snooks or the poems of Pettibone, in preference to those of the great celebrities of our day ? You know well that you do no such thing, — that you have never looked through them, have scarcely given them a thought. You say, very naturally, "They *may* be good; but my time for reading is limited; and I choose to devote it first to those whose works I have already some reason to *know* are good. Snooks and Pettibone may be clever fellows, I dare say they are, but they must await a more convenient season." And in this you talk and act sensibly; quite otherwise when you grumble that more would-be authors do not succeed in getting printed, and that those who do fail to extract more money as copyright from publishers in addition to that which they have already squandered in paper, typography, and binding.

True, there appear at long intervals men decidedly in advance of their time, — who come to their own, and are not recognized and made welcome, — who write, like Wordsworth or Emerson, for a public which their genius must create or their patience await, — authors whose works would sell better if they were less profoundly good. But this class accept their fortune unmurmuringly, and never repine over their inability to serve at once God and Mammon, and so grasp the rewards of both Time and Eternity. They do their own work calmly, uncomplainingly, almost unconsciously, like the stars and the mountains, and are content to gladden and bless as they may, without striking for an advance of wages. They know, without seeking it, that their message of good-will finds its way to the hearts fitted to receive and assimilate it; they would be amazed by an intimation that their efforts were unappreciated and unrewarded. Not laboring mainly for popularity or pelf, they cannot regard the absence of both as an evidence that their effort is defeated and their labor in vain.

"But," says an ingenuous youth, "I aspire to eminence, fame, popularity, — nay, sir, to usefulness, — as an author; which, I trust, is no ignoble aspiration. Then why may I not seek to sell the fruits of my intellectual efforts in order to cultivate and improve my faculties, and qualify me for the career I meditate? Why may I not seek to sell the poem or story I wrote yesterday, in order to win me bread and opportunity to write a better one to-morrow?" The question is a fair one, and shall be fairly answered.

The ever-present and fearful peril of the Literary vocation is compliance, — the sacrifice of the eternal verity to the temporary necessity. To write to-day for to-day's bread involves the necessity of writing what to-day will appreciate, accept, and buy. This is to set your faculty of thought and utterance up at auction to the best cash bidder, agreeing to do whatever Divine or diabolic work he may have in hand; and it is most unlikely that he who bids highest in current coin for to-day's work, payable to-night, will have Divine work for you to do. Of course, it is understood that you do not *directly* sell yourself to whomsoever will pay highest; but that is the palpable *tendency* of going needily into the market to barter brains for bread. You cannot afford to be nice respecting the use to which your mental faculties are to be turned, if you must sell them to-day, or go hungry to-morrow. The natural drift, therefore, of sending your head into the market for sale is toward moral indifference and debasement, — toward the sale of your talents for the most they will fetch, without regard to what use they will be required to subserve. This tendency may be resisted, baffled, overborne; but it can never cease to be a reality and a peril. Sensual appetite is always ready to pay generously for a present gratification; while Virtue is constitutionally austere and provident. And, beside, there is a very great mistake widely prevalent which confounds the continual *use* with the *improvement* of the faculties essential to Authorship; whereas, use is as often exhausting as strengthening. Washington, Bonaparte, Byron, Wellington, — in fact, nearly all the great men of the last age, — evinced qualities as admirable and eminent in the outset as in the maturity of their several careers. Their opportunities, their responsibilities, may have afterward been broader; but Washington on Braddock's fatal field, Bonaparte in Italy, Byron in Childe Harold, Wellington in India, while still young men, evinced the great qualities which have rendered their names immortal. They there gave promise of all that they afterward performed. If such qualities inhere in you, they will find or make their way out; if they do not, you cannot create them by years of imitative, mechanical drudgery as a journeyman in the vocation you are anxious to master.

I would say, then, to aspiring young men : " While you seek the ladder that leads up to renown, preserve, as above all price, your proper independence, mental and physical. Never surrender yourself to what is termed an intellectual vocation until you have first laid the foundations of independence in the knowledge of a good trade or handicraft, to fall back on whenever you shall find yourself unable to maintain at once your position as a brain-worker and your perfect self-respect. Take your place in the field or the shop, and make yourself master of its duties, — fasten yourself to some patch of ground on some slope of the Alleghanies, the Catskills, the Ozarks, — do anything which will make you a self-subsisting, skilful, effective worker with the hands, while you have the full control of your mental powers, and may apply your hours won from toil to their improvement, until you shall be called thence to intellectual pursuits by some other need than your own. Then you may accept the new opportunity in perfect security, and in the proud consciousness that your instructed sinews can earn you a livelihood by manual labor, should it ever happen that you can no longer maintain your integrity and your self-respect in that other vocation to which a hope of wider usefulness, and the request of those you serve, will have drawn you. Now, you need no longer consider how much truth the public will bear, but what is the particular truth it needs to have expounded and enforced to-day. You will serve mankind as a benefactor, not now as a slave.

It is one of the most venerable of jokes, — patronized, I dare say, by Mr. Joseph Miller and other ancient collectors of good things, and yet so pat to my argument that I cannot refrain from quoting it, — that a London ship was once captured off the Spanish coast by an Algerine rover, and her crew and passengers mustered before the Dey, to be put to the best use respectively as slaves. Each, as he entered the immediate presence of the head pirate, was required to name his trade or calling ; which, being duly interpreted, he was assigned to the workshops, the ship-yard, the gardens, or the galleys, according as his past experience had fitted him for efficiency in one vocation or another. At length, there came one who answered the usual question by avowing himself an author, and this was finally translated so as to render it comprehensible to the Dey ; who, after puzzling his brains for some time to devise a better use for so helpless an object, finally ordered him to be provided with a pair of feather inexpressibles, and set to hatching out chickens. Here the story stops, leaving us in tantalizing darkness as to the success of the literary gentleman in this new field of production ; but, as the employment so compelled must have been sedentary and irksome to the last degree, it serves to enforce my moral, that a youth should thoroughly qualify himself to earn his own bread with his hands before he risks himself on the precarious enterprise of ministering to the intellectual needs of others.

Having thus protested, as I could not in conscience fail to do, against the baseness which aspires to authorship as an escape from ruder labor, and then whimpers because its flimsy intellectual wares cannot be exchanged for wholesome bread-corn, or substantial beef, let me not fail to remonstrate also against the crying injustice done, more especially by the laws of *our* country, not to her worthless but to her worthier, nobler Authors, through the denial of International Copyright. We nationally and systematically steal the works of Bulwer, Dickens, Thackeray, Macaulay, Browning, Tennyson ; boldly claiming the right and exerting the power of taking, using, enjoying, their products, without rendering the authors any equivalent ; and we thereby deprive our own authors of the fair and just reward of *their* labor as well. Our Irving, Bryant, Hawthorne, Longfellow, &c., are less widely read and less fully recompensed than they should be, because the works on which they are paid a copyright must be sold in direct competition with those of their European rivals, whom we refuse to pay at all. " Are they not paid by their own countrymen ?" I hear triumphantly asked. "No, sir!" I reply; not paid by Europe for the service they render *us*, not paid by anybody else for the instruction or entertainment *we* derive from their works. This instruction we have no moral right to appropriate without paying for it, any more than we might honestly clothe ourselves in unbought European fabrics which a wrecking storm had strewn along our shores. That we *can* take them without redress, and for the present with impunity, is undoubted ; but *that* no more proves our *right* to do it than the impunity long enjoyed by the corsairs of the Barbary coast in plundering Christian vessels in the Mediterranean, proved the justice of *that* shameful atrocity. The day will yet dawn wherein Man everywhere shall profoundly realize that no essential advantage can ever be obtained through injustice, — that the constitution of the Universe is such that no product of human effort can be obtained cheaper than by honestly buying and fairly paying for it. In that day, it will be felt and admitted that we have seriously injured and imperilled our country, by intrusting the formation of its mind, morals, and manners mainly to Foreign Authors, through the relative cheapening and consequent diffusion of their works inevitably resulting from the denial of International Copyright.

Perhaps there is no chapter in the history of Literature more amusing, and yet none which is essentially more melancholy, than that which acquaints us with the frailties of Authors, and especially of those of decided genius. That Shakespeare was arraigned for deer-stealing, — a most poetical and delicate sort of theft, all admit ; — that the great Bacon, father of modern Philosophy, was disgraced and cashiered for corruption as Lord Chancellor, the most responsible and one of the most lucrative as well as honorable posts in the kingdom ; that Burns was irregular in love and immoderate in drink ; that Byron was a libertine, and Chatterton a cheat ; that some bards have run away with other men's wives, while a good many have run away from their own, — these, and like deplorable facts, are reiterated and gloated over by millions, who are much better acquainted with the vices and errors of the greatly gifted than with their writings. Too many of us find an ignoble, if not malicious, pleasure in reducing those whose intellectual stature threatens to dwarf us at least to our own *moral* level; we catch at the evidences of their frailty, in order to assure ourselves that we too are spiritually deathless as they, or they at least mortal as we are. And their lives are necessarily so public, so transparent, so scrutinized, that the least flaw attracts observation; they seem worse than others at least as bad as they, only because they are better known. How many follies, meannesses, vices, sins, in the lives of the common-place, are charitably hidden from public view by the friendly oblivion which screens the majority from observation in shielding them from public interest or curiosity! How many have stolen deer, and been convicted and whipped or imprisoned for it, and had the matter all over and forgotten within a year or two; while here stands great Shakespeare, still in the stocks for deer-stealing, though he has stood there so patiently — a little disdainfully, perhaps, yet quite exemplarily — for almost three centuries! O, it is a fearful thing for one greatly gifted to cherish vices or yield to temptations! his errors cover and deform him like writhing, hissing snakes, whose scaly sides and gleaming crests shine in the refulgence by which his genius has surrounded him, from the towering height to which his achievements have lifted him, so that the whole world sees them; the good with pitying sorrow, the thoughtless with mirthful levity, the bad with ill-concealed exultation. Vice is lamentable in any, — is the source, not merely of moral degradation, but of physical suffering; but saddest of all are the offences, most signal and enduring the punishments, of those fitted by Nature to be great, — the Kings of the mighty realm of undying Thought!

The necessities, the perplexities, the pecuniary distresses, of authors, — these, too, have afforded the multitude an inexhaustible fund of anecdote and entertainment. In fact, the obvious contrast between the novelist or poet in his garret, lying abed for the day, perhaps, to have his linen washed, while he considers whether to let his hero marry the great heiress and inherit his principality just yet, or tantalize the reader's impatience with new machinations or impediments through two or three chapters more, — this is antithesis too pungent, too comic, not to be enjoyed. The great majority have ceased to read such "slow," tame essays as those of The Spectator and The Tatler; yet the story of Dick Steele's embarrassments, follies, arrests for debt, and irreclaimable prodigalities, have recently been retold to our city audiences by Thackeray with inimitable felicity, and enjoyed with unexampled zest. An author's thoughts, it would seem, may perish or be supplanted, but the mementos of his thoughtlessness will endure forever.

Yet there is exaggeration in the current notion of the constitutional poverty and squalor, the desperate shifts and average seediness, of authors, which ought to be exposed, since there is just truth enough at the bottom of it to render it mischievous. The great, the radical difference between our age and the centuries which preceded the invention of printing, ought to be explained and realized. In those ages, the cost of multiplying books was so great that very few copies, even of the best, were made or could be afforded; and the author's right of property in his work — that is, his rightful control over the privilege of reproducing it — was of slender or doubtful pecuniary value. Homer, of course, received nothing for his masterly and immediately, universally popular works, beyond the few pence flung to him here and there in requital for the pleasure he afforded by singing them. Cicero was paid for his orations by his clients, never by his readers. And thus it chanced that the *dedication* of books, now so absurd and unmeaning, had once a real force and significance. Authors, as a class, were never rich, and those who were poor had yet inherited a prejudice against living on air. And, since their works had no pecuniary value when completed, they were very poor security, while yet unwritten, for the bread that *must* be eaten, and the wine which *would* be drank, by the authors while writing them. So each poor aspirant for literary distinction was obliged, at the outset of his undertaking, to seek and find a *patron*, wealthy, and fond of doing public-spirited acts, or at least of the fame thence arising, who would be willing to subsist him while at his work and reward him at its close. The Dedication, then, was the author's public and formal acknowledgment of his obligation to his patron, —his avowal that the credit of the work ought to be divided between them, — just as to-day the inventor of a mechanical improvement, and the capitalist who supplies the money wherewith to perfect and secure it, often take out a patent jointly. But the Art of Printing, and the general diffusion of knowledge and literary appetite, have abolished patrons, by abolishing the necessity which evoked them; so that there is now but one real patron, The Public, and nearly all dedications to particular individuals are affected, antiquated, and unmeaning.

It is a very common but a very mischievous notion, that the writing of a book is creditable *per se*. On the contrary, I hold it *dis*creditable, and only to be justified by proof of lofty qualities and generous aims embodied therein. To write a book when you have nothing new to communicate, — nothing to say that has not been better said already, — that is to inflict a real injury on mankind. A new book is only to be justified by a new truth. If Jonas Potts, however illiterate and commonplace, has been shipwrecked on Hudson's Bay, and has travelled thence overland to Detroit or Montreal by a route previously unknown, then he may give us a book — if he will attempt no more than to tell us as clearly as possible what he experienced and saw by the way, — which will have a genuine value, and which the world may well thank him for; and so of a man who, having manufactured charcoal all his days, should favor us with a treatise on burning charcoal, showing what was the relative value for that use of the various woods; how long they should be on fire respectively; how much wood should be burned in one pit, and how the burning should be managed. Every contribution, however rude and humble, to our knowledge of nature, and of the means by which her products may most advantageously be made subservient to our needs, is beneficent, and worthy of our regard. But the fabrication of new poems, or novels, or essays, or histories, which really add nothing to our stock of facts, to our fund of ideas, but, so far as they have any significance, merely resay what has been more forcibly, intelligibly, happily, said already, — this is a work which does less than no good, — which ought to be decried and put down, under the general police duty of abating nuisances. I would have every writer of a book cited before a competent tribunal and made to answer the questions: "Sir, what proposition is this book intended to set forth and commend? What fact does it reveal? What is its drift, its purport?" If it embodies a new truth, or even a new suggestion, though it seem a very mistaken and absurd one, make way for it! and let it fight its own battle; but if it has really *no* other aim than to be readable, therefore salable, and thus to win gold for its author and his accomplices, the printer and publisher, then let a bonfire be made of its manuscript sheets, so that the world may speedily obtain from it all the light it is capable of imparting.

I once received a letter from a somewhat noted novelist, pressing me to read thoroughly one of his works just issued, which the cover proclaimed his "greatest novel," and which he wished me to commend to general favor, saying he was anxious to do his part toward the emancipation of the poor from their unmerited degradations and miseries. I was not able to read the book, — editors receive too many requests like this; but I replied to the letter; saying, in substance: "You wish to improve the condition of the poor. Well: allow me to suggest a way. Take hold of the first piece of vacant earth you can gain permission to use, plant an acre with potatoes, cultivate and gather them, give one half to such poor creatures as really need them, and save the balance for your own subsistence while you grow more next year. In this way, you will do more toward meliorating the condition of the poor than you could by writing novels from July to eternity." My philanthropic friend did not take my advice, — he did not even thank me for it; but he soon after started a newspaper, whereof he sent me the first five numbers, in every one of which I received a most unmerciful flagellation. The paper is since dead; but I have no doubt its editor continued his castigations to the last, and died laying it on with whatever vigor he had left. *I* could not help that. I never made any reply; but my convictions, as expressed in my letter to him, remain unchanged to this day.

Yet let us not seem to disparage the Author's vocation; nay: we dare not, we cannot. There is no other earthly exercise of power so Olympian, pervasive, enduring. Reflect how many generations, dynasties, empires, have flourished and vanished since the Book of Job was written; and how many more will rise and fade, leaving that sublime old poem still fresh and living. See Cicero, Virgil, Horace, Livy, still studied and admired by the patrician youth of nations unknown to Rome in her greatness, while all other power pertaining to the Pagan era of the Eternal City has long since passed away forever. Nay: consider how Plutarch, Æschylus, Plato, living in a world so very different from ours, — in many respects, so infantile compared with ours, — can still instruct the wisest and delight the most critical among us, and you may well conclude that to write nobly, excellently, is a far loftier achievement than to rule, to conquer, or to kill, and that the truly great author looks down on the little strifes and agitations of mankind from an eminence which monarchs can but feebly emulate, and the ages can scarcely wear away.

But eminence in any good or great undertaking implies intense devotion thereto, — implies patient, laborious exertion, either in the doing or in the preparing for it. He who fancies greatness an accident, a lucky hit, a stroke of good fortune, does sadly degrade the achievement contemplated, and undervalue the unerring wisdom and inflexible justice wherewith the universe is ruled. Ask who among modern poets have written most admirably, so far as manner and finish are regarded, and the lover of Poetry least acquainted with Literary History will unhesitatingly answer, — Pope, Goldsmith, Gray, Moore, Campbell, Bryant, Longfellow, Tennyson. He may place others above any or all of these in power, in genius, in force; but he cannot doubt that these have most smoothly, happily, faultlessly, sung what they had to sing, — that their thoughts have lost less than almost any others' by inharmony or infelicity of expression. Then let him turn to Biography, and he will find that these men have excelled nearly or quite all others in patient study, in fastidious determination to improve, so long as improvement was practicable; in persistent labor, so long as labor could possibly avail. It was quite easy for Pope to say, "The things I have written fastest have always pleased most"; for he always studied and thought himself full of a subject before he began to write about it, and his composition was merely a setting down and arranging of ideas already present in his mind. And yet I apprehend that Posterity has not ratified his judgment; I mean, that his works which "pleased most" when first published have not stood the test of time as well as some others. The world of letters knew him as a pains-taking, laborious, correct writer, even before he had established his claim to be honored as a great one. And the works he wrote so rapidly he afterward revised, corrected, altered, recast, before allowing the public to see them, to the sad encouragement of blasphemy among his printers, so that on one occasion his publisher decided that it would be easier to compose in type afresh than attempt to correct one of his proofs. No man ever wrote better, so far as style is regarded ; because no man was ever more determined to publish nothing that he could improve. So Goldsmith considered four lines of his "Deserted Village" a good day's work, and the world has ratified his judgment. With the kindred "Elegy" of Gray, this belongs to a school of poetry which I do not transcendently admire ; but its excellence after its kind, I presume, no one has ever doubted. And it is related of Moore, the most fastidious and the most melodious writer of our time, that a friend once travelled with him all day, and was surprised by his taciturn moodiness and abstraction, until, just before night, his face lighted up, and he exclaimed, like the old Greek : " I have it ! That will do !" — then explained to his startled companion that he had been all day trying to adjust a rhyme or counterpart to a line in one of his then unfinished poems, and had but just now succeeded. It is thus that works which the world prizes and embalms are composed. A style termed "easy" is generally obtained at great expense of time and effort, whether in the immediate composition or in the life-long preparation for it ; and he who calculates on storming the ramparts of literary fame by the audacity, the impetuosity, of his genius, will very certainly be repulsed and discomfited. The "kingdom of heaven" may "suffer violence," but the republic of letters resents and repels it.

O, my erring friend ! delighted that your son of fourteen years or your daughter of twelve has written a page of not intolerable verses, I pray you to lay this lesson to heart ! I can sympathize with your paternal partiality ; I do not wonder that you are proud of your child's achievement, — for the writing even of bad verses at so tender an age *is* an achievement in one sense, and may plausibly be deemed by you a sign of promise, — but you are thinking of the figure *those verses* would cut in the Poet's Corner of some journal, of the praises they would elicit and the distinction they would confer on their writer ; and against these fond, foolish, perilous fancies I most earnestly protest and warn you. If your child has any talent — which is possible, though not probable ; for precocity in any but secret authorship argues a low idea of the difficulties of creditable composition, and a taste easily satisfied, because of the poverty of its conceptions of excellence, — still, it is possible your child *has* talent, (which I am confident he did not inherit) ; and, *if* he has, you are taking the very course to ruin him. Puff him up with the conceit that he is an author at fourteen, and he will pretty surely have proved himself a fool before he is twenty-five. But read over his composition with him, and kindly point out its faults or weaknesses ; encourage him to try again, and avoid these errors if possible, but studiously withhold his productions from publicity, and impress him with the truth that to write feebly or badly, — as he cannot now help doing if he writes at all, — is only creditable or noteworthy as it renders possible his writing well after he shall have attained intellectual and physical maturity. Thus cultivate, chasten, and ripen his faculty, but never stimulate it ; and there is a possibility that it may ultimately ally him to the great and good of past ages ; but let him set out with the conceit that he is a prodigy, and his wreck and ruin are inevitable.

It only remains to me to speak more especially of my own vocation, — the Editor's, — which bears much the same relation to the Author's that the Bellows-blower's bears to the Organist's, the Player's to the Dramatist's, Jullien or Listz to Weber or Beethoven. The Editor, from the absolute necessity of the case, cannot speak deliberately ; he must write to-day of to-day's incidents and aspects, though these may be completely overlaid and transformed by the incidents and aspects of to-morrow. He must write and strive in the full consciousness that whatever honor or distinction he may acquire must perish with the generation that bestowed them, — with the thunders of applause that greeted Kemble or Jenny Lind, with the ruffianism that expelled Macready, or the cheerful laugh that erewhile rewarded the sallies of Burton or Placide. No other public teacher lives so wholly in the present as the Editor ; and the noblest affirmations of unpopular truth, — the most self-sacrificing defiance of a base and selfish Public Sentiment that regards only the most sordid ends, and values every utterance solely as it tends to preserve quiet and contentment, while the dollars fall jingling into the merchant's drawer, the land-jobber's vault, and the miser's bag, — can but be noted in their day, and with their day forgotten. It is his cue to utter silken and smooth sayings, — to condemn Vice so as not to interfere with the pleasures or alarm the consciences of the vicious, — to praise and champion Liberty so as not to give annoyance or offence to Slavery, and to commend and glorify Labor without attempting to expose or repress any of the gainful contrivances by which Labor is plundered and degraded. Thus sidling dexterously between somewhere and nowhere, the Able Editor of the Nineteenth Century may glide through life respectable and in good case, and lie down to his long rest with the non-achievements of his life emblazoned on the very whitest marble, surmounting and glorifying his dust.

There is a different and sterner path, — I know not whether there be any now qualified to tread it, — I am not sure that even one has ever followed it implicitly, in view of the certain meagerness of its temporal rewards and the haste wherewith any fame acquired in a sphere so thoroughly ephemeral as the Editor's must be shrouded by the dark waters of oblivion. This path demands an ear ever open to the plaints of the wronged and the suffering, though they can never repay advocacy, and those who mainly support newspapers will be annoyed and often exposed by it; a heart as sensitive to oppression and degradation in the next street as if they were practised in Brazil or Japan ; a pen as ready to expose and reprove the crimes whereby wealth is amassed and luxury enjoyed in our own country at this hour, as if they had only been committed by Turks or Pagans in Asia some centuries ago. Such an Editor, could one be found or trained, need not expect to lead an easy, indolent, or wholly joyous life, — to be blessed by Archbishops or followed by the approving shouts of ascendant majorities ; but he might find some recompense for their loss in the calm verdict of an approving conscience ; and the tears of the despised and the friendless, preserved from utter despair by his efforts and remonstrances, might freshen for a season the daisies that bloomed above his grave.

Let me conclude by restating the main propositions which pervade and vivify this essay. Literature is a noble calling, but only when the call obeyed by the aspirant issues from a world to be enlightened and blessed, not from a void stomach clamoring to be gratified and filled. Authorship is a royal priesthood; but woe to him who rashly lays unhallowed hands on the ark or the altar, professing a zeal for the welfare of the Race only that he may secure the confidence and sympathies of others, and use them for his own selfish ends! If a man have no heroism in his soul, — no animating purpose beyond living easily and faring sumptuously, — I can imagine no greater mistake on his part than that of resorting to authorship as a vocation. That such a one may achieve what he regards as success, I do not deny; but, if so, he does it at greater risk and by greater exertion than would have been required to win it in any other pursuit. No: it cannot be wise in a selfish, or sordid, or sensual man to devote himself to Literature; the fearful self-exposure incident to this way of life, — the dire necessity which constrains the author to stamp his own essential portrait on every volume of his works, no matter how carefully he may fancy he has erased, or how artfully he may suppose he has concealed it, — this should repel from the vestibule of the temple of Fame the foot of every profane or mocking worshipper. But if you are sure that your impulse is not personal nor sinister, but a desire to serve and ennoble your Race, rather than to dazzle and be served by it; that you are ready joyfully to "shun delights, and live laborious days," so that thereby the well-being of mankind may be promoted, — then I pray you not to believe that the world is too wise to need further enlightenment, nor that it would be impossible for one so humble as yourself to say aught whereby error may be dispelled or good be diffused. Sell not your integrity; barter not your independence; beg of no man the privilege of earning a livelihood by Authorship; since that is to degrade your faculty, and very probably to corrupt it; but, seeing through your own clear eyes, and uttering the impulses of your own honest heart, speak or write as truth and love shall dictate, asking no material recompense, but living by the labor of your hands, until recompense shall be voluntarily tendered to secure your service, and you may frankly accept it without a compromise of your integrity or a peril to your freedom. Soldier in the long warfare for Man's rescue from Darkness and Evil, choose not your place on the battle-field, but joyfully accept that assigned you; asking not whether there be higher or lower, but only whether it is here that you can most surely do your proper work, and meet your full share of the responsibility and the danger. Believe not that the Heroic Age is no more; since to that age is only requisite the heroic purpose and the heroic soul. So long as ignorance and evil shall exist, so long there will be work for the devoted, and so long will there be room in the ranks of those who, defying obloquy, misapprehension, bigotry, and interested craft, struggle and dare for the redemption of the world. "Of making many books there is no end," though there is happily a speedy end of most books *after* they are made; but he who by voice or pen strikes his best blow at the impostures and vices whereby our race is debased and paralyzed may close his eyes in death, consoled and cheered by the reflection that he has done what he could for the emancipation and elevation of his kind.

POETS AND POETRY.

WE are all born poets. Not that every tenanted cradle holds an undeveloped Shakespeare, — far from it. *Demonstrated* intellectual greatness is the prerogative of the few; it is "the vision," not "the faculty divine," which is the birthright of the many. The grime of smoke and care and sin heavily inwraps, incases, japans, many souls, even in early childhood, — as we see children of seven years prematurely haggard with suffering, squalor, and vice, — but there was a time when these imps were poets, lacking only the power of expression. The child who conjectured that the stars were but chinks or crannies of heaven, — gimlet-holes bored in the adamantine firmament to let God's glory through; the prattler who watched the darkening evening sky, until, espying the first bright speck through its dusky medium, she rapturously exclaimed, "There! God has made a star!" — were happy only in expressing the common impulses of childhood. As all young children are actually theists, — believers in a veritable, personal, conscious, omniscient, omnipotent Author and Ruler of all things, and utterly averse to substituting for this natural, tangible conception any thin attenuation of Pantheistic fog or "fire-mist," any blank Atheistic assumption, which gives to blind Chance or inexorable Fate the name of Law, — so the uncorrupted child instinctively perceives the poetic element in Nature, realizes that we are not the mere combinations of gases and alkalies to which the chemist's crucible would reduce us, but beings of mysterious origin and untold spiritual force, inhabiting a world only less weird and wondrous than ourselves. The Frenchman, who was astounded by the discovery that he had been talking prose all his life, might have been equally amazed by the assurance that he formerly thought, if he did not utter, poetry, — and this was as true as the other. Every close observer must have noted how naturally the talk of unschooled, unspoiled children takes on poetic vestments, — becomes dramatic not merely, but hyperbolic and imaginative in a high degree. Emerson truly says that the first person who called another *puppy* or *ass* was a poet, — perceiving in the individual contemplated a spiritual aptitude to bark or bray, as the case might be. I only add that the first child who ever saw a man making an ass of himself, — which, with all deference to our common progenitor, I apprehend was the first child that ever clearly saw anything whatever, — at once perceived the spiritual similitude, and probably blurted out the ungracious truth. All savage tribes — that is, all nations still in their mental childhood — have a poetic literature, if any; their legends, their traditions, their romances, their chronicles, are all poetic, alike in substance and in diction. Of this truth our Aborigines afford a ready demonstration. A stagnant or decrepit race, like the Chinese, may have their prosaic ordinances, statutes, records, statistics, philosophies; not so a vigorous, elastic, Teutonic tribe or Saracenic empire.

Thus we naturally find some of the most admired and remarkable poems — the Book of Job, the Hebrew Psalms, the Iliad, and the Bagavhat Geta of the Hindoos — dating back to the infancy of Society, as the Inferno, and Shakespeare's and Milton's masterpieces, ally themselves with the infancy of modern civilization, or of the Protestant development thereof. We laugh at Nimrod Wildfire and kindred etchings of the hyperbolic or exaggerated modes of speech indicative of a new country, — new, that is, to the race now inhabiting it; the story of a Western soil so fertile that a crowbar, carelessly thrust into it overnight, is found bristling with spikes and tenpenny nails next morning; of the pumpkin-vine, that outran the steed of the rather astonished traveller; of the

Vermonter, whose chance companion in the cutter behind a rather lively nag at length perplexedly inquired, "What grave-yard is this we are passing through?" and was answered, "Only the milestones along the road," — but a new people are irresistibly prone to these exaggerations. The young American, who goes abroad, finds himself obliged to moderate and tone down his ordinary conversation to adapt it to the general level; to speak of Niagara, or Lake Superior, or the glaciers of Switzerland, in the language that rises spontane-ously to his lips, would jar the nerves of his polished listeners, and he would very possibly be reminded, by some highly respectable citizen, that the view from the foot of the great cataract at Niagara could not possibly be that of a falling ocean, since the narrowest ocean is three thousand miles across, while Niagara is hardly a mile. The well-bred Eng-lishman of to-day is so fenced in, incrusted, barricaded, with respectabilities, proprieties, decencies, that the poetic element — nay, even the faculty of appreciating it — seems choked out of him; hence, the British poets of to-day find a warmer and more general appreciation with us than at home; and I cannot doubt that there are many more Americans than Britons familiar with the works of Scott, Byron, and I think even Shakespeare. Yet the English are our kinsmen; equal, but dissimilar, in mental capacities and aptitudes, — only we are still in the poetic phase of our national life, out of which they have passed. We are too cultivated and critical to pro-duce a great epic, — our Washington is no Achilles, no Alex-ander, no demigod, but a sensible, conscientious, conservative Virginia planter, heartily loyal to Church and King; yet one whom insane tyranny and regal folly converts at last into a rebel, — of course, a more formidable rebel than any natural agitator, leveller, demagogue, or even philosophizing democrat, could be; for, when *he* draws the sword against the throne he has revered and prayed for from childhood, be sure there are not many left to draw *for* it whose support carries either moral weight or physical power — the weight of numbers — along with it. For Washington, though a model man in his way, is not a representative American. His calm, sedate, orderly frame of mind is not that which is habitual with or prized by the mass of our people. He is such a man as the multitude accept as a leader in a perilous and trying emergency, when they feel a pressing need of the sympathy and aid of the solid "men of property and standing" in their imminent struggle ; but, had not Washington led the army of the Revolution, he would never have been chosen President ; as a plain Virginia gentleman, he would have been beaten in a canvass for the Legislature by some Davy Crockett, Sam Houston, or Larry Keitt of his day, and would thereupon have forsworn politics in disgust, and devoted his after life to his family, his farm, and his stock, and been known only to a hundred or two of the next generation as an upright incorruptible justice of the peace, and a very capable and soldierly captain of the militia company of his neighborhood. No : Washington, in an age of peace and thrift, would never have been "the gray-eyed Man of Destiny," — never been cheered at the theatre, nor glorified in the star-spangled journals. We heap such honors on men of a stamp very different from his.

But to return to Poetry.

The most vulgar error of the vulgar mind with respect to Poetry is that which somehow confounds it with *verse*, and even with *rhyme ;* supposing that a measured distich or quatrain, ending with words of similar but not identical sound, is necessarily poetic. Proud mothers will often draw forth from the deepest recess of closet or bureau some metrical effusion of budding son or daughter, which is supposed to be instinct with poetry, because measured into feet and tagged with rhyme ; when in fact there is no more poetry in it than in the request, "Pass me the baked potatoes." Rhymed couplets of regularly measured and accented lines are a fashion of our poetry, but no more essential to it than a silk or fur hat is to the character of a gentleman. It is barely possible that the child who has an addiction to and knack of making verses may nevertheless possess some share of the poetic faculty, —

the Divine afflatus, — but the presumption against it is almost overwhelming. The poetic genius naturally disdains the fetters of rhyme, or only consents to wear them at the beck of stern necessity. To the fresh, unhackneyed soul, kindling with rapture inspired by its first perceptions of the beauty inhering in the wonder-works of God, rhyme is as unnatural and repulsive as the fool's cap and bells. For, not merely is it true that there have been great poets who never dreamed of such a thing as rhyme, and clever rhymsters who had not the faintest conception of poetry, but there have been genuine poets who failed miserably as rhyming poetasters. John Bunyan, for example, whose Pilgrim's Progress is the epic of Methodism, — (I know, good reader, that he was not technically a Methodist, and that I ought to have said Evangelicalism, had there been such a word,) — and one of the truest, if not the greatest, of British poems, wrote hideous doggerel whenever he attempted verse, as the introduction to that same epic bears testimony. There can hardly be a more certain evidence that a child has ceased to be poetic than the fact that he has begun to rhyme.

The oldest and most natural — I should rather say, the least unnatural — form of poetic expression, when poetry ceased to be a purely spontaneous utterance of exalted and overmastering emotions, and became, in some sense, an art, is that of *parallelism*, or the expression of the same idea or sentiment through two succeeding images or affirmations ; the second being merely cumulative or confirmatory of the former. The Hebrew Scriptures embody some of the earliest and most familiar examples of this parallelism, of which I cite Ruth's appeal to Naomi as a beautiful exemplification : —

> "And Ruth said :
> ' Entreat me not to leave thee,
> Nor to return from following after thee :
> For whither thou goest I will go,
> And where thou lodgest I will lodge :
> Thy people shall be my people,
> And thy God my God :
> Where thou diest will I die,
> And there shall I be buried.' "

I am inclined to deem this parallelism, which informs all the poetry of the Bible, not exclusively Hebrew, but a mode of poetic expression natural to the primitive stages of Society, the intellectual puberty of the Race; though I at this moment recall few examples of it outside of Hebrew lore. Mungo Park, the explorer of Central Africa, relates that, as he lay sick and suffering in the Great Desert, the negro women, who mercifully ministered to his sore necessities, gave utterance to their sympathy in a rude song, of which the burden ran thus : —

> " Let us pity the poor white man :
> He has no mother to bring him milk,
> No wife to grind his corn."

A parallelism as palpable, though not so perfect, as any in Job or Ecclesiastes.

" The Poet," says Emerson, " is the man without impediment." If so, I apprehend that the Poets of our world's infancy enjoyed certain marked advantages over their modern successors. Not only was the whole range of poetic imagery then fresh and unused, so that the bard was never constrained to discard a happy simile occurring to his mind because some other bard had used it before him, but, moreover, his utterance was nowise impeded or shackled by the necessity of obeying the rules or formulæ established by preceding bards and their critics, for the government of the realm of Poetry. If the soul of the universe found expression through his burning words, — if their perusal inspired the reader with a deeper and truer perception of the infinite reason which inheres in seeming dissonance, as well as obvious harmony and good, — if he were impelled by it to love and practise virtue, to loathe vice, yet pity its victims, and to count nothing a defeat or disaster which did not involve a surrender of his own high purpose, his generous aspiration for human well-being, — then was he a true poet, whom the ages were waiting to crown, though Fadladeen should demonstrate unanswerably his ignorance of the first rudiments of the minstrel's art. But the poet of our day must be an obedient vassal to an inexorable rule, — must shun ruggedness or wilfulness of expression as a mortal sin, — must respect the unities, and be loyal to rhythm and rhyme, — or he cannot induce the critics even to blast him with their thunders. True, a wild colt of a bardling will now and then revolt against this despotism, and go prancing and kicking, and displaying his ill-conditioned, shaggy coat across Nature's wide, bare common; but the critical shrug ultimately kills if it does not tame him, and he is left but the sorry choice between subsiding into a patient dray-horse, and being cut up for dog's meat. MacDonald Clarke, twenty years ago, and "Walt. Whitman," just now, undertook to be poets in defiance of the canons of the art; but, though the latter received the unmeasured indorsement of Emerson, and obtained an immediate currency on the strength of it, I doubt whether even he, despite his unquestionable originality, and dazzling defiance of what men have been accustomed to regard as decency, will ever achieve the distinction of being knocked on the head with a volume of the Edinburgh Review.

The earliest poets were, I apprehend, the shepherds of Arabia, Chaldea, and that westernmost jut of the great Asian continent, wherein so large a share of the events memorable in Man's history have transpired. All shepherds are naturally poets; or rather, the loneliness, the silence, and the seriousness, of the shepherd's life naturally predispose him to poetry. He is not necessarily and constantly absorbed in his daily duties, which yet require of him a wakeful, alert understanding, and senses sharpened to acuteness by the necessity of keen perception and watchful observation. When at length his flock have sunk, at early evening, to rest, and the shepherd crouches, wrapped in his blanket-cloak, beside them, his mind awakens to a loftier activity ere his senses are sealed in slumber: from his mountain-side elevation, he looks abroad across rolling river and twinkling city — across valleys where the fog begins to gather and wooded ridges fluttering in the chill night-breeze — to other mountains, vast and towering as

his own, and to heaven, vaster and higher than them all, and
the feelings of immensity, of awe, and of reverence are
stirred within his soul: if of a cold, calculating, mathemati-
cal nature, he becomes an astronomer, and begins to weigh
the stars in his balance; if of a fervid, impulsive genius, his
meditations melt and glow into poetry. From shepherd races
and shepherd climes have come forth the instructors, con-
querors, bards, and civilizers of the barbarian world.

But the mountainous ruggedness, the " cloudless climes and
starry skies," of Chaldea, Syria, and Arabia, so unlike the
vast plains of Sarmatia and Scythia, are especially favorable
to the development of the poetic fire; hence, the Book of Job,
so manifestly pastoral in its origin as well as its imagery, is
one of the sublimest, as it probably is the very oldest, of surviving poems. True, the author is palpably a scholar, an observer, a traveller, who has gathered all the world knew in his
day of astronomic as of terrestrial lore; but his hero is a
Chaldean or Hebrew herdsman, living by the side of the
great Arabian desert, and subject to the mischances and sudden reverses which constantly threaten and frequently befall
the shepherds of that region, even in our own day. In its
magnificent imagery, as well as in its characters and incidents, Job is the simplest and grandest, as well as oldest, of
pastoral poems.

A shepherd boy, keeping his flock on the sterile mountains
of Judea, in constant peril from the savage beasts and not
less savage men of the desert, — " a cunning player on an
harp," sought out by King Saul's servants to expel the evil
spirit which had taken possession of their master (alas that
the evil spirits which gain control of rulers cannot always be.
thus exorcised !), — a battler for his race and faith and native
land, volunteering to encounter, while still a mere lad, the
giant champion of their mortal foe, and vanquishing him in
deadly combat, — a fugitive from the jealous madness of his
royal master, into whom the Evil One seems to have again
entered, and there intrenched himself beyond dislodgement

by the powers of music, — a needy and desperate wanderer
and outlaw for years, carrying his life in his hand, — then
the anointed monarch and idolized hero of his nation, — then
dethroned and put to flight by the ingratitude and perfidy of
his favorite son and the fickle levity of his people, — again
restored to a throne of increasing splendor, and dying peace-
fully and regally in extreme old age, at the summit of his
power and glory, — if I were required to name that one who
of all men had lived the most arduous, stirring, eventful life,
most full of violent contrasts and trying situations, of love
and war, of glory and humiliation, I must say, David, king of
Israel. A life so full of absorbing action would seem to give
little chance for literary culture or achievement; and yet this
warrior king, who could not be permitted to build the Great
Temple to his God, because he had been a man of violence
and blood, has bequeathed us so many Psalms in which the
waiting, contrite souls of ages so remote and races so diverse
as ours from his find a fuller and fitter expression of their
aspirations and their needs than all the piety and genius of
intervening ages have been able to indite. Yes, this untaught
shepherd son of Jesse, this leader in many a sanguinary fight,
this man of a thousand faults and many crimes, knew how
to sweep the chords of the human heart as few or none have
ever touched them before or since, — to take that heart, with
all its frailty, its error, its sin, and lay it penitently, plead-
ingly, at the footstool of its Maker and Judge, and teach it
by what utterances, in what spirit, to implore forgiveness and
help. Other thrones have their successions, dynasties, their
races of occupants; but David reigns unchallenged King
of Psalmody till Time shall be no more.

Of Greek Poetry I have a right to say but little. The
general impression it makes on me is that of youthfulness on
the part of its authors. The most learned among us do not
know those old Greeks very well; and I am often impelled to
wonder whether the versatile, elastic, cheating, unreliable
Greeks of our day are not lineal descendants, not of the

Spartans, perhaps, but of the Athenians and Argives of old;
whether the latter did not hate work and love profit as much
as the Fanariote or the Greek trader of our time ; nay,
whether the Spartans themselves, *plus* a few satisfactory
floggings, are not reproduced in the warrior mountaineers of
Albania and the fierce robber bands which infest the passes
and plains of Thessaly.   True, the Athenian of to-day is
behind the citizens of Western Europe in culture, in courage,
and• in most manly virtues ; but may he not be as far in
advance of the Western Asiatic of Xerxes' or Darius's reign
as were the countrymen of Miltiades or Alexander ?   Europe
north of the Alps has unquestionably advanced ; may not
Greece have simply stood still, instead of retrograding ?   The
solution of this doubt is to be found, not in the prowess nor
the physical achievements of the old Greeks, but in their
literature, and especially their tragedy.

The Greek epic held substantially the place of the modern
novel ; I cannot so confidently say that the novel *fills* the
place of the epic.   The epic embodied and presented human
life under its more heroic and majestic aspects, — the life of
the patriot, ready to seal his devotion with his blood..   Greek
life, as depicted by Homer, is rude and sterile ; its pleasures,
gross and sensual ; its gods, men and women endowed with
supernatural powers, but not at all distinguished by supernatural virtues.   It would be very rash in me to pronounce
Homer monotonous, and at times tedious, when the scholars,
who know him so much better, say exactly the reverse ; so I
will not hazard the criticism, though I shall privately cherish
my own opinion.   I wonder if any one else ever detected or
fancied a resemblance between the roll of Homer's heroes and
Catlin's gallery of Indian portraits ?

The Epic is the utterance of a ruder age than ours.   The
scholar still praises it, — he thinks he delights in it, — but it
is the delight of association, of comparison, of remembrance, —
not of direct and simple enjoyment.   Who ever heard of an
edition of the Iliad in translation being required by the *un*-
classical youth of Great Britain, of this or of any other mod-

ern country ? I apprehend that, for each copy of any great epic to be found in the hands or under the pillow of the youth in all our common schools, you may find ten copies of the Arabian Nights or of certain of Dickens's Novels. Only by those who have been impelled to study them as a task are the great epics still read ; and by these rather as a habit or duty than as a genuine pleasure.

Yet we must be grateful to the creators of the Epic, since to them are we indebted, by direct transmission, by lineal descent, for Tragedy, the broadest, the deepest, the most vivid, expression of human emotions and aspirations. Æschylus is the true child of Homer, and that grand Athenian stage whereon the passions, the impulses, the hopes, the fears, the love, piety, guilt, revenge, remorse, which make up our strangely compounded Human Nature, were depicted so intensely as never before nor since, was the outgrowth of those lofty and stirring narrations wherewith " that blind old man from Scio's rocky isle" was wont to beguile the hours and inspire the hearts of the ancestors of Pericles and Plato. From the goat-song of the Mime, the cart of Thespis, the rude chant of the ballad-singer, the monologue of the legendary, the dialogue of the satirist, was rapidly elaborated that shapely and towering fabric of Grecian Tragedy which must awe, delight, and instruct mankind through ages yet to be.

The argument of Tragedy is the struggle of Man with Misfortune, — the spectacle of Virtue enduring the buffets of Adversity, and of Crime overtaken by the shafts of Retribution. But Greek Tragedy essayed a loftier flight than ours, and presented the suffering but undaunted human soul enduring and defying the bolts of Fate, the anger of the immortal gods. We see there Guilt hurried irresistibly to its awful doom, — inexorable Nemesis visiting the punishment of evil deeds even upon the grandchildren and great-grandchildren of the evil-doer, — the fair, the gentle, and the good, bowing to the destiny invoked by the sin of some progenitor, — and this is not unlike what experience and literature have elsewhere made familiar ; but Prometheus, chained to his rock and suf-

fering the tortures of the damned for having dared to
enlighten and bless mankind, yet calm-souled and defiant,
awaiting the unknown but inevitable hour which shall dethrone his jealous and fearful Olympian tyrant, and bring
him deliverance and recompense, this is a conception peculiar
to Greek Tragedy, and the lesson of stoical endurance and
intellectual force taught by it is without a modern parallel.
Nor must we rashly conclude that the great tragic poets were
irreverent or hostile to the religion of their age and race.
Behind the fable of Prometheus rests the grand, eternal truth,
that all the forces of the universe are subject to the moral
law; that Good is the measure and true end of Power;
that tyranny and cruelty would still be what they are if
their responsible author were armed with celestial thunders;
that, if there could be a more benignant and just being
than the Deity, that being would then be God.

Let me venture to cite one passage from the Agamemnon
of Æschylus as rendered by Bulwer in his Athens, — not one
characteristic of Greek Tragedy, but one which the reader of
poetry will readily contrast with familiar passages of Scott
and Byron. It is that in which Clytemnestra announces to
the chorus the glad tidings of the capture of Troy, — said tidings having been transmitted by the good old fire-telegraph
of primitive times : —

> " A gleam, — a gleam from Ida's height,
>   By the fire-god sent, it came ;
> From watch to watch it leaped, that light,
>   As a rider rode the flame !
> It shot through the startled sky,
>   And the torch of that blazing glory
> Old Lemnos caught on high,
>   On its holy promontory,
> And sent it on, the jocund sign,
>   To Athos, mount of Jove divine.
> Wildly the while it rose from the isle,
>   So that the might of the journeying light
> Skimmed over the back of the gleaming brine !
>   Farther and faster speeds it on,
> Till the watch that keep Macistus' steep, —
>   See it burst like a blazing sun !

Doth Macistus sleep
　On his tower-clad steep?
No! rapid and red doth the wild-fire sweep.
It flashes afar on the wayward stream
Of the wild Euripus, the rushing beam!
It rouses the light on Messapion's height,
And they feed its breath with the withered heath.
　　But it may not stay!
　　And away, — away, —
　It bounds in its freshening might.
　　Silent and soon,
　　Like a broadened moon,
　It passes in sheen, Asopus green,
　And bursts on Cithæron gray.
The warder wakes to the signal rays,
And it swoops from the hill with a broader blaze,
　On — on the fiery glory rode; —
　Thy lonely lake, Gorgŏpis, glowed, —
　To Mĕgara's mount it came;
　　They feed it again,
　　And it streams amain, —
　A giant beard of flame!
The headlong cliffs that darkly down
O'er the Saronic waters frown,
Are passed with the swift one's lurid stride,
And the huge rock glares on the glaring tide,
With mightier march and fiercer power
It gained Arachne's neighboring tower, —
Thence on our Argive roof its rest it won,
Of Ida's fire the long-descended son!
Bright harbinger of glory and of joy!
So first and last, with equal honor crowned,
In solemn feasts, the race-torch circles round.
And these my heralds! this my Sign of Peace!
Lo! while we breathe, the victor lords of Greece
Stalk, in stern tumult, through the halls of Troy!"

The Romans were never a poetic people. Epicureans, who philosophized in verse, like Horace; biting satirists, like Juvenal; happy weavers into verse of legendary lore, like Virgil, the Longfellow of that sole age, the Augustan, in which Roman literature seems to have been at all worthy of the mistress of the civilized world; concise, critical, caustic, pains-taking annalists the Romans were, but not poets. Their best metrical productions have a second-hand flavor; they smell of the lamp; they would have been different, or never have been at all, had there been no Greece.

Brownson says certain ages are termed Dark, because *we* are in the dark with regard to them. Those who will may assign a kindred reason for my assumption, that there was no poetry worth treasuring and praising written between the Augustan age and the time of Dante, and that one needs to be at least as good a Catholic as Dante to appreciate and enjoy the Inferno.

When I assume that English Poetry for us begins with Shakespeare, I must not be misunderstood. That there is merit of a certain kind in Chaucer, in Spenser, and other British rhymers before the age of Queen Bess, is of course manifest. But who in our day ever sat down to read Chaucer or Spenser otherwise than as a task, — something requisite to a competent knowledge of English literature? For my part, I say frankly that I hold The Faery Queene a bore, and never had patience to complete its perusal. Its allegorical representations of our good and evil impulses are tedious, fantastic, unreal, insufferable. They probably instructed and delighted the generation for which they were written; but their fragrance has departed. Lay them respectfully, tenderly down to their long rest, and let the gathering dust slowly bury them out of sight!

But of that vast, "myriad-minded" Shakespeare, what shall I say? True, I do not love him; but do I the less appreciate and admire his intellectual force and grandeur? Because I profoundly hate his Toryism, shall I disparage his unquestioned and, in its way unequalled, genius? Because I am compelled to perceive that his jokes are often sorry and his puns mainly detestable, must I be presumed to deny that his humor is delicious and his imaginative faculty beyond that of any other mortal? By no means.

I am provoked by his ingrain Toryism, because it seems at once unnatural and irrational. I will not deny that the mass of men are base, — possibly *as* base as he represents them, — I will only insist that there are capacities, possibilities, in this abused nature of ours, beyond our actual achievement, or beyond his apprehension of that achievement. Even if it were otherwise, he, a child of the people, the son of a woollen-draper, should not have been first to discover and proclaim the deplorable fact. Yet, no autocrat born in the purple nourished a more profound contempt for the rabble, the canaille, the *oi polloi,* than this vagabond by statute and venison-thief by conviction. In his game, only the court-cards count; all the rest go for nothing. We, the untitled, undistinguished masses, are not merely clowns and poltroons, fit only for butts for knightly jests, and hardly good enough to be meat for knightly swords, but there is a constant, though quiet, assumption that this, as it ever has been, must continue to be forever. You would naturally suppose that grandest event in modern history, the discovery of the Western continent, which was still recent in his day, and which must have been the theme of many a conversation in his presence among the Raleighs, Drakes, and other daring spirits of that stirring time, who had personally visited the New World, would have inspired even in his breast some hope of a fairer future for Humanity on earth, — some aspiration, at least, for a Social Order wherein Rank and Wealth should not be everything, and Man nothing, — but no : I cannot recall even a passing allusion to America, save that most inaccurate one, "the still vext Bermoothés," and never once an intimation, a suspicion, that the common lot might be meliorated through the influence of the settlement and civilization of this side of the globe. Of course, the actor-manager-author meant no disrespect to us Anglo-Americans in prospect, nor yet to our Franco-American neighbors just north, nor to the Spanish and Portuguese Americans south of us ; it was only a way he had of viewing everything with an eye which, though it oft, " in fine frenzy rolling," might " glance from heaven to earth, from earth to heaven," never penetrated laterally much beyond the fogs of London and the palace of Whitehall, and not only saw in the million merely the counters wherewith kings and nobles played their gallant game, but refused to see in them the possibility of becoming anything better.

Whether Shakespeare the monarchist or Milton the republican were intellectually the greatest Englishman who ever lived, I will not judge; but none can doubt that, morally, Milton was by far the superior. His purity of life and nobleness of aim; his constancy to the republican cause after it had been irretrievably ruined; in short, his every act and word, prove his immeasurably the nobler nature. Shakespeare, the Tory and Courtier, had he lived an age later, could never have dared and suffered for his convictions as Milton did for his. Nor, though he has written many finer passages, which have found ten times as many delighted readers as aught of Milton's has found, or perhaps will ever find, can I recall one passage from Shakespeare, which does his manhood such honor as is reflected on Milton's by his two sonnets on his blindness, which, however familiar, I shall make no apology for citing:—

ON HIS BLINDNESS.

When I consider how my light is spent
Ere half my days, in this dark world and wide,
And that one talent which is death to hide,
Lodged with me useless, though my soul more bent
To serve therewith my Maker, and present
My true account, lest he returning chide;
"Doth God exact day-labor, light denied?"
I fondly ask: But Patience, to prevent
That murmur, soon replies, "God doth not need
Either man's work or His own gifts; who best
Bear His mild yoke, they serve Him best: His state
Is kingly; thousands at His bidding speed,
And post o'er land and ocean without rest;
They also serve who only stand and wait."

TO CYRIAC SKINNER.

Cyriac, this three years, day these eyes, though clear,
To outward view, of blemish or of spot,
Bereft of light, their seeing have forgot,
Nor to their idle orbs doth sight appear
Of sun, or moon, or star, throughout the year,
Or man, or woman. Yet I argue not

Against Heaven's hand or will, nor bate a jot
Of heart or hope; but still bear up and steer
Right onward. What supports me, dost thou ask?
The conscience, Friend, t' have lost them overplied
In Liberty's defence, my noble task,
Of which all Europe rings from side to side.
This thought might lead me through the world's vain mask
Content, though blind, had I no better guide.

Such sentiments, not only uttered but *lived,* the efflux of a serene, majestic soul, which calamity could not daunt, nor humiliation depress, not merely honor our common nature, — they exalt and ennoble it. Shakespeare could no more have written thus of himself than Milton could have created and gloated over the character of Falstaff.

Of later English poets, prior to those of the reign of George III., I regard Pope alone as deserving of remark; and he mainly because of the unmeasured eulogies of Byron and others, who certainly should be judges of poetry. For myself, while esteeming him a profound philosopher and moralist, and the king of verse-makers, I should hardly account him a poet at all. "The Rape of the Lock" is undoubtedly a clever poem of the slighter or secondary order; but very much of Pope's verse, had it been cast in the mould of prose, would never have struck us as essentially poetic. For all the poetry they contain, some of his satirical verses might better have taken the form of prose, not to speak of those which, for the sake of decency, had better not been written at all. And so I say of Goldsmith, Thomson, Cowper, Young, and their British cotemporaries: they understood the knack of verse-writing; they did well what they undertook; their effusions — "The Deserted Village," especially — may still be read with a mild and temperate enjoyment; but a thousand such bards would never have created a National Poetry, — never have produced anything which other nations would eagerly translate and delightedly treasure. Essentially, they are not poets, but essayists, sometimes moralists or sermonizers; at others, romancers or story-tellers; but they produced nothing which mankind could not easily spare. Let them glimmer awhile in their decent, inoffensive mediocrity, then sink into a kind of oblivion.

The credit of ushering in the brightest era of British Poetry belongs to the Scotch ploughman and rustic, Robert Burns. This man of many faults and sins, who little deemed himself summoned to do the work of a literary reformer, was yet fated to brush aside the sickly sentimentalisms and fantastic conceits of an artificial age, and teach Poetry to speak once more to the soul in accents of Truth and Nature. At the sound of his honest, manly, burly voice, the nymphs and goddesses, the Chloes and Strephons, of a dawdling and unreal generation vanished, and Poetry once more spoke from heart to heart in her own unmuffled, undisguised voice, and was joyfully recognized and welcomed. I know that citations may be made from Burns which would seem to contradict this statement; but they prove only that he was at times fitfully ensnared by the Delilahs whose sorceries he was nevertheless destined to vanquish and conclude. "A man's a man for a' that," "The Twa Dogs," "The Cottar's Saturday Night," and many more such, will for generations be read and admired in the gas-lighted drawing-room, and by the log-cabin fireside, as vindications of the essential and proper nobility of Human Nature, and of the truth that virtue and vice, worth and worthlessness, fame and shame, are divided by no pecuniary, no social, line of demarcation, but may each be found in the palace and in the hovel, — under the casque of a noble or the cap of a boor. In the character and works of Robert Burns is the first answer of the dumb millions to the taunts and slurs of Shakespeare.

The great French Revolution — if I should not rather say, the great mental world-revolution which preceded and impelled the French — ushered in a new era in Literature, and especially in Poetry. Burns was the herald or forerunner of this era, but he did not live to mark its advent.

I do not rank Walter Scott with the poets of our century. Though chronologically his place is among them, he belongs essentially to another epoch, or at least to the period of transition. The morning-star of this era was Keats; its lurid and oft-clouded sun was Byron. Keats was a dreamy and sensitive youth, whose soul found in poetry its natural expression; but who had not attained the maturity of his genius, the perfection of his utterance, when a harsh and withering criticism killed him. Byron was a wild and dissolute young lord, who had made one tolerably good, and many weak, if not inexcusably bad, attempts at poetry, when a severe but just critique stung him to madness, and his wrath and bitterness flashed and glowed into enduring verse. His indignation was volcanic; but the lava it ejected was molten gold, — sulphurous, as volcanic discharges are apt to be. As the death-freighted thunderbolt, which often stuns and slays, has been known to unseal the ears of the deaf and the reason of the idiot, so the harsh discipline which crushed the poet Keats made a poet of the second-rate poetaster Byron.

When I assign to Byron a very high, if not the highest, place among modern English poets, I will only ask those who differ from me to instance another whose writings have been so widely read, or have exerted so marked an influence on the age in which they appeared and the generation then in their teens. I do not commend that influence, — I realize that it does not, on the whole, conduce to a more confiding faith in either God or man. Byron's poems, equally with his life, letters, and conversation, excuse, if they do not justify, De Staël's savage characterization, "He is a demon." Read Cain and Manfred considerately, then take up Goethe's "Faust," and study the *rôle* of Mephistopheles, and you will be tempted to guess, since Goethe could not well have modelled his demon after Byron's life, that Byron must have modelled his character on that of Goethe's devil.

It would be a difficult task to write an honest life of Byron that would be adapted to the use of Sunday schools, unless you were to do as he promised in the opening of Don Juan, but failed to perform, when he gave out that his story would be a moral one, because, before he ended it, he meant —

" to show
The very place where wicked people go."

Yes, this sceptical, cynical, irreverent, law-deriding libertine Byron has made his mark deeply on our century, and not wholly for evil. His honest, profound, implacable hatred of tyranny in every shape, where has it been surpassed, either in intensity or in efficacy? Do you believe Holy Inquisitions and other machinery for torturing and killing men and women for the honest avowal of their religious convictions could endure another year, if every one had read " The Prisoner of Chillon ? " You or I may loathe his way of looking at the great problem of Evil; but tell me who ever presented the argument against what is currently termed the Evangelical view of this problem more tersely, strongly, startlingly, than he has done in " Cain, a Mystery " ? And his remark that, " if Satan is to be allowed to talk at all, you must not expect him to talk like a clergyman," is obviously just. You must let him fairly present his view of " the great argument," as Milton does not, as Byron does, but with too manifest a leaning to the infernal side. Bind up " Paradise Lost " and " Cain " in one volume, and you will have therein the best condensed statement of the pro and con of the theology currently accounted Orthodox or Evangelical that can be found in the English language.

I think Moore has somewhere said before me, that the Third Canto of Childe Harold contains some of the noblest poetry we have. Waterloo, the Alpine thunder-storm, and scores of passages equally vivid, will at once present themselves to the reader's mind. " Description is my forte," said Byron; and Bayard Taylor, sailing through the Adriatic and the Ægean, along the rugged coast of Dalmatia, and among the ruin-strown, yet flower-mantled, " Isles of Greece," remarks that he finds himself continually recalling or repeating the descriptive stanzas of Childe Harold, suggested by a similar voyage; for nothing else could so truly, forcibly, aptly, embody his own impressions and emotions. Remember that Homer and Æschylus had gazed on much of this same panorama, and written from minds full of the thoughts it excited, and you are prepared to estimate the tribute paid by our American traveller to the genius of Byron. Let me quote one familiar passage — how could I quote any that is *not* familiar? — from Manfred. I cite that respecting the Coliseum, because, having myself seen the moon rise through its ruined arches while Italian devotees were praying and chanting within, and French cavalry prancing and manœuvring without, its enormous walls, I feel its force more vividly than though I had seen this mightiest monument of ancient Rome in imagination only. Yet what could I say of that grandest of ruins to equal this?

> "MANFRED.
>
> " The stars are forth, the moon above the tops
>   Of the snow-shining mountains. — Beautiful!
> I linger yet with Nature, for the night
> Hath been to me a more familiar face
> Than that of man; and in her starry shade
> Of dim and solitary loveliness,
> I learned the language of another world.
> I do remember me, that in my youth,
>   When I was wandering, — upon such a night
> I stood within the Coliseum's walls,
> Midst the chief relics of almighty Rome;
> The trees which grew along the broken arches
> Waved dark in the blue midnight, and the stars
> Shone through the rents of ruin : from afar,
> The watch-dog bayed beyond the Tiber; and,
> More near, from out the Cæsars' palace came
> The owl's long cry, and, interruptedly,
> Of distant sentinels the fitful song
> Began and died upon the gentle wind.
> Some cypresses beyond the time-worn breach
> Appeared to skirt the horizon; yet they stood
> Within a bowshot. — Where the Cæsars dwelt,
> And dwell the tuneless birds of night, amidst
> A grove which springs through level battlements,
> And twines its roots with the imperial hearths,
> Ivy usurps the laurel's place of growth; —
> But the gladiator's bloody circus stands,
> A noble wreck, in ruinous perfection!
> While Cæsar's chambers, and the Augustan halls,
> Grovel on earth in indistinct decay.—
> And thou didst shine, thou rolling moon, upon

All this, and cast a wide and tender light,
Which softened down the hoar austerity
Of rugged desolation, and filled up,
As 't were anew, the gaps of centuries;
Leaving that beautiful which still was so,
And making that which was not, till the place
Became religion, and the heart ran o'er
With silent worship of the great of old ! —
The dead but sceptred sovereigns, who still rule
Our spirits from their urns."

Of Coleridge, Southey, Campbell, Rogers. and other cotemporaries of Byron, Wordsworth excepted, I shall say very
little. Each did some things well; but, beyond a few stirring
lyrics by Campbell, and perhaps the Christabel and Gene-
vieve of Coleridge, I think our literature could spare them all
without irreparable damage.

Wordsworth's ultimate triumph is a striking proof of the
virtue of tenacity. Here is a studious, meditative man, of no
remarkable original powers, who quietly says to himself, " Intensity of expression, vehemence of epithet, volcanic passion,
profusion of superlatives, are out of place in Poetry, which
should embody the soul's higher and purer emotions in the
simplest and directest terms which the language affords." So
he begins to write and the critics to jeer, but he calmly per-
severes ; and, when it is settled that he *won't* stop writing, the
critics conclude to stop jeering, and at length admit that he
was a poet all the while, but that their false canons or perverted tastes precluded their discovery of the fact for a quarter of a century. I do not accept Wordsworth's theory, — I
believe there are ten persons born each year who are fitted to
derive both pleasure and instruction from the opposite school
to one who can really delight in and profit by the bare, tame
affirmations which are characteristic of Wordsworth (for he,
like the founders of other schools, is not always loyal to his
own creed), — but that Wordsworth's protest against the intensity of the Byronic school was needed and wholesome, I
cannot doubt.

Yet it was not Wordsworth, not "the Lake school," as it

was oddly designated, that led and inspired the reaction against "the Satanic school," so called, of Poetry, by which the later morning of the XIXth century was so mildly irradiated. The credit of that reaction is primarily due to a woman, — to Felicia Hemans. When Byron, still young, was dying in Greece of disappointment, and the remorse which a wasted life engenders, she was just rising into fame among the purest and happiest homes of England, like a full moon rising calmly, sweetly, at the dewy close of a torrid and tempestuous day. It was *her* influence that hushed the troubled waves of doubt and defiance and unrest, and soothed the heaving breast into renewed and trusting faith in virtue, eternity, and God.

I apprehend that Mrs. Hemans finds fewer readers, with far fewer profound admirers, to-day than she had thirty years ago; and in this fact there is a strong presumption that we, who so admired her then, assigned her a higher station than her writings will maintain. A pure and lovely woman, unhappy in her domestic relations, and nobly struggling by literature to subsist and educate her children, is very apt to arouse a chivalry, among readers not only, but critics, that is unfavorable to sternness of judgment. I would gladly believe that the girls of 1868 read Mrs. Hemans as generally, and esteem her as highly, as their mothers did in *their* girlhood.; but I fear their brothers, for the most part, neither read nor admire her. Let me venture, therefore, for the sake of my older readers, to cite one of her minor poems, which must recall to many minds hours of pure and tranquil pleasure passed in the perusal of the author's fresh effusions. Forty years ago, had you opened a thousand American weekly newspapers, — presuming that so many then existed, — you would have found the "Poet's Corner" of at least one third of them devoted to one of the latest productions of Mrs. Hemans, and not one fourth so many given up to the verses of any other person whatever. Now, you might open three thousand journals without discovering therein even her name. Bryant, Tennyson, Longfellow, Whittier, Lowell, Holmes, now fill her accustomed place; as, forty years hence, alas! some fresher favorites will fill *their* places. So flows and ebbs this transitory world! But let not us, her old admirers, suffer her name to drift by us into Oblivion's murky sea without a parting cup of remembrance. We will recall

THE ADOPTED CHILD.

"Why wouldst thou leave me, O gentle child?
Thy home on the mountain is bleak and wild, —
A straw-roofed cabin, with lowly wall;
Mine is a fair and pillared hall,
Where many an image of marble gleams,
And the sunshine of picture forever streams."

"O, green is the turf where my brothers play,
Through the long, bright hours of the Summer's day!
They find the red cup-moss where they climb,
And they chase the bee o'er the scented thyme,
And the rocks where the heath-flower blooms they know;
Lady, kind lady, O let me go."

"Content thee, boy! in my bower to dwell;
Here are sweet sounds which thou lovest well:
Flutes on the air in the stilly noon,
Harps which the wandering breezes tune,
And the silvery wood-note of many a bird,
Whose voice was ne'er in thy mountain heard."

"O! my mother sings at the twilight's fall,
A song of the hills far more sweet than all;
She sings it under our own green tree,
To the babe half slumbering on her knee;
I dreamt last night of that music low, —
Lady, kind lady! O, let me go."

"Thy mother is gone from her cares to rest;
She hath taken the babe on her quiet breast;
Thou wouldst meet her footstep, my boy, no more,
Nor hear her song at the cabin door.
Come thou with me to the vineyards nigh,
And we 'll pluck the grapes of the richest dye."

"Is my mother gone from her home away?
But I know that my brothers are there at play:
I know they are gathering the foxglove's bell,
Or the long fern-leaves by the sparkling well;

Or they launch their boats where the bright streams flow,
Lady, kind lady ! O, let me go."

" Fair child, thy brothers are wanderers now ;
They sport no more on the mountain's brow ;
They have left the fern by the spring's green side,
And the streams where the fairy barks were tied.
Be thou at peace in thy brighter lot ;
For thy cabin home is a lonely spot."

" Are they gone, *all* gone, from the sunny hill ?
But the bird and the blue-fly rove over it still ;
And the red-deer bound in their gladness free ;
And the heath is bent by the singing bee,
And the waters leap, and the fresh winds blow :
Lady, kind lady ! O, let me go ! "

I do not know how many ever suspected, during his life,
that THOMAS HOOD was a poet of rare and lofty powers. I
apprehend, however, that they were, at least till near the close
of his career, a "judicious few," — fewer, even, than the judicious are apt to be. For this true bard was nevertheless a
man, — though delicate in frame, and for the most part frail
in health, he had physical needs, — more than all, he had a
wife and children, who looked to him for daily bread, and
must not look in vain. Poet as he was, he knew that mankind not only stone their prophets before building their tombs,
but starve their poets before glorifying them ; and he declined
to sacrifice his children's bread to his own glory. The world
would not pay cash down for poems, but freely would for fun ;
so he chose to mint his golden fancies into current coin that
would pass readily at the grocer's and baker's, rather than
fashion it daintily into cameos and filigree-work, which he
must have pledged at ruinous rates with the pawnbroker.
And we, generation of blockheads ! thought him a rare buf-
foon, because he sported the cap and bells in our presence,
knowing this, though by no means the best thing he could do,
decidedly that for which we would pay him best. If his
" Whims and Oddities " imply the degradation of a great faculty, is not the fault, the shame, rather ours than his ? If
a modern Orpheus could only find auditors by fiddling for

bacchanal dancers in bar-rooms, could *we* justly reproach him for his vulgar tastes and low associations ?

We who so long read and laughed at Hood's puns and quips, — read and only laughed, when we should have thought and sighed, — we might have seen, if we had sought instruction, and not mere recreation, that a great moralist, teacher, philanthropist; an earnest hater of tyranny and wrong; a warrior, with Damascus blade, on cant, and meanness, and servility, — was addressing us in parables which were only wasted, as others' parables have been, because our ears were too gross, our understandings too dull and sordid, to perceive, or even seek, their deeper meaning. We might have discerned the lesson, but did not, because the laugh sufficed us.

Have I seemed to regret or condemn the law whereby the true poet is divorced from the hope of gain by his faculty ? I surely did not mean it. Wisely, kindly devised is that Divine ordinance, "Ye cannot serve God and Mammon." The law is steadfast and eternal, — the seeming exceptions few and factitious. The greatest benefactors of mankind have waited till after death for the recognition of their work and their worth. If to speak the highest truths and do the noblest deeds were the sure way to present fame and pelf, what merit would there be in virtue, what place for heroism on earth ? If Poetry were the Pennsylvania Avenue to fortune and present fame, how could our earth upbear the burden of her poets ? No : it were better for Poetry that there had never been a Copyright Law, so that the Poet's utterances were divorced from all hope of pecuniary recompense. We should then have had far fewer poems, perhaps, but not half the trouble in unburying them from the avalanche of pretentious rhythmical rubbish whereby they are overlaid and concealed. Let aspiring youth evermore understand that writing Poetry is not among the Divinely appointed means for overcoming a dearth of potatoes. I do not say that potatoes were never gained in this way, though I doubt that any were ever thus *earned.* Be this as it may, I am quite sure that no one ever undertook to write Poetry *for* potatoes, — to satisfy his personal need of potatoes by writing Poetry, — who thereby truly succeeded. He may have achieved the potatoes, but not the Poetry. So Hood did manfully and well in writing "Whims and Oddities" for a livelihood, and Poetry for fame alone. Do you suppose the hope of money could ever have impelled any man to write "The Song of the Shirt"?

Let us refresh our remembrance of him with the simplest and best-known of his minor effusions, — one ten thousand times quoted, familiar to almost every school-child, yet not worn out, because it cannot be : —

I REMEMBER, I REMEMBER.

I remember, I remember
The house where I was born,
The little window where the sun
Came peeping in at morn ;
He never came a wink too soon,
Nor brought too long a day ;
But now I often wish the night
Had borne my breath away !

I remember, I remember
The roses, red and white,
The violets, and the lily-cups, —
Those flowers made of light !
The lilacs where the robin built,
And where my brother set
The laburnum on his birthday, —
The tree is living yet !

I remember, I remember
Where I was used to swing,
And thought the air must rush as fresh
To swallows on the wing ;
My spirit flew in feathers then,
That is so heavy now,
And summer-pools could hardly cool
The fever on my brow !

I remember, I remember
The fir-trees dark and high ;
I used to think their slender tops
Were close against the sky.
It was a childish ignorance,
But now 't is little joy
To know I 'm farther off from heaven
Than when I was a boy.

How many years is it since he who is England's Laureate first dawned upon us ? It seems to me scarcely twenty; yet he must have been writing and printing for nearly twice that period. It is a slow as well as arduous labor for even excellence to make itself felt across an ocean; yet I believe there are to-day as many Americans as Englishmen who honor and delight in the poems of Alfred Tennyson. One of their best characteristics is the carefulness, the evident labor and extreme polish, with which they are produced. After thirty years devoted to Poetry, — almost exclusively, I believe, — his writings may all be compressed within a moderate volume. In an age when many a by no means old man has turned out his twenty volumes, and many a Miss in her teens has nearly finished her third novel, this is a virtue indeed to be commended. To one who has achieved the public ear — for whose future issues eager publishers have checks of generous amount ready to be exchanged for the unread manuscript — the temptation to overwrite is hard to be resisted. Poets are popularly supposed to be, as a class, neither rich nor frugal; the more honor, then, to one who refuses to dilute his nectar like a milkman to whom the pump is convenient. I was deeply interested in Bayard Taylor's anecdote of the German poet Uhland, when in a green old age, who, to the traveller's natural inquiry as to what work he was now composing or meditating, replied that he had not recently felt constrained to write anything, — in other words, that nothing now pressed upon his mind for utterance with irresistible force. Would that authors, as a class, could truly say that they write only under the spur of thoughts burning for expression, — not of appetites clamoring for satisfaction.

Though Tennyson has written sparingly, he has yet covered much ground. "In Memoriam," "The Princess," "Maud," — I hardly know who in our day has produced three poems so unlike, yet each so excellent. "In Memoriam" is probably the best expression of a profound and lasting, yet temperate and submissive, sorrow to be found in our language. Yet his minor poems had made him a world-wide reputation

— made him the Queen's Laureate — before one of these was written, at least before it was published. And they are worthy of their fame. So rich and pure in imagery, so dainty and felicitous in expression, so musical and mellifluous in their rhythm and cadence, — they are rightly ranked among the gems of English literature. Let me cite a part of one of them which is not the most popular, but which seems to me among the happiest. The fable, if fable it be, that eating the lotus brings forgetfulness of care, answering almost to the old Greek's draught from Lethe, is not novel ; but who before has ever treated it so well as this ?

THE LOTUS-EATERS.

I.

" Courage ! " he said, and pointed tow'rd the strand ;
" This mounting wave will roll us shoreward soon."
In the afternoon, they came unto a land
In which it seeméd always afternoon.
All 'round the coast, the languid air did swoon,
Breathing like one that hath a weary dream.
Full-faced above the valley stood the moon ;
And, like a downward smoke, the slender stream
Along the cliff to fall and pause and fall did seem.

II.

A land of streams ! some, like a downward smoke,
Slow-dropping vails of thinnest lawn, did go ;
And some through wav'ring lights and shadows broke,
Rolling a slumb'rous sheet of foam below.
They saw the gleaming river seaward flow
From th' inner land : far off, three mountain-tops,
Three silent pinnacles of aged snow,
Stood sunset-flushed : and, dewed with showery drops,
Up-clomb the shadowy pine above the woven copse.

III.

The charméd sunset lingered low adown
In the red West : through mountain-clefts, the dale
Was seen far inland, and the yellow down
Bordered with palm, and many a winding vale
And meadow, set with slender galingale ;
A land where all things always seem'd the same !
And 'round about the keel, with faces pale,
Dark faces pale against that rosy flame,
The mild-eyed, melancholy Lotus-eaters came.

IV.

Branches they bore of that enchanted stem,
Laden with flower and fruit, whereof they gave
To each; but whoso did receive of them,
And taste, to him the gushing of the wave
Far, far away did seem to moan and rave
On alien shores; and if his fellow spake,
His voice was thin, as voices from the grave;
And deep-asleep he seemed, yet all awake,
And music in his ears his beating heart did make.

V.

They sat them down upon the yellow sand,
Between the sun and moon, upon the shore;
And sweet it was to dream of Father-land,
Of child and wife and slave; but evermore
Most weary seemed the sea, weary the oar,
Weary the wandering fields of barren foam.
Then some one said, " We will return no more";
And all at once they sang, " Our island home
Is far beyond the wave; we will no longer roam."

*   *   *   *   *

Of Robert Browning the reading public knows too little; it shall yet know more. Even in England, I found few whose delight in him equalled my own; and I fairly startled judicious friends by insisting that he is not inferior, on the whole, to Tennyson. But there are obvious reasons why *this* prophet should be denied honor in his own country of all others. For Browning's verse too often lacks clearness; his fancies are piled one upon another in wild confusion; he is fitfully fantastic and mystical; and John Bull has, of all men, the most intense aversion to what is called Transcendentalism. There is an anecdote afloat of Douglas Jerrold meeting a friend in the street soon after Browning's " Sordello " was issued, and thrusting the book into his hands with the fierce command, rather than entreaty, " Read that!" The puzzled friend read a few lines of the opening, and desisted, with the remark, " Why, this is rank nonsense!" "'O, thank God!" exclaimed Jerrold; " then I am not mad! I was sure, if that was sense, that I ought to be sent to Bedlam at once." Another anecdote makes Browning gravely relate to an intimate friend that he had tested in Sordello a favorite theory, by omitting in the published copy each alternate line of the poem as written; but he candidly added, the experiment was a failure.

Browning's best issue was that which opens with "The Blot on the Scutcheon," and contains "Pippa Passes," "Luria," and "Paracelsus." The first-named is one of the purest, sweetest, most affecting dramatic poems in our literature; the action hastens to its catastrophe as resistlessly as, and more naturally than, that of Hamlet or Macbeth; and the heroine's dying wail over her lost innocence, her early doom, —

> " I had no mother, — God
> Forsook me, — and I fell,"

has a condensed force and pathos rarely exceeded.

I am apt to have little sympathy with the complaint that an author is obscure. It very often implies only indolence and lack of earnestness in the complainant. We are prone to read too drowsily, and expect writers to spell out their meaning to us, as if we were four-year-olds, still busy with our " a-b-abs " and " baker." There is an anecdote current to this effect, that when Emerson first began to lecture transcendental-wise in Boston, one of his most constant auditors was the able and veteran conservative lawyer, Jeremiah Mason, accompanied by his daughters. His brethren at the bar were puzzled by this addiction on the part of so distinguished a conservative, and wonderingly inquired of him whether he understood what Emerson uttered. He candidly responded that he did not; but added that his daughters (girls of thirteen and fifteen) understood it perfectly. There was probably more truth in this reply than was intended. The kingdom of heaven stands not alone in being easier of access to little children than to adults. Comprehension is not the result of knowledge solely, but of receptivity, of sympathy. It was not nearly so easy for the old lawyer as for the young damsels to attain the same plane of thought with the lecturer, and to travel in the same direction. He might possibly have learned more had he been less wise.

Yet it is deplorably true that our newest literature too often lacks simplicity, lucidity, straightforwardness. It speaks in riddles, when it should be natural, direct, and open as the day. Carlyle is not half so obscure as his contemners declare him; yet his "Sartor Resartus" cannot be thoroughly mastered and enjoyed by the average reader short of three or four perusals; and how many will have patience to give it that number? Whatever requires so many involves the pursuit of knowledge under difficulties. Emerson, though he is no longer opaque, did formerly try the patience, as well as the discernment, of his admirers; and I can quite credit the story told of one who stopped him in the street and recited a passage from one of his essays, asking what he meant by it; to which the author of "Brahma" and "The Sphinx," after pondering the passage a moment, calmly replied that he certainly *had* a meaning in his mind when he wrote that sentence, though it had now unfortunately escaped him. But Browning's fault seems to inhere rather in utterance than in conception; his mind is full of materials ill stowed, which come rushing against and trampling over each other when summoned to daylight, and so choke the aperture and prevent egress, or rush forth an incongruous, confused mass, muddily sweeping all before them. His later writings are half spoiled by this chaotic whirl, and are thence inferior on the whole to their immediate predecessors. Yet what a wealth of allusion, a mine of meaning, a daguerreotype of the intellectual tendencies of the age, are found in "Bishop Blougram's Apology"! And what have we clearer and purer in our language than this? —

EVELYN HOPE.

Beautiful Evelyn Hope is dead!
  Sit and watch by her side an hour.
That is her book-shelf, this her bed;
  She plucked that piece of geranium flower,
Beginning to die, too, in the glass.
  Little has yet been changed, I think;
The shutters are shut; no light may pass,
  Save two long rays through the hinges' chink.

Sixteen years old when she died!
  Perhaps she had scarcely heard my name, —

It was not her time to love; beside,
　　Her life had many a hope and aim;
Duties enough, and little cares,
　　And now was quiet, now astir,
Till God's hand beckoned unawares,
　　And the sweet white brow is all of her.

Is it too late, then, Evelyn Hope?
　　What! your soul was pure and true;
The good stars met in your horoscope,
　　Made you of spirit, fire, and dew, —
And, just because I was thrice as old,
　　And our paths in the world diverged so wide,
Each was nought to each, must I be told?
　　We were fellow-mortals, nought beside?

No, indeed! for God above
　　Is great to grant, as mighty to make,
And creates the love to reward the love, —
　　I claim you still, for my own love's sake!
Delayed, it may be, for more lives yet,
　　Through worlds I shall traverse, not a few;
Much is to learn and much to forget,
　　Ere the time be come for taking you.

But the time *will* come, — at last it will,
　　When, Evelyn Hope, what meant, I shall say,
In the lower earth, in the years long still,
　　That body and soul so pure and gay;
Why your hair was amber, I shall divine,
　　And your mouth of your own geranium's red, —
And what you would do with me, in fine,
　　In the new life come in the old one's stead.

I have lived, I shall say, so much since then,
　　Given up myself so many times;
Gained by the gains of various men,
　　Ransacked the ages, spoiled the climes:
Yet one thing — one — in my soul's full scope,
　　Either I missed or itself missed me, —
And I want and find *you*, Evelyn Hope!
　　What is the issue? let us see!

I loved you, Evelyn, all the while,
　　My heart seemed full as it could hold, —
There was place and to spare for the frank young smile,
　　And the red young mouth, and the hair's young gold.
So, hush! — I will give you this leaf to keep —
　　See, I shut it inside the sweet, cold hand;
There — that is our secret! go to sleep;
　　You will wake, and remember, and understand.

I envy the biographer of Robert and Elizabeth Barrett Browning. Twenty years ago they were poets, unknown to each other, undistinguished; he poor, and each by no means young. I have heard that their first acquaintance came through their published works, which revealed a sympathy destined to make them one forever. Reversing the usual order, they loved, they became personally acquainted, and were married. Thenceforward, each wrote better, more acceptably, — in the main, more lucidly, — than before; wrote, doubtless, by the help of the other's happy suggestions as well as loving criticisms. And so each won larger and still widening audience, and more generous appreciation, and ampler recompense; and a fair son was born to them; and a wealthy friend, nowise related to either, left them a modest fortune; and they spent their wedded years partly in their native England and partly in their beloved Florence, which inspired both of them, but especially the wife, with some of her noblest and most enduring poems, — "Casa Guidi Windows" for instance, and "Aurora Leigh," — and there, I believe, she died, leaving her husband and son not to lament, but to rejoice over and thank God for, the abiding memory of her worth and her love.

I close this hurried survey without having attempted to consider the claims of any among our countrymen to the character and designation of Poets. I should prefer to consider American Poetry by itself, and in its relations to that which preceded and that which is cotemporary with it. In so doing, we should find, I judge, that, while it has grave faults, — faults of imitation, of poverty, of crudity, of exaggeration, — it has decided merits and excellences also, — merits not only eminent in themselves, but such as give promise of still loftier achievement in the future. If we have contributed our full share to the bounteous Anglo-Saxon stock of shallow and sham poetry, we have also contributed our full quota — considering our youth as ● nation, and our prosaic preoccupations, our lack of leisure, and of the highest intellectual culture — to that which the world will not willingly let die. I waive this discussion for the present, however, and close with a more direct consideration of the problem, " What is the essential nature and true office of Poetry ? "

Of course, I need waste no more time on the pitiable ignorance which confounds Poetry with Verse, — the eternal essence with the occasional form or garb, — though this delusion has still many votaries, — I might say, victims. The young lady who corrected a friend's allusion to Shakespeare as a Poet with the smilingly confident assurance that his plays were not poetry, not being rhymed, has still sharers in her sad misapprehension. Poetry is at least four thousand years old, — as old as extant literature, if not older ; while Rhyme, I suspect, can hardly be traced beyond the time of the Troubadours of western and southern Europe, in the days of the Crusades. Verse, Metre, or Rhythm is of course much older. I presume some rude trace of this may be found in the very oldest writings extant, — the chant or speech in Genesis of Lamech to his wives, for instance, and the oldest Hindoo or Chinese Poems. But, though it may seem natural, and almost necessary, that poetic utterances should flow into harmonious or rhythmical numbers, this is not inevitable. Chateaubriand, one of the greatest poets of the last generation, wrote rarely in verse. Willis has written good verses, but his finest poem is " Unwritten Music,"— in structure, a prose essay. That Rhyme is not essential to Poetry, all probably know who clearly know anything ; but that measured and duly accented lines, each beginning with a capital letter, do not constitute Poetry, though it may be generally, is by no means universally understood. But we cannot define by negations alone ; and the question still recurs, What *is* Poetry ?

I understand by Poetry that mode of expression or averment which lifts the soul above the region of mere sense, — which reaches beyond the merely physical or mechanical aspects of the truth affirmed, and apprehends that truth in its universal character and all-pervading relations, so that our own natures are exalted and purified by its contemplation. For instance, I affirm that the Creation was a wondrous, beneficent work, which all intelligent, moral beings cognizant thereof must have regarded with admiration, but that the plans and purposes of God are entirely above the comprehension of Man, — that is plain prose.   Now let us see a poetic statement of that same truth, and mark its immensely superior vividness and force : —

> " Then the Lord answered Job out of a whirlwind, and said, —
> Where wast thou when I laid the foundations of the earth ?
> Declare, if thou hast understanding !
> Who hath laid the measures thereof ? if thou knowest ?
> Or who hath stretched the line upon it ?
> Whereupon are the foundations thereof fastened ?
> Or who laid the corner-stone thereof, —
> When the morning stars sang together,
> And all the sons of God shouted for joy ? "

Or I am impelled to observe that the creations of the mind, unlike all corporeal existences, are essentially indestructible, and so fitted to abide and exert influence forever, — that is a prosaic statement of an obvious fact ; let us note how Byron presents it in poetry : —

> " The beings of the mind are not of clay ;
> Essentially immortal, they create
> And multiply in us a brighter ray,
> And more beloved existence — that which Fate
> Prohibits to dull life in this our state —
> Of mortal bondage, by these spirits supplied
> First exiles, then replaces, what we hate,
> Watering the hearts whose early flowers have died,
> And with a greener growth replenishing the void."

Or I observe that the midnight thunder, during a violent Summer tempest, is echoed from mountain-top to mountain-top, forming a chorus of awful sublimity ; but the poet seizes the thought, and fuses it in the glowing alembic of his numbers thus : —

> " Far along,
> From crag to crag the rattling peaks among,
> Leaps the live thunder, — not from one lone cloud,
> But *every* mountain now hath found a tongue ;
> And Jura answers, through his misty shroud,
> Back to the joyous Alps, that call to her aloud."

Such instances speak more clearly than the plainest or the subtlest definitions. They show that, to the poetic conception, Nature is no huge aggregation of senseless matter, warmed into fitful vitality by sunbeams only to die and be resolved into its elements, but a living, conscious, vital universe, quivering with deathless aspiration because animated by the breath of God.

Nor must we regard Poetry merely as an *intellectual* achievement, — a trophy of human genius, an utterance from the heart of Nature, fitted to solace its votaries and strengthen them for the battle of Life. Poetry is essentially, inevitably, the friend of Virtue and Merit, the foe of Oppression and Wrong, the champion of Justice and Freedom. Wherever the good suffer from the machinations and malevolence of the evil, — wherever Vice riots, or Corruption festers, or Tyranny afflicts and degrades, there Poetry is heard as an accusing angel, and her breath sounds the trump of impending doom. She cannot be suborned nor perverted to the service of the powers of darkness : a Dante or a Körner, lured or bribed to sing the praises of a despot, or glorify the achievements of an Alva or a Cortes, could only stammer out feeble, halting stanzas, which mankind would first despise, then compassionately forget. But to the patriot in his exile, the slave in his unjust bondage, the martyr at the stake, the voice of Poetry comes freighted with hope and cheer, giving assurance that, while Evil is but for a moment, Good is for ever and ever ; that all the forces of the Universe are at last on the side of Justice ; that the seeming triumphs of Iniquity are but a mirage, Divinely permitted to test our virtue and our faith ; and that all things work together to fulfil the counsels and establish the kingdom of the all-seeing and omnipotent God.

REFORMS AND REFORMERS.

THIS hard, cold, rocky planet, on whose surface we exist, toward whose centre we gravitate, seems to evince but a rugged and wayward kindness for her step-child, Man. Even to the savage, whom she takes to her rough breast with some show of maternal fondness, she says, · "Take your chance with my varying moods, — to-day, sunshine, flowers, and bounty; to-morrow, wintry blasts, bare hills, and destitution." What wonder if the poor Esquimaux, shivering in his foodless lodge, which bleak wastes of drifting snow environ, should misread even the serenely benignant skies, and fancy that diabolic was at least equally potent with Divine agency in creating such a world?

To civilized man, unless fenced about and shielded by that purely artificial creation we term Property, Nature presents a still sterner aspect. He may know, even better than the savage, how to extract sustenance and comfort from the elements everywhere surrounding him; but he finds those elements appropriated, — monopolized, — *tabooed*, — the private, exclusive possessions of a minority. To cut in the forest a dead, decaying tree, wherewith to warm his shivering, scarce-clad limbs, — to dig edible roots from the swamp, or gather berries from the beetling crag to stay his gnawing hunger, — is a trespass on the rights of some proprietor, property-owner, landlord, which legally subjects him to the assiduous but disagreeable attentions of the justice and the constable. Doomed to fight his way through this thorny jungle, he finds the weapons all chained out of his reach, or pointed against him. Born into a state of war, he must first forge or buy the requisite implements for the fray, though his adversaries are under no sort of obligation to wait till he is ready. The fertile prairie often produces sour, ungenial grasses ; and the giant forest, so luxuriant in its panoply of tender foliage, affords but a grudging subsistence to the few birds and animals which inhabit or traverse it. Everywhere is presented the spectacle of diverse species of animated beings struggling desperately for subsistence, and often devouring each other for food.

Into this unchained menagerie Man is thrust, to fight his way as best he can. The forest, the prairie, the mountain, the valley, the lakes, and the ocean, must be tamed to hear and heed his voice ere they can be relied on to satisfy his urgent needs. The river long obstructs his progress ere he learns the secret of making it bear him swiftly and cheaply on his course ; the soil that shall ultimately yield him the amplest harvests is a quaking bog, useless, and hardly passable, until he succeeds in draining and tilling it. The lion or tiger, whom he ultimately regards as a raree-show, and carts about for his diversion, is primarily quite other than amusing, and, though exhibiting himself at less than the "half price" at which children are elsewhere admitted to the spectacle, attracts no curious children of Adam to any exhibition but that of their own heels. The waterfall that propels the civilizee's mill arrests the savage's canoe. In short, Nature, though complaisant at seasons, is yet, in the larger view, grudging and stern toward our race, until transformed and vivified by Labor and Science.

Man, therefore, is by primal necessity a Transformer, — in other words, a Reformer. He must first, by resolute effort, fix his bit in the mouth of Nature, his saddle on her back, and his spurs in her sides, ere he is prepared to run his nobler race and achieve his higher destiny. Though mental development and moral culture be the admitted *ends* of his mundane existence, yet to *begin* with the pursuit of these is to court and insure defeat, by invoking frost and starvation. If the philosopher or divine were to visit the pioneer just slashing together his log hut in the wilderness, and accost him with, "Why wear out your life in such sordid, grovelling, material drudgery, when the gorgeous canopy of heaven overarches you, the glad sun'irradiates and warms you, and all Nature, ministering gratuitously to your gross, bodily wants, invites to meditation and elevating self-communion?" the squatter's proper answer, should he deign to give any answer at all, would be: "Sir, I provide first for my bodily needs, and against the fitful inclemencies of the now genial skies, in order that I may by and by have leisure and opportunity for those loftier pursuits you eulogize so justly, though inappositely. I could not fitly meditate on God, the Universe, and Human Destiny, with a shivering wife looking me sadly in the face, nor with the cries of hungry children ringing in my ears. Nay: I could not so meditate this balmy June morning, in full view of the truth that, if I were content with meditation to-day, such *would be* the appeals of those dependent on me ere June should greet us again. What you suggest, then, is excellent in its time and place; but I must hew and delve to-day, in order that my season for contemplation and culture may ultimately come."

Now, this obvious response of the pioneer to the philosopher is in essence the material or circumstantial Reformer's answer to the Stoic and the Saint. "Wealth is dross; Power is anxiety, — is care; Luxury enervates the body and debases the soul," these remonstrate in chorus: "Know thyself, and be *truly* wise; chasten your appetites, and be rich in the *moderation* of your physical wants," adds the Stoic; "Know God, and find happiness in adoring and serving Him," echoes the Saint. "True, O Plato! true, divinest Cecilia! but everything in its order. To render fasting meritorious, one'should have meat at command; and great spiritual exaltation springs not naturally from a body gaunt with enforced hunger. Let me surround myself with what is needful for me and mine in the way of food, and clothing, and shelter; not forgetting meantime the nobler ends of my existence, but looking also to these; thus will I achieve for myself Opportunity for that loftier plane of being whereto you so justly invite me. I am not forgetting nor disobeying the injunction to ' Seek first the kingdom of God and His righteousness " ; I am only affirming that, until the legitimate physical needs of those dependent on my exertions are provided for, it would not be righteous in me to surrender myself to contemplation, nor even to devotion." And this is substantially the answer of the Reformer of Man's external circumstances to those who insist that the end he meditates is to be attained from *within*, rather than from *without*, — in the apt phrase of Charles Lane, by improvement, not of this or that *circum*stance, but of the vital *centre*-stance. We readily admit this ; but what then ? The question still recurs, " How is the desired end to be attained ? " and we hold that there is no practical cure for the vital woes of the pitiable which does not involve a preliminary change in their outward conditions. You may shower precepts and admonitions, tracts and Bibles, on the squalid, filthy, destitute thousands who tenant, thick as knotted adders, the cellars and rookeries of our great cities, and all will run off them like water from a duck's back, leaving them exactly as it found them. But first take them out of these lairs and lazar-houses, wash them, clothe them decently, and place them where they may, by honest, useful labor, earn a fair subsistence ; *now* you may ply them with catechisms and exhortations with a rational hope of advantage. To attempt it sooner, even with seeming success, is only to cover their filthiness with a tenacious varnish of hypocrisy, rendering it less hateful to the eye, but more profound and ineradicable.

But not the Worker only — the robust, earnest Thinker also — is of necessity a Radical. He sees his less fortunate brethren oppressed and degraded, debased and enslaved, through the malign influences of selfish Cunning and despotic Force ; and his very soul is stirred within him as was that of Moses by the spectacle of his people's sufferings under the rule of their Egyptian taskmasters. No matter what is the extent or nature of Man's abstract, inherent depravity, he cannot fail to see that men are actually better or worse as they have better or worse instructors, rulers, and institutions. Before condemning Human Nature as incorrigible, and thereupon justifying those who nevertheless contrive to make its guidance and government a gainful trade, he inquires whether this same abused Nature has not done better under other auspices, and becomes satisfied that it has. Then he says to the banded decriers of Human Nature and to the conservatives of old abuses who take shelter under their wing: " You say that Man cannot walk erect ; remove your bandages from his feet, your shackles from his limbs, and let us see ! You say that he cannot take care of himself ; then why compel him, in addition, to take such generous care of *you ?* You say he is naturally dishonest and thievish ; but how could he be otherwise, when he cannot fail to perceive that you, who set yourselves up for his guides and exemplars, are perpetually and enormously robbing him ? Begin by giving back to him the earth which you have taken from under his feet, the knowledge you have monopolized, the privileges you have engrossed ; and we can better determine whether he needs anything, and what, from your charity, after he shall have recovered what is rightfully his own."

It is a fearful gift, this of moral prescience, — the ability and the will to look straight into and through all traditions, usages, beliefs, conventionalities, garnitures, and ask : What is this *for ?* What does it signify ? If it were swept away, what would be really lost to mankind ? This baptism, or whatever may be the appliance, — does it really cleanse ? Does it even tend to the desiderated result ? or does it not rather fortify with a varnish of hypocrisy and a crust of conceit the preëxisting impurity and vice ? Is there the old unrighteousness left, with only self-righteousness superadded? Well does a deep thinker speak of the spirit of reform as walking up and down, " paving the world with eyes," — eyes which not merely inquire and pierce, but challenge, accuse, arraign also. Happily was the prophet of old named a *seer ;* for he who rightly and deeply sees thence foresees. Your brawling demagogue is a very empty and harmless personage, —"a voice, and nothing more"; but a silent, unimpassioned thinker, though uttering only the most obvious and universal truths, sets the social caldron furiously seething and bubbling. "Think not that I am come to send peace on earth," says the Prince of Peace; "I am not come to send peace, but a sword." All the rebels, conspirators, Messianic impostors, of that turbulent age, were not half so formidable to Judean conservatism, Roman despotism, as the Sermon on the Mount. And so in our day, a genuine, earnest reformer, no matter in what manger cradled, in what Shaker garb invested, sets all things spinning and tilting around him.

The true Reformer turns his eyes first inward, scrutinizing himself, his habits, purposes, efforts, enjoyments, asking, What signifies this? and this? and wherein is its justification? This daily provision of meat and drink, — is its end nourishment and its incident enjoyment? or are the poles reversed, and do I eat and drink for the gratification of appetite, hoping, or trusting, or blindly guessing, that, since it satiates my desires, it must satisfy also my needs? Is it requisite that all the zones and continents should be ransacked to build up the fleeting earthly tabernacle of this immortal spirit? Is not the soul rather submerged, stifled, drowned, in this incessant idolizing, feasting, pampering of the body? These sumptuous entertainments, wherein the palate has everything, the soul nothing, — what faculty, whether of body or mind, do they brighten or strengthen? Why should a score of animals render up their lives to furnish forth my day's dinner, if my own life is thereby rendered neither surer nor nobler? Why gorge myself with dainties which cloud the brain and clog the step,. if the common grains and fruits and roots and water afford precisely the same sustenance in simpler and less cloying guise, and are far more conducive to health, strength, elasticity, longevity? Can a man worthily surrender his life to the mere acquiring and absorbing of food, thus alternating only from the state of a beast of burden to that of a beast of prey? Above all, why should I fire my blood and sear my brain with liquors which give a temporary exhilaration to the spirits at the cost of permanent depravation and disorder to the whole physical frame? In short, why should I live for and in my appetites, if these were Divinely created to serve and sustain, not master and dethrone, the spirit to which this earthly frame is but a husk, a tent, a halting-place, in an exalted, deathless career? If the life be indeed more than meat, why shall not the meat recognize and attest that fact? And thus the sincere Reformer, in the very outset of his course, becomes a "tee-total" fanatic, represented by the knavish and regarded by the vulgar as a foe to all enjoyment and cheer, insisting that mankind shall conform to his crotchets, and live on bran-bread and blue cold water.

Turning his eyes away from himself, he scans the relations of man with man, under which labor is performed and service secured, and finds, not absolute Justice, much less Love, but Necessity on the one hand, Advantage on the other, presiding over the general interchange of good offices among mankind. In the market, on the exchange, we meet no recognition of the brotherhood of the human race. A famine in one country is a godsend to the grain-growers and flour-speculators of another. An excess of immigration enhances the cost of food while depressing the wages of labor, adding in both ways to the wealth of the forehanded, who find their only drawback in the increased burdens of pauperism. Thus the mansion and the hovel rise side by side, and where sheriffs are abundant is hanging most frequent. One man's necessity being another's opportunity, we have no right to be surprised or indignant that the general system culminates, by an inexorably logical process, in the existence and stubborn maintenance of Human Slavery.

Yes, I insist that Slavery is a logical deduction from principles generally accepted, and almost universally accounted sound and laudable. For, once admit the premises that I have a right to seek profit from my neighbor's privations and calamities ; that I have a right to consume in idleness the products or earnings of half a dozen workers, if my income will justify the outlay; and that it is better to live indolently on others' earnings than industriously from the proceeds of my own, — and the rightfulness of Slavery is a logical deduction, as plain as that two and two make four. Hence the gambler, the swindler, the pander for gain to others' vices, is always pro-Slavery, or is only withheld from that side by fear of being himself enslaved. You would not on three continents find a pirate or gaming-house bully who would not gladly tramp five miles on a dark, stormy night, to help lynch an Abolitionist. And thus not only have all Reforms a sympathetic, even if ill-understood, relationship, but the *enemies* of reforms are united by a free-masonry equally potent and comprehensive. The negro-trader of Charleston or New Orleans would always help to mob a Temperance lecturer, even though he did not himself drink; for he hated and dreaded the application of ethical laws to practical life. This particular reform did not interfere with his pursuits or his gains ; but he felt instinctively that all other reforms were just behind it, — that they were peering over its shoulder, and ready to rush in if this one succeeded in opening the door. So he put his shoulder against it, and held fast, — not that he objected specially to this, but that he would make seasonable resistance to the crowd that came trooping in its train.

It was very common, of old, for the members of diverse parties and sects to protest that they were not Abolitionists, — a most superfluous assurance. Essentially, radically, there are just so many Abolitionists as comprehend that it is better for themselves, better also for their children, to earn their subsistence by fair, honest service to their kind, than to have it supplied them for nothing. He only is truly, inflexibly an Abolitionist who realizes that the faculty of producing or earning bread is as much an element of man's happiness as the ability to consume and relish it. He who idly wishes that Providence had made him heir of a fortune, so that he might have fared sumptuously and lived idly, might just as well sigh outright for John Mitchell's coveted Alabama plantation and fat negroes.

Whether it shall ever be found practicable to substitute a more trustful and beneficent social order for that which now prevails, the sceptics are fully justified in doubting. So many experiments — fairly tried, so far as *they* can see — have resulted in so many failures, that they quite rationally conclude that the Family is the only, or at least the highest, social organization whereof poor, depraved human nature is capable. It is all very well, they fairly say, to talk of the great economies of some theoretic social system, — how much could be saved in fences and fuel, stowage and lights, production and distribution, by uniting five hundred families in one household, on a common domain, rather than scattering them over twice as many acres or twenty-score farms ; but, since it is proved that families *cannot* or will not live and labor in this way, what use in commending it ? You might as well talk of the superior pavement of the New Jerusalem seen in St. John's vision to that of Broadway or Chestnut Street, and insist that our cities shall henceforth use the former exclusively.

There is much force in this view ; but there is more force in one higher and nobler. It is true that men and women educated in the selfish isolation and antagonism of our current households are not qualified — at least, the great mass of them are not — for any better form of society. It is true that this knowledge has been attained through years of patient exertion and sacrifice, — attained by earnest, ardent, self-denying men and women, who would have given their lives to perfect conclusively a contrary demonstration. And, though it is truly urged that these demonstrations were made under very imperfect and unfavorable circumstances, it is equally true that they were the most favorable that could be, and better than can now be, obtained.

We stand, then, in the presence of this state of facts :

On the one hand, it is proved difficult to create and maintain a more trustful and harmonious social structure out of such materials as the old social machinery has formed, — or rather, we may say practically, out of such materials as the old machinery has expelled and rejected; yet we know, on the other hand, that a more — yes, I will say it — Christian Social Order is not impossible. For it is more than half a century since the first associations of the gentle ascetics contemptuously termed Shakers were formed; and no one will pretend that *they* have failed. No : they have steadily and eminently expanded and increased in wealth, and every element of material prosperity, until they are at this day just objects of envy to their neighbors. They produce no paupers; they excrete no beggars; they have no idlers, rich or poor; no purse-proud nabobs, no cringing slaves. So far are they from pecuniary failure, that they alone have known no such word as fail since, amid poverty and odium, they laid the foundations of their social edifice, and inscribed " Holiness to the Lord " above their gates. They may not have attempted the highest nor the wisest achievement; but what they attempted they have accomplished. And, if there were no other success akin to theirs, — but there *is*, — it would still be a demonstrated truth that men and women can live and labor for general, not selfish, good, — can banish pauperism, servitude, and idleness, and secure general thrift and plenty, by moderate coöperative labor and a complete identity of interests. Of this truth, each year offers added demonstrations; but, if all were to cease to-morrow, the fact that it *had* been proved would remain. Perhaps no Plato, no Scipio, no Columbus, no Milton, now exists; but the capacity of the Race is still measured and assured by the great men and great deeds that have been. Man *can* work for his brother's good as well as his own : an unbroken, triumphant experience of half a century has established the fact, so that fifty centuries of contrary experience would not disprove it.

But we are not required to prove the capacity, the adaptability, of Man to a social accord so extreme as Communism.

The practicability of this involves that of every social reconstruction less radical, just as a bushel of grain contains every lesser measure thereof; but the truth of the reverse does not follow. A bank on which every human being, or even every stockholder, might fill up and draw checks at discretion, would soon be broken; but it does not follow that a well-managed joint-stock bank must inevitably fail. Man may yet, in far distant ages, become wise enough, good enough, to realize that Labor is needful to him as food, and that frugality and temperance are essential to long life and sustained enjoyment. But, far this side of that, he may become convinced that he wars on himself in seeking a selfish good, and that only in conjunction with others' happiness can his own be secured. It needs not that he be willing to share his earnings with others, in order that he may realize that every involuntary idler saps the general well-being, and that it is the interest of each to see that there is work and fair recompense for all.

I write in sad and chill November. The skies are sullen and weeping; the ground is reeking mire; and the fierce northwester lingers just behind the Highlands, ready to rush upon the tattered and thin-clad like a pack of famished wolves. Adown the street pace crowds of weary seekers, — seekers once of fame, perhaps, or power, or wealth; but now of food and raiment, — of work and wages. The shop-windows and doors are choked with ship-loads of wares adapted to their urgent physical needs, — everything requisite to eat, and burn, and wear. All these were produced by labor; and the needy are most willing to give labor in exchange for them. The owners, on the other hand, want to sell them, — bought them for that purpose, and must break if the end is not attained. Yet here the two classes stand facing, eyeing each other, — a thin plate of glass dividing them, — the man within anxious to sell, and he without eager to buy, — yet some malignant spell seems to keep them still blankly, helplessly staring at each other. Perhaps a mere combination of the hungry, thin-clad thousands who wishfully, fruitlessly gaze into those windows, would secure the desired result; for here are persons of all kinds as well as grades of ability anxiously seeking work, — that is, seeking opportunity to coin their own exertions into the bread and clothes and shelter they so pressingly need. Say there is no work for them, and their own hunger and rags give you the lie : they themselves collectively afford that very market for their labor for want of which they severally shiver and famish. But the carpenter cannot live on timber, even if he had it; he cannot even build himself the dwelling for want of which his children shiver in some damp basement; and thus the seedy tailor grows daily more ragged, and the unemployed shoemaker despairingly sees his own feet come more and more fully in contact with the frosty, flinty pavement; while the seamstress out of work creeps to her bare garret and prays God that starvation, rather than infamy, may end her long battle, now so nearly lost, for the coarsest and scantiest bread. Legislators! philanthropists! statesmen! there *must* be some way out of this social labyrinth; for God is good, and has not created men and women to starve for want of work. The precept " Six days *shalt* thou labor" implies and predicts work for all; where is it? and what shall supply it? If you cannot or will not solve this problem, at least do not defame or impede those who earnestly seek its solution!

The great, the all-embracing Reform of our age is therefore the SOCIAL Reform, — that which seeks to lift the Laboring Class, as such, — not out of labor, by any means, — but out of ignorance, inefficiency, dependence, and want, and place them in a position of partnership and recognized mutual helpfulness with the suppliers of the Capital which they render fruitful and efficient. It is easily said that this is the case now; but, practically, the fact is otherwise. The man who has only labor to barter for wages or bread looks up to the buyer of his sole commodity as a benefactor; the master and journeyman, farmer and hired man, lender and borrower, mistress and servant, do *not* stand on a recognized footing of reciprocal benefaction. True, self-interest is the acknowledged impulse of either party; the lender, the employer, parts with his money only to increase it, and so, it would seem, is entitled to prompt payment or faithful service, — not, specially, to gratitude. He who pays a bushel of fair wheat for a day's work at sowing for next year's harvest has simply exchanged a modicum of his property for other property, to him of greater value ; and so has no sort of claim to an unreciprocated obeisance from the other party to the bargain. But so long as there shall be ten who would gladly borrow to one disposed and able to lend, and many more anxious to be hired than others able and willing to employ them, there always will be a natural eagerness of competition for loans, advances, employment, and a resulting deference of borrower to lender, employed to employer. He who may hire or not, as to him shall seem profitable, is independent ; while he who must be hired or starve exists at others' mercy. Not till Society shall be so adjusted, so organized, that whoever is willing to work shall assuredly *have* work, and fair recompense for doing it, as readily as he who has gold may exchange it for more portable notes, will the laborer be placed on a footing of justice and rightful independence. He who is able and willing to give work for bread is not essentially a pauper ; he does not desire to abstract without recompense from the aggregate of the world's goods and chattels ; he is not rightfully a beggar. Wishing only to convert his own muscular energy into bread, it is not merely his but every man's interest that the opportunity should be afforded him, — nay, it is the clear *duty* of Society to render such exchange at all times practicable and convenient.

A community or little world wherein all freely serve and all are amply served, — wherein each works according to his tastes or needs, and is paid for all he does or brings to pass, — wherein education is free and common as air and sunshine, — wherein drones and sensualists cannot abide the social atmosphere, but are expelled by a quiet, wholesome fermentation, — wherein humbugs and charlatans necessarily find their level, and nought but actual service, tested by the severest ordeals, can secure approbation, and none but sterling qualities win esteem, — such is the ideal world of the Socialist. Grant that it is but a dream, — and such, as yet, it for the most part has been, — it by no means follows that it has no practical value. On the contrary, an ideal, an illusion, if a noble one, has often been the inspirer of grand and beneficent efforts. Moses was fated never to enter the Land of Promise he so longingly viewed from afar ; and Columbus never found — who can now wish that he had ? — that unimpeded sea-route westward to India that he sought so wisely and so daringly. Yet still the world moves on, and by mysterious and unexpected ways the great, brave soul is permitted to subserve the benignant purposes of God contemplating the elevation and blessing of Man. And so, I cannot doubt, the unselfish efforts in our day for the melioration of social hardships, though their methods may be rejected as mistaken or defective, will yet signally conduce to their contemplated ends. Fail not, then, humble hoper for " the Good Time Coming," to lend *your* feeble sigh to swell the sails of whatever bark is freighted with earnest efforts for the mitigation of human woes, nor doubt that the Divine breath shall waft it at last to its prayed-for haven !

Time will not suffice to speak fully of the efforts, but yesterday so earnest and active, now so languid and unapparent, for the abolition of the legal penalty of Death. Perhaps this effort has already succeeded so far as it was best it should succeed at present, — that is, so far that some States in the West, as others in the East, have absolutely, and others virtually, abolished the Death Penalty. If we could now forget the whole subject for ten years, we might, at the close of that period, compare carefully and searchingly the prevalence of capital crime in the States respectively which have abolished and those which have retained the Gallows, and strike an instructive balance between them. For the present, let it suffice that no one appears now to be seriously contending that life is less safe or crime more prevalent in the States which destroy no human lives than in others. And, when Society shall for a generation have set a consistent example of reverencing the inviolability of this life, regarding it as a sacred gift from God, which He only may warrantably take away, — we may rationally hope that the example will not be lost, even on those constitutionally prone to outrage, violence, and crime.

Nay, let me venture one more suggestion. The nations, races, ages, most advanced in civilization and knowledge have ever been most reluctant to quench the light of life. Despots and oligarchies have mowed down men by wholesale, where republics and popular governments have generally been for-bearing and humane. Every trial of popular sovereignty in Europe has been attended or followed by a mitigation or diminution of sanguinary penalties ; and the glorious uprising of '48 would ere this have nearly dismissed the hangman or headsman from the public service, if Royal treachery, courtly conspiracy, and popular levity had not crushed it. And now, in the heyday of Reaction, we hear from time to time of one despot after another, having recovered his throne and his presence of mind, reëstablishing or reinvigorating the Gallows. I rejoice in the hope that the progress of Christianity, civilization, and liberty, will yet drive it altogether from the earth.

I will barely glance at the great problem of Educational Reform, — of the blending of Labor with Study, so as to preserve health of body and vigorous activity of mind, enable the student nearly or quite to work his way through academy and college, and send him out better qualified to wrestle with adversity, instruct the uneducated, and maintain a healthful independence, than he otherwise could be. Not to argue or commend, but simply to state the position of the Reformers, shall be the point of my aim.

The old division of mankind into a numerous, unlearned, or working, and a thinly sown but powerful thinking, directing, educated, governing class, is no longer possible, save in approximation. The principle underlying the Brahminical system of caste is alien to our laws and our intellectual condition. The masses have at least a smattering of knowledge, and more than a shadow of power. They may be educated badly, imperfectly, superficially; they will never again consent to be not educated at all. Ever-increasing millions will be spent on their instruction: shall they thereby be taught what they need to know, or what is adapted to other needs than theirs? An argument will hardly be necessary to show that the training required to make an able and efficient doctor, lawyer, or clergyman, is not that which is essential to the development of a capable and well-informed farmer, mechanic, or civil engineer. Nobody contends that the routine of our colleges is that which is best calculated to fit a youth for eminence as a military or naval commander: why, then, should it be deemed appropriate for our embryo captains of industry? None are more apt to inveigh against the shallowness or quackery of our current applications of science to agriculture, than they who bar the way to our advance to the acquisition of a science of agriculture which shall be neither shallow nor empirical.

The time when to know how to read was proof presumptive of an education for the priesthood can never be recalled. The supposition that methodized knowledge is not as important to the cultivator as to the clergyman is no longer entertained. No wise champion of classical education to-day sadly or sneeringly inquires, with the Apocryphal writer of Ecclesiasticus, "How can *he* get wisdom that holdeth the plough, that glorieth in the goad, that driveth oxen, and is occupied with the care of bullocks?" The spirit that dictated those questions may still linger in some cloistral recesses, some sepulchral caverns, but it no longer stalks abroad outspoken and defiant. It is in our age a thing of night, and must vanish with the dawning of the day.

Well, then: we need and must have a system of higher education which recognizes the truth that Man is by nature a worker, — a fashioner and ruler of matter, — that to be industrious is dictated to him by a beneficent law of his being, and that daily muscular as well as mental effort is among the conditions of his healthful and joyful existence. We need an education which recognizes that God has placed men on earth that they may work, and that every attempt to escape this destiny parallels the original offence of Jonah, and subjects the offender to calamities like to his. We need an education which shall not only regard as an end the forming of more instructed and efficient farmers and artisans than we now have, but the ultimate training of the great mass of our youth to degrees of skill in the choice and use of implements hitherto unknown. To this end, we must have seminaries which not merely provide work for their pupils, but *require* it inflexibly from all, — which educate the head and the hand together, each to be the ally and the complement of the other; which shall teach our aspiring youth, not only *how* to do better than their fathers did in every field of blended intellectual and industrial effort, but *why* this way is better than any other, and in what direction further improvement is to be made. Thus, and thus only, may we expect to elevate our industrial pursuits to that position which they are justly entitled to hold, and render them attractive to our aspiring and noble youth. Every useful vocation is respected in proportion to the measure of intellect it requires and rewards, and never can rise above this level. You may eulogize the Dignity of Labor till doomsday, without making a boot-black's calling as honorable as that of an engineer or a draughtsman; and, so long as an ignorant and stupid boor shall be esteemed wise enough, learned enough, for a competent farmer or mechanic, all spread-eagle glorification of Manual Labor will be demagogue cant and office-seeking hypocrisy. Only through a truer and nobler education can the working masses ever attain the position and the respect which the genius of our institutions predicts and requires for them. And that Education has yet its seminaries to found and its professors to train or discover.

But I must not dwell longer on special Reform movements, though many others challenge our attention. If the few bricks taken almost at random give any fair idea of the character and proportions of the edifice, you will thence perceive, — what many of you, doubtless, have not waited till now to learn, — that what the Reform Spirit of our age labors primarily and generally to establish is the equality of Human Rights, regardless of all disparities of strength, or knowledge, or caste, or creed, or color, — an equality based on the all-embracing moral obligation to consecrate every faculty, every impulse, to the highest good of Humanity. Through all its selfishness, rapacity, folly, and sin, the Genius of our Age speaks to us in tones which the discerning hear and the thoughtful heed; and the burden of its message runs thus: "It is nobler and better to teach the child than to hang the man; — it is wiser to remove temptation from the path of the weak than to punish them because they have stumbled and fallen, — easier to find the vagrant orphan a home, and teach him a trade, than to watch him as a rogue and punish him as a thief, — cheaper and better for Society to find work for all who need and seek it than to support the needy in idleness as paupers, vagrants, or criminals, — nobler to warn than to doom, — more godlike to lift up than to crush down, — and far safer to be surrounded and shielded by gratitude and love than to be walled in with batteries and hedged about by spears." Thus testifies the age of Steam-Presses, Railroads, and Lightning Telegraphs to Statesmen, Legislators, and Rulers; when shall it be fully understood and heeded ?

But I have proposed to speak, not only of Reforms, but of Reformers, — a theme somewhat less grand and inspiring. For, indeed, the contrast between the work proposed and the man who proposes and undertakes it is often so broad as to partake of the ludicrous. I have met several in my day who were quite confident of their ability to correct Euclid's Geometry or upset Newton's theory of Gravitation; but I doubt whether one of them could have earned or borrowed two hundred dollars in the course of a year, and nothing stumps an average Reformer of things in general so complete-ly as to be asked to settle his board-bill. I can guess with what awed apprehension the green disciple comes up from some rural hamlet or out-of-the-way village to the metropolis, there to meet for the first time the oracle of some great move-ment for the regeneration of the world, whose writings he has devoured with wondering admiration; and with what blank surprise he finds himself introduced, at some club-house or restaurant, to said oracle, — a spindling, chattering, personally insignificant entity, who discourses volubly and disjointedly of the times, the crops, and the weather; and never even blunders on a pithy saying, unless when, in the fervor of good fellowship, he orders "Pork Chops for two." But it were hardly fair to ride down Reformers in a body, as a brigade of heavy cavalry might sweep over a pulk of Cos-sacks; let us analyze the mass with searching and patient discrimination.

The first or lowest class among them I take to be the *envious.* The wide disparity between most men's estimate of themselves respectively, and their neighbors' valuation of the very same article, has been abundantly observed. The num-ber who suppose themselves enormously underrated in the world's opinion is very great; and each believes that he would have long since acquired a fortune or achieved eminence if he had only passed current for all he was worth. The ambitious and conceited, thus stamped in the mint of Society at what they consider a ruinous depreciation, are naturally rebels against the authority which thus disranks and degrades them, — they know that the Social edifice is wrong end up, from the fact that they are so near the bottom of it. And thus thousands fancy themselves Reformers, while their real ob-jection to the world as it is relates not at all to the fashion of the structure, but solely to their own place in it.

Akin to this class is that of the devotees of Sensual Appetite, whose prospective millennium is a period of general license, wherein everybody may do with impunity whatsoever his desires may prompt, — or, at least, *they* may. This class sees the Social world so covered, fettered, interpenetrated, by laws, customs, beliefs, which plant themselves firmly across the path whereon its members are severally pressing forward to the gratification of every impulse, that it is plain that either Society is or they are sadly in the wrong; and imperious Appetite forbids the conclusion that *they* are. If the world as it is would only concede them wealth without industry, enjoyment without obedience, respect without virtue, it would be as good a world now as they could ask for; but since it will not (indeed, cannot) do thus, they make desperate fight against it, just as a vicious and indiscreet bull, it is said, will sometimes butt heads with a locomotive. Byron speaks to us out of the heart of this class, and so forcibly that his statement will hardly be improved. The diction of this school is often nervous; its logic invincible, if only its premises be granted; and its rhetoric really fascinating to those who are in the heyday of youth and its passions; but the understanding is only clouded, it is not convinced, by the inculcations thus incited, and the cooling of the blood gives conscience an opportunity to reassert her long-ignored sovereignty. The free songs, so deliciously warbled and heartily delighted in by bachelor Little, become a scandal and a nuisance to respectable Mr. Thomas Moore, husband of a worthy wife, and father of piano-playing daughters; and thus Social Order, without directly replying to the sophistries or resisting the vagaries of her revolting sons, awaits patiently the inevitable hour when they shall voluntarily kneel at her feet to abjure their treason, beg her forgiveness, and seek absolution.

I think there is a small class whom mere force of will, or, rather, a spirit of antagonism, impels into the service of Reform. These mark how unequal is the battle ever waged between the contending hosts, and are prompted by a chivalrous sentiment to couch a lance on the weaker side. They see how royalties, hierarchies, aristocracies, bourgeoises, all support each other and overbear the opposing array, — how the victory so grandly won by Radicalism to-day only results at last in widening the base and increasing the power of Conservatism; and they mentally say, "Here goes for the side which must triumph, if at all, against immense odds, yet can never enjoy the fruits of a victory !" — and so rush in, to be cut down, thrust back, or metamorphosed, as chance or Providence may determine.

For indeed the argument for Conservatism is intrinsically so strong, that only the maddest unwisdom, the most preposterous displays of selfishness, on the part of its champions, could possibly overthrow it. No monarchy was ever undermined or overturned except through some monarch's own blunders or crimes, and none ever will be. If ever man of wealth were so timorous as to fear that the houseless, shivering wretches in the streets would eject the possessors of stately, comfortable mansions, and sit down securely in their places, he evinced a want of sagacity at least equal to his want of nerve. If a city could be sacked by its desperate denizens, the first set who effected a lodgement in its palaces would make haste to shoot the residue of the rabble horde for their own security, and so would weaken themselves beyond the possibility of maintaining their dizzy altitude. Radicalism is the tornado, the earthquake, which comes, acts, and is gone for a century ; Conservatism is the granite, which may be chipped away here or there to build a new house, or let a railroad pass, but which will substantially abide forever.

The argument for Conservatism appeals resistlessly to all who have good digestive organs which they cherish, with anything satisfactory whereon to employ them. The natural presumption that whatever has stood the shocks and mutations of centuries is deeply grounded in Nature and the Divine purpose, is wellnigh invincible. " I grant you," says the Conservative, " that many things seem rather out of tune ; but what then ? Is it *my* duty to upset what so many great and good men have left untouched, and some of them have expressly commended? That the world is full of ignorance and wrong, crime and woe, is very true; but *I* cannot help that; and it will do no good to shed gallons of tears over it, and try to put others into mourning. No: let us take things as we find them; relieve distress when we can afford it, and float along as nearly with the current as will answer. Bad as the world is, a man with good fortune, (which includes health,) a reasonable self-control, a tolerably clear conscience, a well-filled store-house, and a fair balance with his banker, may extract a good deal of enjoyment from it, if he will wisely improve his opportunities, and not insist on making himself miserable by dabbling too deeply in the miseries of others." Millions *live* all of this, who do not *say* more than half of it.

Perhaps one of the most instructive spectacles is that of the impulsive young Radical undergoing a gradual transformation, or cooling off, into a staid, respectable Conservative, with property to care for, a position to maintain, and a reputation to cherish. He was honest of yore, and is honest (as the world goes) now; but circumstances alter cases. When he declaimed against the monopoly or aggregation of lands, he had none of his own; but he has since become "seized," as the lawyers say, of a snug estate, and he would not like to have any one seize it away from him. It may be larger than one man absolutely needs; but he wants to improve it, and it will cut up nicely among his rather numerous children or nephews. So he builds him an elegant mansion, surrounds and fills it with evidences of taste and ministers to luxury, and sits down to contemplate matters in general more calmly and philosophically than he did in his impulsive, headlong youth. And the great world without takes on a very different aspect when viewed through his elegant shrubbery, adown his velvet lawn, and colored rosily by the bumper of generous juice which often gets between his eyes and the distant prospect, from that it wore when viewed with naked optics, or with only a cup of crystal water between him and the sun. " Yes," he says, slowly and languidly, " there *is* need of Reform ; but let it be effected prudently and decorously. These *modern* Radicals are different from those of *my* young days : they are rash, reckless, destructive, infidel ; I can have no sympathy, no fellowship, with such." True, O Plutus ! you can have none. But " prudently," did you say, sir ? Ah no ! Reforms of any depth will *never* be urged prudently and cautiously ; for, if their advocates were prudent, they would not be Reformers at all. Very likely, Prudence may step in at the opportune moment, and mediate successfully between heedless Innovation and stubborn Reaction ; but to wait for Prudence to *impel* a Reform is to wait for Death to originate Life.

And, indeed, the embarrassment of headlong allies is one of the chief sorrows of the Reformer's lot. He can never say " A " without some one else following with a " B " which he is sure does not belong to the same alphabet ; but this the other as confidently denies ; and the whole Conservative party backs the latter with all its force. Luther's career was perpetually made thorny by this sort of unwelcome allies, and Bossuet knew exactly from what armory to draw the most deadly shafts to hurl against the advancing hosts of the Reformation. " If you assert this, how will you defend your position against him who will manifestly assert that ? If you put the Bible above the Church, how answer him who puts Reason above the Bible ? If you insist that every *man* shall be allowed to vote, how resist the demand that every *woman* be equally enfranchised ? If you repudiate *vindictive* punishments, how justify punishment at all ? " I think it was Brougham who observed, that there never yet was a Reform proposed that might not have been defeated by giving adequate weight to the question, " If you go so far, why not farther ? If this be right, is not more equally right ? And where can you consistently stop ? " And thus many a fiery Radical has been cooled down into placid (or acrid) Conservatism, by discovering that the character of his associates,

the tendency of their doctrines, the ends which they contemplated, were such as he could never approve.

I presume there are not many Reformers worthy of the
designation who ever anticipated fame or wealth as a result
of their labors in the cause of Humanity. Yet I recollect
an application once made to me by a particularly green
youth, who wished employment as a writer or journalist,
urging as an inducement that he thought he could indite
some forcible essay in favor of the Reforms wherein I was
deeply interested. " My friend," I felt constrained to reply,
" I can very easily write myself quite as much in favor of
those Reforms as the public will bear; another such hand at
the bellows would ruin me." Conservatism has many faults,
but it is a good paymaster; while Radicalism is constitutionally out at the elbows, and may toss you its purse with ever
so lordly an air, but all you take by the motion is a poor six-
penny worth of dried eelskin. True, now and then a Reformer lives to fight out *his* special battle, and secure the
hard-won triumph of his well-directed, persistent effort. But
by this time Conservatism has taken the bantling into *her*
snug house, there to fondle and cherish it as her own; while
Radicalism has swept on to new efforts, new struggles, perhaps ultimately new triumphs : so the forlorn Reformer
stands shivering at the remorseless door which has en-
gulfed *his* darling; he cannot hope to overtake the rushing
host, which is now far on its eager way, and indeed he has
no heart for the attempt; so he commonly ends by begging
admittance into the mansion, and the privilege of now and
then fondling the baby, which coolly eyes the queer, old,
seedy codger, and wonders how *he* ever wormed his way into
the hallowed precincts of Respectability and Elegance. *He*
says nothing, for his heart is too full; but gathers up his
tattered garments and dies, looking fondly, sadly, on that cold,
averted face to the last.

To the earnest, true Reformer, life is indeed no holiday

feast, and earth no Eden garnished with singing-birds and flowers. The most sanguine, buoyant soul, once fairly entered on this career, is not long in learning how much stronger is old Adam than young Melancthon. Not merely that his bread is apt to be coarse and his couch somewhat rugged, — he was prepared for this, — but the intractability of ignorance, the stubbornness of prejudice, the thanklessness of those arrested in a downhill career, the inefficiency of effort, and "the heart-sickness of hope deferred," are indeed appalling. Doubting, irresolute Hamlet may well be distracted, not so much by the fact that "the times are out of joint," as that *he* seems to have been "born to set things right." For the moral dangers of the Reformer's calling are even more disheartening than its pecuniary discouragements. "Do you know," said a broken-down ex-lecturer for Temperance, Anti-Slavery, &c., &c., once to me, in a tone and with a look of deep meaning, "that there is no life so *unhealthy* as that of a popular agitator?" The "patriot to a brewery" may even enjoy it; but for the proud, shy, home-bred man, who would rather see the smile on the face of the loved one than be the subject of a civic ovation, and rather hear the idle prattle of his babes than the shouts of clustered thousands responsive to his burning words, it is a cold, stern life that he leads; and he labors under constant apprehensions that, while he is striving to diffuse sentiments of benignity, generosity, and mercy, the milk of human kindness, by reason of those very efforts, is slowly drying up in his own breast, and he, while still struggling earnestly, though somewhat mechanically, to redeem the human race, is coming gradually to dislike and despise them.

The most striking, perhaps the only general, tribute ever paid to the position and merits of the true Reformer is that embodied in the universal jeer and shout which announces the exposure of the fallen aspirant or false pretender. As there was never a villain who did not hail with hearty exultation the exposure of a priest's lechery or a moralist's knavery, so the lazy, sensual, luxury-loving, money-grasping million enjoy nothing more keenly than the tidings that one who has reproved their selfishness and made them uncomfortable by his projects of social melioration or homilies on human brotherhood has at length been tempted into sin, or turned inside out by some casual revelation, and proved as selfish and venal as themselves. As the news is rapidly disseminated, the face of sensualism and self-seeking broadens into one universal grin, — peal after peal of "unextinguished laughter" disturbs the serenity of the atmosphere, — you might suspect from hearing it that everybody's uncle had died, and left him heir to a bounteous fortune. The grandest Hebrew prophet, looking on such a spectacle, might forcibly say, as of old : " Hell from beneath is stirred up to meet thee ; it stirreth up its denizens to inquire exultingly, ' Art thou also become as one of us ? ' " And thus the Reformer who, while he stood erect, seemed beneath the meanest, — more hated, reviled, and despised, — shall prove by his fall that he was dreaded, and really honored, as well ; that the devils contemplated .his efforts in the spirit which believes and trembles ; that those who most defamed and misrepresented, yet secretly respected and wished themselves virtuous enough to be almost, if not altogether, such as he. And thus a career which in its progress seemed despised and reprobated shall yet in its defeat and ruin prove to have been really admired and honored, even by those who lacked virtue to imitate or even commend it.

Yet this shout from the nethermost *hades* is by no means justified by the fact on which it is based. Men are often weak and fallible in action, even though their intellectual perception of the right is of the deepest and clearest. Bacon's philosophy is sound and valuable, though Bacon was a corrupt chancellor, a bribed judge. The earth *does* move, in accordance with Galileo's hypothesis, though Galileo himself was induced by ghostly fulminations and personal perils to recant it. Peter might have denied and blasphemed till doomsday without belittling or confounding that salvation of which he had been chosen a witness and an apostle. Few men are equal in their daily lives to the moral altitude of their highest perceptions; and all the confessors and martyrs might apostatize, and heap shame on their own heads, without detracting one iota from the worth of philanthropy or Christianity. Man is a reed which the slightest breeze deflects, the feeblest step prostrates; but Truth is adamant and eternal.

Yes, it is a great thing to be truly a Reformer, even one misinterpreted and scorned through life, as what genuine Reformer ever failed to be. The tombs of the dead prophets are built only of the stones hurled at them while living; and thus may we accurately measure the greatness of their daring, the force and truth of their unprecedented utterances. To speak firmly the word destined ultimately to heal Man's deadliest maladies, yet certain instantly to evoke his direst curses — this is a heroism whereof no other forlorn hope than that of Humanity is capable. Idly, weakly, shall the timidly perspicacious hope to speak the great truth, yet not offend the beneficiaries of current falsehoods; to declare the true God, yet excite no uproar among Diana's silversmiths. The world was never created, and is not governed, so that Policy and Principle, Time and Eternity, God and Mammon, can all be served together. If they could be, Virtue would be merely shrewdness, and blindness the physical synonyme of evil.

But what then? Do we say that the path of Rectitude is thorny and craggy, and that the only verdure and balmy sunshine that approach it are those of the adjacent, alluring by-ways of Luxury and Ease, leading down to the garden of Sensual Pleasure? By no means. What is affirmed is not that Truth's service is necessarily one of privation and suffering, but that the true soldiers never choose it as the way of ease, of ambition, or from any selfish consideration whatever, but because it is the way of Right. " Necessity is upon me," says the true Apostle; his course is one dictated to him by considerations higher than any hopes of heaven, deeper than any fears of hell. Doubtless, to the eye of sense, his career seems dwarfish, his aspirations baffled, his life a defeat and a failure. But he has never appealed to the ordeal of sense, and feels under no obligation to accept its judgments. Who shall say that Nebuchadnezzar on his throne is happier than Daniel in his prison? or that Herod in his palace, gorged with Epicurean dainties, and gloating over voluptuous music and dancing, is more blest than the uncouth, stern-souled Baptist, striding in solitary hunger over sun-scorched deserts of rock and sand, — very far from luxury, but very near to God, — or contemplating his swiftly approaching death in a malefactor's dungeon? Jerusalem and the Temple, the Palace and its gardens, are the possessions of the former; but what are they to the celestial splendors, the eternal verities, which are present to the rapt, adoring gaze of the latter, and gild the visions of his rocky couch with a glory inconceivable to the apprehension of the Sadducee?

These two can never understand each other while they remain essentially as now. The unbelief that questions, and cavils, and scruples, and doubts, and denies, seems to him incomparably less virulent and fearful than that which makes mitres and triple-crowns counters of a sordid ambition, and shakes the keys of eternal bliss or woe in the face of long-suffering millions, to make them bow their necks passively to the yoke of a soul-crushing despotism.

For, indeed, to the Reformer's apprehension, nothing can be more absurd than the dread of irreligion professed by men whose daily lives are a proclamation of indifference to the wants and wrongs of the benighted and destitute, — who are so intent on having the Poor evangelized, that they do not ask how they are to be fed, — and who act as though a plentiful distribution of tracts and Bibles would alone suffice to banish evil from the earth.

To the Conservative, Religion would seem often a part of the subordinate machinery of Police, having for its main object the instilling of proper humility into the abject, of contentment into the breasts of the down-trodden, and of enduing with a sacred reverence for Property those who have no personal reason to think well of the sharp distinction of Mine and Thine. The Reformer, on the other hand, insists on Humanity as the inevitable manifestation of all true Religion, presses the best-beloved Apostle's searching question, " If a man love not his brother, whom he *has* seen, how can he love God, whom he has *not* seen " ? or, as a poet of our own day has phrased it, affirms that there

> "are infidels to Adam worse than infidels to God,"

and that the effective answer to an imperfect, halting faith, is a devoted, loving life.

This earnest, angry strife shall yet be composed, — this stormy clamor be hushed, — not through the absolute defeat of either party, but through the recognition by each of the truth affirmed by the other, so that Conservatism and Reform shall take their places side by side on the same platform, and Faith and Life, Humanity and Christianity, be recognized by our enlarged vision as halves of the same unit, planets revolving around and lighted in turn by the same sun of Everlasting Truth. Meantime, let us cherish the Reformer! for his, and not the Conservative's, is the active, aggressive force through which this ultimate harmonization of the Real with the Ideal is to be achieved. Harsh and sweeping, rash and destructive, he may seem, and often is ; but his fire, however blind and indiscriminate its rage, will be found at last to have left unconsumed all that was really worth preserving. With him, while we respect the proper force and legitimate function of Conservatism, we must say —

> " Standing still is childish folly ;
> Going backward is a crime ;
> None should patiently endure
> *Any* ill that he can cure :
> ONWARD ! keep the march of Time !
> ONWARD ! while a wrong remains
> To be conquered by the right,

> While Oppression lifts a finger
>   To affront us by his might,
> While an error clouds the reason
>   Of the universal heart,
> Or a slave awaits his freedom,
>   ACTION is the wise man's part."

And *to* him our final word of gratitude and cheer shall fitly be—

> " We thank thee, watcher on the lonely tower,
>   For all thou tellest of the coming hour
> When Error shall decay and Truth grow strong,
>   And Right shall rule supreme and vanquish Wrong."

And, indeed, though the life of the Reformer may seem rugged and arduous, it were hard to say considerately that any other were worth living at all. Who can thoughtfully affirm that the career of the conquering, desolating, subjugating warrior, — of the devotee of Gold, or Pomp, or Sensual Joys; the Monarch in his purple, the Miser by his chest, the wassailer over his bowl, — is not a libel on Humanity and an offence against God ? But the earnest, unselfish Reformer, — born into a state of darkness, evil, and suffering, and honestly striving to replace these by light, and purity, and happiness, — he may fall and die, as so many have done before him, but he cannot fail. His vindication shall gleam from the walls of his hovel, his dungeon, his tomb ; it shall shine in the radiant eyes of uncorrupted Childhood, and fall in blessings from the lips of high-hearted, generous Youth. As the untimely death of the good is our strongest moral assurance of the Resurrection, so the life wearily worn out in doubtful and perilous conflict with Wrong and Woe is our most conclusive evidence that Wrong and Woe shall yet vanish forever. Luther, dying amid the agonizing tears and wild consternation of all Protestant Germany, — Columbus, borne in regal pomp to his grave by the satellites of the royal miscreant whose ingratitude and perfidy had broken his mighty heart, — Lovejoy, pouring out his life-blood beside the Press whose freedom he had so gallantly defended, — yes, and not less majestic, certainly not less tragic, than either, the lowly and lonely couch of the dying 'Uncle Tom,' whose whole life had been a brave and Christian battle against monstrous injustice and crime, — these teach us, at least, that all true greatness is ripened, and tempered, and proved, in life-long struggle against vicious beliefs, traditions, practices, institutions ; and that not to have been a Reformer is not to have truly lived. Life is a bubble which any breath may dissolve ; Wealth or Power a snow-flake, melting momently into the treacherous deep across whose waves we are floated on to our unseen destiny ; but to have lived so that one less orphan is called to choose between starvation and infamy, — one less slave feels the lash applied in mere wantonness or cruelty, — to have lived so that some eyes of those whom Fame shall never know are brightened and others suffused at the name of the beloved one, — so that the few who knew him truly shall recognize him as a bright, warm, cheering presence, which was here for a season and left the world no worse for his stay in it, — this surely is to have really *lived*, — and not wholly in vain.

THE GROUNDS OF PROTECTION.*

Mr. President and Respected Auditors : —

IT has devolved on me, as junior advocate for the cause of
Protection, to open the discussion of this question. I do
this with less diffidence than I should feel in meeting able
opponents and practised disputants on almost any other topic,
because I am strongly confident that you, my hearers, will
regard this as a subject demanding logic rather than rhetoric,
the exhibition and proper treatment of homely truths, rather
than the indulgence of flights of fancy. As sensible as you can
be of my deficiencies as a debater, I have chosen to put my
views on paper, in order that I may present them in as concise a manner as possible, and not consume my hour before
commencing my argument. You have nothing of oratory to
lose by this course ; I will hope that something may be gained
to my cause in clearness and force. And here let me say that,
while the hours I have been enabled to give to preparation
for this debate have been few indeed, I feel the less regret in
that my *life* has been in some measure a preparation. If there
be any subject to which I have devoted time, and thought, and
patient study, in a spirit of anxious desire to learn and follow
the truth, it is this very question of Protection ; if I have
totally misapprehended its character and bearings, then am

* Speech at the Tabernacle, New York, February 10, 1843, in public debate
on this resolution : —
Resolved, That a Protective Tariff is conducive to our National Prosperity.
Affirmative : Joseph Blunt,   Negative : Samuel J. Tilden,
    Horace Greeley.   Parke Godwin.

I ignorant, hopelessly ignorant indeed. And, while I may not hope to set before you, in the brief space allotted me, all that is essential to a full understanding of a question which spans the whole arch of Political Economy, — on which abler men have written volumes without at all exhausting it, — I *do* entertain a sanguine hope that I shall be able to set before you considerations conclusive to the candid and unbiassed mind of the policy and necessity of Protection.

Let us not waste our time on non-essentials. That unwise and unjust measures have been adopted under the *pretence* of Protection, I stand not here to deny; that laws *intended* to be Protective have sometimes been injurious in their tendency, I need not dispute. The logic which would thence infer the futility or the danger of Protective Legislation would just as easily prove *all* laws and all policy mischievous and destructive. Political Economy is one of the latest-born of the Sciences; the very fact that we meet here this evening to discuss a question so fundamental as this proves it to be yet in its comparative infancy. The sole favor I shall ask of my opponents, therefore, is that they will not waste their efforts and your time in attacking positions that we do not maintain, and hewing down straw giants of their own manufacture, but meet directly the arguments which I shall advance, and which, for the sake of simplicity and clearness, I will proceed to put before you in the form of Propositions and their Illustrations, as follows : —

Proposition I. A NATION WHICH WOULD BE PROSPEROUS, MUST PROSECUTE VARIOUS BRANCHES OF INDUSTRY, AND SUPPLY ITS VITAL WANTS MAINLY BY THE LABOR OF ITS OWN HANDS.

Cast your eyes where you will over the face of the earth, trace back the History of Man and of Nations to the earliest recorded periods, and I think you will find this rule uniformly prevailing, that the nation which is eminently Agricultural and Grain-exporting, — which depends mainly or principally on other nations for its regular supplies of Manufactured fabrics, — has been comparatively a *poor* nation, and ultimately a *dependent* nation. I do not say that this is the *instant* result of exchanging the rude staples of Agriculture for the more delicate fabrics of Art ; but I maintain that it is the inevitable *tendency.* The Agricultural nation falls in debt, becomes impoverished, and ultimately subject. The palaces of "merchant princes" may emblazon its harbors and overshadow its navigable waters ; there may be a mighty Alexandria, but a miserable Egypt behind it ; a flourishing Odessa or Dantzic, but a rude, thinly peopled southern Russia or Poland ; the exchangers may flourish and roll in luxury, but the producers famish and die. Indeed, few old and civilized countries become largely exporters of grain until they have lost, or by corruption are prepared to surrender, their independence ; and these often present the spectacle of the laborer starving on the fields he has tilled, in the midst of their fertility and promise. These appearances rest upon and indicate a law, which I shall endeavor hereafter to explain. I pass now to my

Proposition II. THERE IS A NATURAL TENDENCY IN A COMPARATIVELY NEW COUNTRY TO BECOME AND CONTINUE AN EXPORTER OF GRAIN AND OTHER RUDE STAPLES AND AN IMPORTER OF MANUFACTURES.

I think I hardly need waste time in demonstrating this proposition, since it is illustrated and confirmed by universal experience, and rests on obvious laws. The new country has abundant and fertile soil, and produces Grain with remarkable facility ; also, Meats, Timber, Ashes, and most rude and bulky articles. Labor is there in demand, being required to clear, to build, to open roads, &c., and the laborers are comparatively few ; while, in older countries, Labor is abundant and cheap, as also are Capital, Machinery, and all the means of the cheap production of Manufactured fabrics. I surely need not waste words to show that, in the absence of any counteracting policy, the new country will import, and continue to import, largely of the fabrics of older countries, and to pay for them, so far as she may, with her Agricultural staples. I will endeavor to show hereafter that she will continue to do this long after she has attained a condition to manufacture them as cheaply for herself, even regarding the *money* cost alone. But that does not come under the present head. The whole history of our country, and especially from 1782 to '90, when we had no Tariff and scarcely any Paper Money, — proves that, whatever may be the Currency or the internal condition of the new country, it will continue to draw its chief supplies from the old, — large or small according to its measure of ability to pay or obtain credit for them ; but still, putting Duties on Imports out of the question, it will continue to buy its Manufactures abroad, whether in prosperity or adversity, inflation or depression.

I now advance to my

Proposition III. IT IS INJURIOUS TO THE NEW COUNTRY THUS TO CONTINUE DEPENDENT FOR ITS SUPPLIES OF CLOTHING AND MANUFACTURED FABRICS ON THE OLD.

As this is probably the point on which the doctrines of Protection first come directly in collision with those of Free Trade, I will treat it more deliberately, and endeavor to illustrate and demonstrate it.

I presume I need not waste time in proving that the ruling price of Grain (as of any Manufacture) in a region whence it is considerably exported, will be *its price at the point to which it is exported, less the cost of such transportation.* For instance: the cost of transporting Wheat hither from large grain-growing sections of Illinois was last fall sixty cents ; and, New York being their most available market, and the price here ninety cents, the market there at once settled at thirty cents. As this adjustment of prices rests on a law obvious, immutable as gravitation, I presume I need not waste words in establishing it.

I proceed, then, to my next point. The average price of Wheat throughout the world is something less than one dollar per bushel ; higher where the consumption largely exceeds the adjacent production, — lower where the production largely exceeds the immediate consumption (I put out of view in this statement the inequalities created by Tariffs, as I choose at this point to argue the question on the basis of universal Free Trade, which is of course the basis most favorable to my opponents). I say, then, if all Tariffs were abolished to-morrow, the price of Wheat in England — that being the most considerable ultimate market of surpluses, and the chief supplier of our manufactures — would govern the price in this country, while it would be itself governed by the price at which that staple could be procured in sufficiency from other grain-growing regions. Now, Southern Russia and Central Poland produce Wheat for exportation at thirty to fifty cents per bushel; but the price is so increased by the cost of transportation that at Dantzic it averages some ninety and at Odessa some eighty cents per bushel. The cost of importation to England from these ports being ten and fifteen cents respectively, the actual cost of the article in England, all charges paid, and allowing for a small increase of price consequent on the increased demand, would not, in the absence of all Tariffs whatever, exceed one dollar and ten cents per bushel; and this would be the average price at which we must sell it in England in order to buy thence the great bulk of our Manufactures. I think no man will dispute or seriously vary this calculation. Neither can any reflecting man seriously contend that we could purchase forty or fifty millions' worth or more of Foreign Manufactures per annum, and pay for them in additional products of our Slave Labor — in Cotton and Tobacco. The consumption of these articles is now pressed to its utmost limit, — that of Cotton especially is borne down by the immense weight of the crops annually thrown upon it, and almost constantly on the verge of a glut. If we are to buy our Manufactures principally from Europe, we must pay for the additional amount mainly in the products of Northern Agricultural industry, — that is universally agreed on. The point to be determined is, whether we could obtain them abroad cheaper — *really* and positively cheaper, all Tariffs being abrogated — than under an efficient system of Protection.

Let us closely scan this question. Illinois and Indiana, natural grain-growing States, need Cloths; and, in the absence of all Tariffs, these can be transported to them from England for two to three per cent. of their value. It follows, then, that, in order to undersell any American competition, the British Manufacturer need only put his cloths at his factory *five* per cent. below the wholesale price of such cloths in Illinois, in order to command the American market. That is, allowing a fair broadcloth to be manufactured in or near Illinois for three dollars and a quarter per yard, cash price, in the face of British rivalry, and paying American prices for materials and labor, the British manufacturer has only to make that same cloth at three dollars per yard in Leeds or Huddersfield, and he can decidedly undersell his American rival, and drive him out of the market. Mind, I do not say that he *would* supply the Illinois market at that price *after* the American rivalry had been crushed; I know he *would not;* but, so long as any serious effort to build up or sustain Manufactures in this country existed, the large and strong European establishments would struggle for the additional market which our growing and plenteous country so invitingly proffers. It is well known that in 1815 – 16, after the close of the Last War, British Manufactures were offered for sale in our chief markets at the rate of *"pound for pound,"* — that is, fabrics of which the first cost to the manufacturer was $ 4.44 were offered in Boston market at $ 3.33, duty paid. This was not sacrifice, — it was dictated by a profound forecast. Well did the foreign fabricants know that their self-interest dictated the utter overthrow, at whatever cost, of the young rivals which the war had built up in this Country, and which our Government and a majority of the People had blindly or indolently abandoned to their fate. William Cobbett, the celebrated Radical, but with a sturdy English heart, boasted upon his first return to England that he had been actively engaged here in promoting the interests of his country by compassing the destruction of

American Manufactories in various ways which he specified, — "*sometimes* (says he) *by Fire.*" We all know that great sacrifices are often submitted to by a rich and long-established stage-owner, steamboat proprietor, or whatever, to break down a young and comparatively penniless rival. So in a thousand instances, especially in a rivalry for so large a prize as the supplying with Manufactures of a great and growing Nation. But I here put aside all calculations of a temporary sacrifice; I suppose merely that the foreign manufacturers will supply our Grain-growing States with Cloths at a trifling profit so long as they encounter American rivalry; and I say it is perfectly obvious that, if it cost three dollars and a quarter a yard to make a fair broadcloth in or near Illinois, in the infancy of our arts, and a like article could be made in Europe for three dollars, then the utter destruction of the American manufacture is inevitable. The Foreign drives it out of the market and its maker into bankruptcy; and now our farmers, in purchasing their cloths, " buy where they can buy cheapest," which is the first commandment of Free Trade, and get their cloth of England at three dollars a yard. I maintain that this would not last a year after the American factories had been silenced, — that then the British operator would begin to think of *profits* as well as bare cost for his cloth, and to adjust his prices so as to recover what it had cost him to put down the dangerous competition. But let this pass for the present, and say the Foreign Cloth is sold to Illinois for three dollars per yard. We have yet to ascertain how much she has gained or lost by the operation.

This, says Free Trade, is very plain and easy. The four simple rules of Arithmetic suffice to measure it. She has bought, say a million yards of Foreign Cloth for three dollars, where she formerly paid three and a quarter for American; making a clear saving of a quarter of a million dollars.

But not so fast, — we have omitted one important element of the calculation. We have yet to see what effect the purchase of her Cloth in Europe, as contrasted with its manufacture at home, will have on the price of her Agricultural staples. We have seen already that, in case she is forced to sell a portion of her surplus product in Europe, the price of that surplus must be the price which can be procured for it in England, *less* the cost of carrying it there. In other words : the average price in England being one dollar and ten cents, and the average cost of bringing it to New York being at least fifty cents and then of transporting it to England at least twenty-five more, the net proceeds to Illinois cannot exceed thirty-five cents per bushel. I need not more than state so obvious a truth as that the price at which the surplus can be sold governs the price of the whole crop; nor, indeed, if it were possible to deny this would it at all affect the argument. The real question to be determined is, not whether the American or the British manufacturers will furnish the most cloth for the least *cash*, but which will supply the requisite quantity of Cloth for the least *Grain in Illinois.* Now we have seen already that the price of Grain at any point where it is readily and largely produced is governed by its nearness to or remoteness from the market to which its surplus tends, and the least favorable market in which any portion of it must be sold. For instance : if Illinois produces a surplus of five million bushels of Grain, and can sell one million of bushels in New York, and two millions in New England, and another million in the West Indies, and for the fifth million is compelled to seek a market in England, and that, being the remotest point at which she sells, and the point most exposed to disadvantageous competition, is naturally the poorest market, that farthest and lowest market to which she sends her surplus will govern, to a great extent if not absolutely, the price she receives for the whole surplus. But, on the other hand, let her Cloths, her Wares, be manufactured in her midst, or on the junctions and waterfalls in her vicinity, thus affording an immediate market for her Grain, and now the average price of it rises, by an irresistible law, nearly or quite to the average of the world. Assuming that average to be one dollar, the price in Illinois, making allowance for the fertility and cheapness of her soil, could not fall below an average of seventy-five cents. Indeed, the experience of the periods when her consumption of Grain has been equal to her production, as well as that of other sections where the same has been the case, proves conclusively that the average price of her Wheat would exceed that sum.

We are now ready to calculate the profit and loss. Illinois, under Free Trade, with her "workshops in Europe," will buy her cloth twenty-five cents per yard cheaper, and thus make a nominal saving of two hundred and fifty thousand dollars in her year's supply; but, she thereby compels herself to pay for it in Wheat at thirty-five instead of seventy-five cents per bushel, or to give over *nine* and one third bushels of Wheat for every yard under Free Trade, instead of *four* and a third under a system of Home Production. In other words, while she is making a quarter of a million dollars by buying her Cloth "where she can buy cheapest," she is losing nearly Two Millions of Dollars on the net product of her Grain. The striking of a balance between her profit and her loss is certainly not a difficult, but rather an unpromising, operation.

Or, let us state the result in another form : She can buy her cloth a little cheaper in England, — Labor being there lower, Machinery more perfect, and Capital more abundant; but, in order to pay for it, she must not merely sell her own products at a correspondingly low price, but enough lower to overcome the cost of transporting them from Illinois to England. She will give the cloth-maker in England less Grain for her Cloth than she would give to the man who made it on her own soil; but for every bushel she sends him in payment for his fabric, she must give two to the wagoner, boatman, shipper, and factor, who transport it thither. On the whole product of her industry, two thirds is tolled out by carriers and bored out by Inspectors, until but a beggarly remnant is left to satisfy the fabricator of her goods.

And here I trust I have made obvious to you the law which dooms an Agricultural Country to inevitable and ruinous disadvantage in exchanging its staples for Manufactures, and involves it in perpetual and increasing debt and dependence. The *fact*, I early alluded to; is not the *reason* now apparent? It is not that Agricultural communities are more extravagant or less industrious than those in which Manufactures or Commerce preponderate, — it is because there is an inevitable disadvantage to Agriculture in the very nature of all distant exchanges. Its products are far more perishable than any other; they cannot so well await a future demand; but in their excessive bulk and density is the great evil. We have seen that, while the English Manufacturer can send his fabrics to Illinois for less than five per cent. on their first cost, the Illinois farmer must pay two hundred per cent. on his Grain for its transportation to English consumers. In other words : the English manufacturer need only produce his goods five per cent. below the American to drive the latter out of the Illinois market, the Illinoian must produce wheat for *one third* of its English price in order to compete with the English and Polish grain-grower in Birmingham and Sheffield.

And here is the answer to that scintillation of Free Trade wisdom which flashes out in wonder that *Manufactures* are eternally and especially in want of Protection, while Agriculture and Commerce need none. The assumption is false in any sense, — our Commerce and Navigation cannot live without Protection, — never did live so, — but let that pass. It is the interest of the whole country which demands that that portion of its Industry which is *most exposed* to ruinous foreign rivalry should be cherished and sustained. The wheat-grower, the grazier, is protected by ocean and land ; by the fact that no foreign article can be introduced to rival his except at a cost for transportation of some thirty to one hundred per cent. on its value ; while our Manufactures can be inundated by foreign competition at a cost of some two to ten per cent. It is the grain-grower, the cattle-raiser, who is protected by a duty on Foreign Manufactures, quite as much as the spinner or shoemaker. He who talks of Manufactures being protected and nothing else, might just as sensibly complain that we fortify Boston and New York, and not Pittsburg and Cincinnati.

Again : You see here our answer to those philosophers who modestly tell us that their views are liberal and enlightened, while ours are benighted, selfish, and un-Christian. They tell us that the foreign factory-laborer is anxious to exchange with us the fruits of his labor, — that he asks us to give him of our surplus of grain for the cloth that he is ready to make cheaper than we can now get it, while we have a superabundance of bread. Now, putting for the present out of the question the fact that, though *our* Tariff were abolished, *his* could remain, — that neither England, nor France, nor any great manufacturing country, would receive our Grain untaxed though we offered so to take their goods, — especially the fact that they never *did* so take of us while we were freely taking of them, — we say to them, " Sirs, we are willing to take Cloth of you for Grain : but why prefer to trade at a ruinous disadvantage to both ? Why should there be half the diameter of the earth between him who makes coats and him who makes bread, the one for the other ? We are willing to give you bread for clothes ; but we are not willing to pay two thirds of our bread as the cost of transporting the other third to you, because we sincerely believe it needless and greatly to our disadvantage. We are willing to work for and buy of you, but not to support the useless and crippling activity of a falsely directed Commerce : not to contribute by our sweat to the luxury of your nobles, the power of your kings. But come to us, you who are honest, peaceable, and industrious ; bring hither your machinery, or, if that is not yours, bring out your sinews; and we will aid you to reproduce the implements of your skill. We will give you more bread for your cloth here than you can possibly earn for it where you are, if you will but come among us and aid us to sustain the policy that secures steady employment and a fair reward to Home Industry. We will no longer aid to prolong your existence in a state of semi-starvation where you are ; but we are ready

to share with you our Plenty and our Freedom here." Such
is the answer which the friends of Protection make to the
demand and the imputation : judge ye whether our policy be
indeed selfish, un-Christian, and insane.

I proceed now to set forth my

Proposition IV. THAT EQUILIBRIUM BETWEEN AGRICULTURE,
MANUFACTURES AND COMMERCE, WHICH WE NEED, CAN ONLY BE
MAINTAINED BY MEANS OF PROTECTIVE DUTIES.

You will have seen that the object we seek is not to make
our country a Manufacturer for other nations, but for herself,
— not to make her the baker and brewer and tailor of other
people, but of her own household. If I understand at all
the first rudiments of National Economy, it is best for each
and all nations that each should mainly fabricate for itself,
freely purchasing of others all such staples as its own soil or
climate proves ungenial to. We appreciate quite as well as
our opponents the impolicy of attempting to grow coffee in
Greenland or glaciers in Malabar, — to extract blood from a
turnip or sunbeams from cucumbers. A vast deal of wit has
been expended on our stupidity by our acuter adversaries, but
it has been quite thrown away, except as it has excited the
hollow laughter of the ignorant as well as thoughtless. All
this, however sharply pushed, falls wide of our true position.
To all the fine words we hear about "the impossibility of
counteracting the laws of Nature," "Trade regulating itself,"
&c., &c., we bow with due deference, and wait for the sage to
resume his argument. What we *do* affirm is this, *that it is
best for every nation to make at home all those articles of its
own consumption that can just as well — that is, with nearly
or quite as little labor — be made there as anywhere else.* We
say it is not wise, it is not well, to send to France for boots,
to Germany for hose, to England for knives and forks, and so
on ; because the real cost of them would be less, — even
though the nominal price should be slightly more, — if we
made them in our own country ; while the facility of paying

for them would be much greater. We do not object to the occasional importation of choice articles to operate as specimens and incentives to our own artisans to improve the quality and finish of their workmanship, — where the home competition does not avail to bring the process to its perfection, as it often will. In such cases, the rich and luxurious will usually be the buyers of these choice articles, and can afford to pay a good duty. There are gentlemen of extra polish in our cities and villages who think no coat good enough for them which is not woven in an English loom, — no boot adequately transparent which has not been fashioned by a Parisian master. I quarrel not with their taste : I only say that, since the Government *must* have Revenue and the American artisan *should* have Protection, I am glad it is so fixed that these gentlemen shall contribute handsomely to the former, and gratify their aspirations with the least possible detriment to the latter. It does not invalidate the fact nor the efficiency of Protection that foreign competition with American workmanship is not entirely shut out. It is the *general* result which is important, and not the exception. Now, he who can seriously contend, as some have seemed to do, that Protective Duties do not aid and extend the domestic production of the articles so protected might as well undertake to argue the sun out of the heavens at mid-day. All experience, all common sense, condemn him. Do we not know that our Manufactures first shot up under the stringent Protection of the Embargo and War ? that they withered and crumbled under the comparative Free Trade of the few succeeding years ? that they were revived and extended by the Tariffs of 1824 and '28 ? Do we not know that Germany, crippled by British policy, which inundated her with goods yet excluded her grain and timber, was driven, years since, to the establishment of her " Zoll-Verein " or Tariff Union, — a measure of careful and stringent Protection, under which Manufactures have grown up and flourished through all her many States ? She has adhered steadily, firmly, to her Protective Policy, while we have faltered and oscillated ; and what is the result ? She has created and established her Manufactures ; and in doing so has vastly increased her wealth and augmented the reward of her industry. Her public sentiment, as expressed through its thousand channels, is almost unanimous in favor of the Protective Policy ; and now, when England, finding at length that her cupidity has overreached itself, — that she cannot supply the Germans with clothes yet refuse to buy their bread, — talks of relaxing her Corn-Laws in order to coax back her ancient and profitable customer, the answer is, "No ; it is now too late. We have built up Home Manufactures in repelling your rapacity, — we cannot destroy them at your caprice. What guaranty have we that, should we accede to your terms, you would not return again to your policy of taking all and giving none so soon as our factories had crumbled into ruin ?" Besides, we have found that we can make cheaper — really cheaper — than we were able to buy, — can pay better wages to our laborers, and secure a better and steadier market for our products. We are content to abide in the position to which you have driven us. Pass on !"

But this is not the sentiment of Germany alone. All Europe acts on the principle of self-Protection ; because all Europe sees its benefits. The British journals complain that, though they have made a show of relaxation in their own Tariff, and their Premier has made a Free Trade speech in Parliament, the chaff has caught no birds ; *but six hostile Tariffs* — all Protective in their character, and all aimed at the supremacy of British Manufactures — were enacted within the year 1842. And thus, while schoolmen plausibly talk of .the adoption and spread of Free Trade principles, and their rapid advances to speedy ascendency, the practical man knows that the truth is otherwise, and that many years must elapse before the great Colossus of Manufacturing monopoly will find another Portugal to drain of her life-blood under the delusive pretence of a commercial reciprocity. And, while Britain continues to pour forth her specious treatises on Political Economy, proving Protection a mistake and an impossibility through her Parliamentary Reports and Speeches in praise of Free Trade, the shrewd statesmen of other nations humor the joke with all possible gravity, and pass it on to the next neighbor ; yet all the time take care of their own interests, just as though Adam Smith had never speculated nor Peel soberly expatiated on the blessings of Free Trade, looking round occasionally with a curious interest to see whether anybody was really taken in by it.

I have partly anticipated, yet I will state distinctly, my

Proposition V. PROTECTION IS NECESSARY AND PROPER TO SUSTAIN AS WELL AS TO CREATE A BENEFICENT ADJUSTMENT OF OUR NATIONAL INDUSTRY.

" Why can't our Manufacturers go alone ? " petulantly asks a Free-Trader; "they have had Protection long enough. They ought not to need it any more." To this I answer that, if Manufactures were protected as a matter of special bounty or favor to the Manufacturers, a single day were too long. I would not consent that they should be sustained one day longer than the interests of the *whole* Country required. I think you have already seen that, not for the sake of Manufacturers, but for the sake of all Productive Labor, should Protection be afforded. If I have been intelligible, you will have seen that the purpose and essence of Protection is LABOR-SAVING, — the making two blades of grass grow instead of one. This it does by " planting the Manufacturer as nearly as may be by the side of the Farmer," as Mr. Jefferson expressed it, and thereby securing to the latter a market for which he had looked to Europe in vain. Now, the market of the latter is certain as the recurrence of appetite ; but that is not all. The Farmer and the Manufacturer, being virtually neighbors, will interchange their productions directly, or with but one intermediate, instead of sending them reciprocally across half a continent and a broad ocean, through the hands of many holders, until the toll taken out by one after another has exceeded what remains of the grist. " Dear-bought and far-fetched" is an old maxim, containing more *essential* truth than many a chapter by a modern Professor of Political Economy. Under the Protective policy, instead of having one thousand men making Cloth in one hemisphere, and an equal number raising Grain in the other, with three thousand factitiously employed in transporting and interchanging these products, we have over two thousand producers of Grain, and as many of Cloth, leaving far too little employment for one thousand in making the exchanges between them. This consequence is inevitable : although the production on either side is not confined to the very choicest locations, the total product of their labor is twice as much as formerly. In other words, there is a double quantity of food, clothing, and all the necessaries and comforts of life, to be shared among the producers of wealth, simply from the diminution of the number of non-producers. If all the men now enrolled in Armies and Navies were advantageously employed in Productive Labor, there would doubtless be a larger dividend of comforts and necessaries of life for all, because more to be divided than now and no greater number to receive it : just so in the case before us. Every thousand persons employed in needless Transportation and in factitious Commerce are so many subtracted from the great body of Producers, from the proceeds of whose labor all must be subsisted. The dividend for each must, of course, be governed by the magnitude of the quotient.

But, if this be so advantageous, it is queried, why is any legislation necessary ? Why would not all voluntarily see and embrace it ? I answer, because the apparent individual advantage is often to be pursued by a course directly adverse to the general welfare. We know that Free Trade asserts the contrary of this ; maintaining that, if every man pursues that course most conducive to his individual interest, the general good will thereby be most certainly and signally promoted. But, to say nothing of the glaring exceptions to this law which crowd our statute-books with injunctions and penalties, we are everywhere met with pointed contradictions of its assumption, which hallows and blesses the pursuits of the gambler, the distiller, and the libertine, making the usurer a saint and the swindler a hero. Adam Smith himself admits that there are avocations which enrich the individual but impoverish the community. So in the case before us. A B is a farmer in Illinois, and has much grain to sell or exchange for goods. But, while it is demonstrable that, if *all* the manufactures consumed in Illinois were produced there, the price of grain must rise nearly to the average of the world, it is equally certain that A B's *single act*, in buying and consuming American cloth, will not raise the price of grain generally, nor of *his* grain. It will not perceptibly affect the price of grain at all. A solemn compact of the whole community to use only American fabrics would have some effect; but this could never be established, or never enforced. A few Free-Traders standing out, selling their grain at any advance which might accrue, and buying "where they could buy cheapest," would induce one after another to look out for No. 1, and let the public interests take care of themselves : so the whole compact would fall to pieces like a rope of sand. Many a one would say, "Why should I aid to keep up the price of Produce ? I am only a *consumer* of it," — not realizing or caring for the interest of the community, even though it less palpably involved his own ; and that would be an end. Granted that it is desirable to encourage and prefer Home Production and Manufacture, a Tariff is the obvious way, and the only way, in which it can be effectively and certainly accomplished.

But why is a Tariff necessary after Manufactures are once established ? "You say," says a Free-Trader, "that you can Manufacture cheaper if Protected than we can buy abroad : then why not do it *without* Protection, and save all trouble ? " Let me answer this cavil : —

I will suppose that the Manufactures of this Country amount in value to One Hundred Millions of Dollars per annum, and those of Great Britain to Three Hundred Millions. Let us suppose also that, under an efficient Protective Tariff,

ours are produced five per cent. cheaper than those of England, and that our own markets are supplied entirely from the
Home Product. But at the end of this year, 1843, we, — concluding that our Manufactures have been protected long
enough and ought now to go alone, — repeal absolutely our
Tariff, and commit our great interests thoroughly to the guidance of "Free Trade." Well: at this very time the British
Manufacturers, on making up the account and review of their
year's business, find that they have manufactured goods cost-
ing them Three Hundred Millions, as aforesaid, and have sold
to just about that amount, leaving a residue or surplus on
hand of Fifteen or Twenty Millions' worth. These are to be
sold; and their net proceeds will constitute the interest on
their capital and the profit on their year's business. But
where shall they be sold? If crowded on the Home or their
established Foreign Markets, they will glut and depress those
markets, causing a general decline of prices and a heavy loss,
not merely on this quantity of goods, but on the whole of
their next year's business. They know better than to do any
such thing. Instead of it, they say, "Here is the American
Market just thrown open to us by a repeal of their Tariff: let
us send thither our surplus, and sell it for what it will fetch."
They ship it over accordingly, and in two or three weeks it is
rattling off through our auction stores, at prices first five, then
ten, fifteen, twenty, and down to thirty per cent. below our
previous rates. Every jobber and dealer is tickled with the
idea of buying goods of novel patterns so wonderfully cheap;
and the sale proceeds briskly, though at constantly declining
prices, till the whole stock is disposed of and our market is
gorged to repletion.

Now, the British Manufacturers may not have received for
the whole Twenty Millions' worth of Goods over Fourteen or
Fifteen Millions; but what of it? Whatever it may be is
clear profit on their year's business in cash or its full equivalent. All their established markets are kept clear and eager;
and they can now go on vigorously and profitably with the
business of the new year. But more: they have crippled an

active and growing rival; they have opened a new market, which shall erelong be theirs also.

Let us now look at our side of the question:—

The American Manufacturers have also a stock of goods on hand, and they come into our market to dispose of them. But they suddenly find that market forestalled and depressed by rival fabrics of attractive novelty, and selling in profusion at prices which rapidly run down to twenty-five per cent. below cost. What are they to do? They cannot force sales at any price not utterly ruinous; there is no demand at any rate. They cannot retaliate upon England the mischief they must suffer,—her Tariff forbids; and the other markets of the world are fully supplied, and will bear but a limited pressure. The foreign influx has created a scarcity of money as well as a plethora of goods. Specie has largely been exported in payment, which has compelled the Banks to contract and deny loans. Still, their obligations must be met; if *they* cannot make sales, *the Sheriff* will, and must. It is not merely their surplus, but their whole product, which has been depreciated and made unavailable at a blow. The end is easily foreseen: our Manufacturers become bankrupt and are broken up; their works are brought to a dead stand; the Laborers therein, after spending months in constrained idleness, are driven by famine into the Western wilderness, or into less productive and less congenial vocations; their acquired skill and dexterity, as well as a portion of their time, are a dead loss to themselves and the community; and we commence the slow and toilsome process of rebuilding and rearranging our industry on the one-sided or Agricultural basis. Such is the process which we have undergone twice already. How many repetitions shall satisfy us?

Now, will any man gravely argue that we have *made* Five or Six Millions by this cheap purchase of British goods,—by "buying where we could buy cheapest?" Will he not see that, though the *price* was low, the *cost* is very great? But the apparent saving is doubly deceptive; for the British manufacturers, having utterly crushed their American rivals by one or two operations of this kind, soon find here a market, not for a beggarly surplus of Fifteen or Twenty Millions, but they have now a demand for the amount of our whole consumption, which, making allowance for our diminished ability to pay, would probably still reach Fifty Millions per annum. This increased demand would soon produce activity and buoyancy in the general market; and now the foreign Manufacturers would say in their consultations, "We have sold some millions' worth of goods to America for less than cost, in order to obtain control of that market; now we have it, and must retrieve our losses,"—and they *would* retrieve them, with interest. They would have a perfect right to do so. I hope no man has understood me as implying any infringement of the dictates of honesty on their part, still less of the laws of trade. They have a perfect right to sell goods in our markets on such terms as we prescribe and they can afford; it is *we*, who set up our own vital interests to be bowled down by their rivalry, who are alone to be blamed.

Who does not see that this sending out our great Industrial Interests unarmed and unshielded to battle against the mail-clad legions opposed to them in the arena of Trade is to insure their destruction? It were just as wise to say that, because our people are brave, therefore they shall repel any invader without fire-arms, as to say that the restrictions of other nations ought not to be opposed by us because our artisans are skilful and our manufactures have made great advances. The very fact that our manufactures are greatly extended and improved is the strong reason why they should not be exposed to destruction. If they were of no amount or value, their loss would be less disastrous; but now the Five or Six Millions we should make on the cheaper importation of goods would cost us One Hundred Millions in the destruction of Manufacturing Property alone.

Yet this is but an item of our damage. The Manufacturing classes feel the first effect of the blow, but it would paralyze every muscle of society. One hundred thousand artisans and laborers, discharged from our ruined factories, after being some time out of employment, at a waste of millions of the National wealth, are at last driven by famine to engage in other avocations, — of course, with inferior skill and at an inferior price. The farmer, gardener, grocer, lose them as customers to meet them as rivals. They crowd the labor-markets of those branches of industry which we are still permitted to pursue, just at the time when the demand for their products has fallen off, and the price is rapidly declining. The result is just what we have seen in a former instance: all that any man may make by buying Foreign goods cheap, he loses ten times over by the decline of his own property, product, or labor; while to nine tenths of the whole people the result is unmixed calamity. The disastrous consequences to a nation of the mere derangement and paralysis of its Industry which must follow the breaking down of any of its great Producing Interests have never yet been sufficiently estimated. Free Trade, indeed, assures us that every person thrown out of employment in one place or capacity has only to choose another; but almost every working-man knows from experience that such is not the fact, — that the loss of a situation through the failure of his business is oftener a sore calamity. I know a worthy citizen who spent six years in learning the trade of a hatter, which he had just perfected in 1798, when an immense importation of foreign hats utterly paralyzed the manufacture in this country. He travelled and sought for months, but could find no employment at any price, and at last gave up the pursuit, found work in some other capacity, and has never made a hat since. He lives yet, and now comfortably, for he is industrious and frugal; but the six years he gave to learn his trade were utterly lost to him, — lost for the want of adequate and steady Protection to Home Industry. I insist that the Government has failed of discharging its proper and rightful duty to that citizen, and to thousands and tens of thousands who have suffered from like causes. I insist that, if the Government had permitted without complaint a foreign force to land on our shores and plunder that man's house of the savings of six years of faithful industry, the neglect of duty would not have been more flagrant. And I firmly believe that the people of this country are One Thousand Millions of Dollars poorer at this moment than they would have been had their entire Productive Industry been constantly protected, on the principles I have laid down, from the formation of the Government till now. The steadiness of employment and of recompense thus secured, the comparative absence of constrained idleness, and the more efficient application of the labor actually performed, would have vastly increased the product, — would have improved and beautified the whole face of the country; and the Moral and Intellectual advantages thence accruing would alone have been inestimable. A season of suspension of labor in a community is usually one of aggravated dissipation, drunkenness, and crime.

But let me more clearly illustrate the effect of foreign competition in raising prices to the consumer. To do this, I will take my own calling for an example, because I understand that best; though any of you can apply the principle to that with which he may be better acquainted. I am a publisher of newspapers, and suppose I afford them at a cheap rate. But the ability to maintain that cheapness is based on the fact that I can certainly sell a large edition daily, so that no part of that edition shall remain a dead loss on my hands. Now, if there were an active and formidable Foreign competition in newspapers, — if the edition which I printed during the night were frequently rendered unsalable by the arrival of a foreign ship freighted with newspapers early in the morning, — the present rates could not be continued: the price must be increased or the quality would decline. I presume this holds equally good of the production of calicoes, glass, and penknives as of newspapers, though it may be somewhat modified by the nature of the article to which it is applied. That it does hold true of sheetings, nails, and thousands of articles, is abundantly notorious.

I have not burdened you with statistics, — you know they are the reliance, the stronghold, of the cause of Protection, and that we can produce them by acres. My aim has been to exhibit not mere collections of facts, however pertinent and forcible, but the *laws* on which those facts are based, — not the immediate manifestation, but the ever-living necessity from which it springs. The contemplation of these laws assures me that those articles which are supplied to us by Home Production alone are relatively cheaper than those which are rivalled and competed with from abroad. And I am equally confident that the shutting out of Foreign competition from our markets for other articles of general necessity and liberal consumption which can be made here with as little labor as anywhere would be followed by a corresponding result, — a reduction of the price to the consumer at the same time with increased employment and reward to our Producing Classes.

But, Mr. President, were this only on one side true, — were it certain that the price of the Home product would be permanently higher than that of the Foreign, I should still insist on efficient Protection, and for reasons I have sufficiently shown. Grant that a British cloth costs but $ 3 per yard, and a corresponding American fabric $ 4, I still hold that the latter would be decidedly the cheaper for us. The Fuel, Timber, Fruits, Vegetables, &c., which make up so large a share of the cost of the Home product, would be rendered comparatively valueless by having our workshops in Europe. I look not so much to the nominal price as to the comparative facility of payment. And, where cheapness is only to be attained by a depression of the wages of Labor to the neighborhood of the European standard, I prefer that it should be dispensed with. One thing must answer to another ; and I hold that the farmers of this country can better afford, as a matter of pecuniary advantage, to pay a good price for manufactured articles than to obtain them lower through the depression and inadequacy of the wages of the artisan and laborer.

You will understand me, then, to be utterly hostile to that idol of Free Trade worship, known as Free or unlimited Competition. The sands of my hour are running low, and I cannot ask time to examine this topic more closely; yet I am confident I could show that this Free Competition is a most delusive and dangerous element of Political Economy. Bear with a brief illustration: At this moment, common shirts are made in London at the incredibly low price of *three cents per pair.* Should we admit these articles free of duty and buy them because they are so cheap? Free trade says Yes; but I say No! Sound Policy as well as Humanity forbids it. By admitting them, we simply reduce a large and worthy and suffering class of our population from the ability they now possess of procuring a bare subsistence by their labor to unavoidable destitution and pauperism. They must now subsist upon the charity of relatives or of the community, — unless we are ready to adopt the demoniac doctrine of the Free Trade philosopher Malthus, that the dependent Poor ought to be rigorously starved to death. Then what have we gained by getting these articles so exorbitantly cheap? or, rather, what have we not lost? The labor which formerly produced them is mainly struck out of existence; the poor widows and seamstresses among us must still have a subsistence; and the imported garments must be paid for: where is the profits of our speculation?

But even this is not the worst feature of the case. The labor which we have here thrown out of employment by the cheap importation of this article is now ready to be employed again at any price, — if not one that will afford bread and straw, then it must accept one that will produce potatoes and rubbish; and with the product some Free-Trader proceeds to break down the price and destroy the reward of similar labor in some other portion of the earth. And thus each depression of wages produces another, and that a third, and so on, making the circuit of the globe, — the aggravated necessities of the Poor acting and reacting upon each other, increasing the omnipotence of Capital and deepening the dependence of Labor, swelling and pampering a bloated and factitious Commerce, grinding down and grinding down the destitute,

until Malthus's remedy for Poverty shall become a grateful
specific, and, amid the splendors and luxuries of an all-
devouring Commercial Feudalism, the squalid and famished
Millions, its dependants and victims, shall welcome death as a
deliverer from their sufferings and despair.

I wish time permitted me to give a hasty glance over the
doctrines and teachings of the Free Trade sophists, who esteem
themselves *the* Political Economists, christen their own views
liberal and enlightened, and complacently put ours aside as
benighted and barbarous. I should delight to show you how
they mingle subtle fallacy with obvious truth, — how they
reason acutely from assumed premises, which, being mistaken or incomplete, lead to false and often absurd conclu-
sions, — how they contradict and confound each other, and
often, from Adam Smith, their patriarch, down to McCulloch
and Ricardo, either make admissions which undermine their
whole fabric, or confess themselves ignorant or in the dark on
points the most vital to a correct understanding of the great
subject they profess to have reduced to a Science. Yet even
Adam Smith himself expressly approves and justifies the
British Navigation Act, the most aggressively Protective
measure ever enacted, — a measure which, not being understood and seasonably counteracted by other nations, changed
for centuries the destinies of the World, — which silently
sapped and overthrew the Commercial and Political greatness of Holland, — which silenced the thunder of Van
Tromp, and swept the broom from his mast-head. But I
must not detain you longer. I do not ask you to judge
of this matter by authority, but from facts which come
home to your reason and your daily experience. There
is not an observing and strong-minded mechanic in our
city who could not set any one of these Doctors of the Law
right on essential points. I beg you to consider how few
great practical Statesmen they have ever been able to win to
their standard, — I might almost say none ; for Huskisson
was but a nominal disciple, and expressly contravened their

whole system upon an attempt to apply it to the Corn Laws ;
and Calhoun is but a Free-Trader by location, and has never
yet answered his own powerful arguments in behalf of Protection. On the other hand, we point you to the long array
of mighty names which have illustrated the annals of Statesmanship in modern times, — to Chatham, William Pitt, and
the Great Frederick of Prussia ; to the whole array of memorable French Statesmen, including Napoleon the first of them
all; to our own WASHINGTON, HAMILTON, JEFFERSON, and
MADISON; to our two CLINTONS, TOMPKINS, to say nothing of
the eagle-eyed and genial-hearted LIVING master-spirit* of our
time. The opinions and the arguments of all these are on
record ; it is by hearkening to and heeding their counsels that
we shall be prepared to walk in the light of experience and
look forward to a glorious National destiny. My friends ! I
dare not detain you longer. I commit to you the cause of
the Nation's Independence, of her Stability and her Prosperity.
Guard it wisely and shield it well ; for it involves your own
happiness and the enduring welfare of your countrymen !

* Henry Clay.

SUNDRY LECTURING REMINISCENCES.

A DAY'S RIDE IN MAINE.

Augusta, Maine, March 24, 1849.

THREE days had glided away rapidly, and pleasantly, and not very idly, among the heartiest of friends in Bangor, — days bright as Italy, and pure as the breath of mountains. The still abundant snow gradually melted into the rivulets from the streets, the adjacent roads, and the southern exposures, in the beams of the ascendant sun; but the nights were crisp and bracing, and the frequent appearance of lighter sleighs in the streets bespoke the obstinacy with which Winter's fleecy mantle still held its ground in the surrounding country. The ice still bound the Penobscot nearly to Frankfort, fourteen miles below; holding the business of Bangor and vicinity in its rugged embrace, and even tempting the foolhardy to travel with teams on its now treacherous surface. But on Tuesday the clear azure of several preceding days was gradually obscured by the portents of a coming storm, which, in the course of the following night, became quite unequivocal, and the pattering of rain on the roof of the Hatch House through the small hours gave premonition of a moist ride to Waterville on the morrow. It was not, however, till the stage-coach (a naked, open wagon) drew up at the door, between six and seven in the morning (Wednesday, 21st), that the fun of it became entirely palpable. The wind came strong from the southwest; the skies were black; the rain was coming faster and faster; in short, a Down-East Equinoctial was upon us.

There were six of us passengers, not forgetting the driver, the best roadsman of all, whom no obstacle could daunt and no botheration disconcert, and who, protected in part by his rubber over-all, looked the day's driving wind and driven rain in the face with buoyant philosophy. The six amused themselves, when they could stay in the wagon, by turning a part of the water from one to the other by means of four umbrellas, which would have been of some account had not the course of the descending fluid been so greatly deflected from the perpendicular by the sweeping gale, and had there not been entirely too much of it. Even as it was, the man in a red-flannel shirt and glazed outer garments, who occupied the most sheltered position (leeward of the umbrellas), and seemed to have been taught by some bird the secret of oiling himself, contrived to maintain a comparatively dry look to the end.

Ten miles — mainly of mud — had slid rapidly and merrily behind us, before we encountered the first formidable snow-drift still occupying the road, over which hundreds of teams had travelled securely for weeks, but into which, softened by the rain, ours plunged, and in it wallowed. The next moment, the leaders were down in a tangled pile; the off one rolled clear over the nigh one, and was extricated, and got up on the near side. The passengers (the heaviest having been thrown out rather suddenly as we came to a halt, the wagon barely not upsetting) walked ahead in quest of help and shelter; (perhaps it did n't pour!) the wheel-horses were also taken off, and four oxen obtained to draw the wagon out of the drift, and on to the changing-place, not far distant.

Soon, all were on board again, — all as good as before, except that the buffaloes were wet on both sides, and the seats had rather a clammy feeling; and we went on merrily as ever — meeting few decided obstacles for the next twelve miles — to the second changing-place (North Dixmont).

So far, we had made good time, in spite of wind and weather. "And now," said the driver, "you may expect to see some bad going." The testimony was confirmed by others, but we did not need their assurance. Two miles more were got over pretty well, one bad place being avoided by letting down the fence, and making a detour through the field; but soon we were brought to a dead halt again. The horses were floundering in a rather profound drift; the wagon was "stuck"; and no resource remained but to beat up the neighborhood for oxen to draw it on, while the passengers went ahead in quest of dinner. The portliest of the number (weighing good two hundred), who had already twice taken his own portrait by a flying-leap into a snow-drift, and had received some severe contusions and a hard wrench in the later operation, when he narrowly missed breaking a leg in clearing the wagon, alone lingered behind to pick up some bits of rides between the worst snow-drifts, of which, I think, there were a hundred within that next two miles. Yet, the wagon was, by six oxen, got through or around them somehow in a little more than two hours, — the horses following behind, and coming through with a beaten and sorry look. I had no idea it could be done so soon by an hour.

Dinner (at Troy) in a hurry, and all aboard again; and henceforward to Waterville we were enabled to take the rain sitting instead of walking for nearly all the time. Some drifts had to be walked over, of course; some snow had to be shovelled away from before the wheels; once or twice, we had to take hold and help propel the wagon through a drift, that need not have been so deep, so far as any practical utility was regarded in its construction; and twice more our solid friend was half thrown, half jumped, into the snow-drifts, as the wagon keeled up on one side, and seemed intent on going over. The last time, one arm went through the drift into about two feet of coolish water, and he, already racked and sore, was on the point of losing temper. The others were more nimble, or, rather, more lucky; generally making a clean jump, and alighting perpendicularly and right end up. Finally, at 6 p. m., we drove rapidly into Waterville, — fifty good miles from Bangor, — and found warm rooms and various comforts awaiting us. Lecturing that evening was a little up hill; but, since the hearers did not audibly complain, I sha' n't. I thought the village dancing-school at our hotel ought to have broken up at midnight, considering that some of us were to be called for the Augusta stage at 5 A. M.; but the young folks seemed to enjoy it to a much later hour; and, if their parents don't object, I probably should be quiet. Still, I *do* say that dancing — which ought to be a healthful, innocent, and approved recreation for all — is made unpopular with the grave and devout by the outrageously late hours to which mere infants in years are kept up by it, in hot and crowded rooms, whence they are suddenly transferred, when utterly exhausted, to the outdoor cold and their fireless homes. It was not the creaking of that fiddle, the heavy pounding of unskilled feet on the ball-room floor, and the annoying rattle of my door-latch in consequence, till some time this morning, that put this into my head; but these served to confirm me in my earlier conviction.

A RIDE ACROSS THE ALLEGHANIES.

WASHINGTON, Monday, December 3, 1851.

IT was 10 o'clock on Saturday morning when our steamboat reached Wheeling, in two days from Cincinnati. That was a bad sample of Western steamboat management. I had promised at home to be here the evening before the Session opened; and it was essential that I should be punctual. I ought to have stopped but one day instead of two at Cincinnati. I ought to have travelled by land from that city, and so been at Wheeling six hours sooner. The boat ought to, and might have been there some hours earlier. But here it was 10 o'clock, and the stages to connect at Cumberland with the Baltimore and Ohio train next morning had all been gone some four hours. No other train would leave Cumberland till Monday morning, — twenty-four hours later. I jumped ashore with my baggage, and sped to the stage-office. One

of the Members of Congress, for self and company, got there
at the same moment, and spoke: "Can you send us through
to Cumberland in time for to-morrow's train?" "No, sir, it
is too late." The Congressman returned to report progress.
Not comprehending the impossibility of driving 193 miles in
22 hours, even over a hilly road, with relays of good horses
every ten or twelve miles, I hung on, and had the resident
proprietor summoned. I put the question to him, varied as
follows: "Will money put us through to Cumberland in
time for to-morrow's cars?" "Yes, money will, — money
enough.". "How much?" "If five of you will pay for a full
stage (nine seats) and twenty dollars extra, you shall be
taken through." I hurried down to the boat in search of the
Congressmen, but looked it over without finding them. At
last, I discovered one of the Senators: "Mr. R., call your
friends; we can be taken to Cumberland in season, for about
twenty dollars each."

He would not listen, — said it could not be done, — he had
tried it once, and failed. (I suspect he did not try the extra
price, "No cure, no pay.") He turned away, and the boat
put off. I went back to the stage-office alone. "Mr. S., what
is your price for taking me through to Cumberland in season?" "Regular fare to Baltimore, eleven dollars; forty
dollars extra for gaining time, — in all, $ 51." I put down
the change, and he got up his horses. In ten minutes we
were on the road. The gentleman who drove stands at the
head of his profession. He understood, by experience or instinct, that the perfection of driving is not to seem or need to
drive at all. By a slight and easy motion of his wrist, he
thridded his way through a drove of cattle, around a carriage,
and among the piles of broken or to be broken stone everywhere encumbering the road, now on one side, then on the
other, and again in the middle or on both. He knew just
when to hold in, and when to let out, but seemed to do more
of the former than of the latter; hardly using a persuasion
to speed in the course of the ride. He drove at no time over
eleven, nor under ten, miles per hour. The day was bright,

though cool; the air crisp and bracing. We had a light carriage, with fresh horses every ten to twelve miles. Whatever craft we espied ahead was sure to be hull down astern in the course of five minutes. We drove sixty-two miles in a trifle short of six hours, but lost nearly an hour more in making changes, as we were not expected at the stations. It was 10.40 (Baltimore time) when we started. At half past 5 we overhauled the Mail Stages half-way between Brownsville and Uniontown, Pa., 62 miles from Wheeling. I threw my baggage upon one, and followed it; bidding a hearty farewell to my driver, who turned back to Brownsville for the night, on his way to Wheeling. We were in Uniontown to tea 15 minutes past 6; left at 7; and drove straight ahead over the Alleghanies, only stopping to change or water, and making the five changes in less than twenty minutes, all told. The night was cold, and snow contrived to fall from about midnight, though less profusely than on the plains this side. I think the cold prevented. But each stage was just full of passengers, and little discomfort was felt from the cold. I don't consider riding through a cold night without a halt the summit of human felicity; but it does very well, if you don't waste your time and strength in trying to go to sleep. That is absurd. We drove into Cumberland at 7 A. M.; had breakfast, and abundant time for outward renovation, before the cars started at half past 8. The storm continued through the day, changing from snow to sleety hail and almost rain as we neared the coast. We met with a bad accident at 4 P. M., — when 45 miles from Baltimore, our snow-scraper catching against some part of the track, so that it was broken and turned under the forward engine, which was thrown off the track, and the one behind it partly followed the example. Both were disabled and considerably injured. Happily, we had still a third engine, pushing behind, which was detached and run back to Frederick for help to clear away the wreck and mend the track, which had been torn up by our disaster. After four hours' delay, we got under headway again, but came on very slowly, and only made the Relay House at

11 P. M., — too late for any chance to reach this city till morning. But we were in here before 9 A. M., three hours before Congress convened, and in ample season to look into whatever was going on. Governor Brown of Mississippi, whom I left on the boat at Wheeling, incredulous as to the practicability of getting through to Cumberland in season, was of course not here to vote for his friend, Howell Cobb, when even one vote was no slight consideration. I presume he is in, *via* Pittsburg, to-night.

A NIGHT-RIDE ACROSS THE PRAIRIES.

SOUTH BEND, INDIANA, October 18, 1853.

I LEFT New York on Monday morning of last week, reached Lafayette, *via* Erie Railroad, Buffalo City, the steamboat Queen of the West to Cleveland, and the railroad thence by Galion, Bellefontaine, and Indianapolis, at noon on Wednesday. Having given the residue of that day and all the next to the State Agricultural Fair, and fulfilled the engagement that drew me to Indiana, I returned to Indianapolis on Friday morning, spoke there in the evening, and started back *via* Lafayette, on Saturday morning, to fulfil a promise to speak on the evening of that day at Laporte, where I should reach the Northern Indiana and Southern Michigan Road, and set my face homeward. How we were delayed on our way back to Lafayette, and how, on reaching that smart young village, I was misled, by the kind guidance of a zealous friend, into waiting for the Northern cars at a place half a mile distant from that where they then actually were; how I at last broke over all assurances that they always started from this point, and must come here before leaving, and made for their out-of-the-way station just in time to be too late, — it were a fruitless vexation to recall. Suffice it that at noon I stood on the platform where I might and should have been twenty minutes before, just in time to see the line of smoke hovering over the rapidly receding train, to realize that any seasonable fulfilment of my promise to Laporte was now impossible, and to learn that the next regular train would leave on Monday, and take me to Laporte just two days after I should have been there. I wandered back to the village, in no enviable mood, to telegraph my mishap to Laporte, and had the privilege of cooling my heels for an hour and a quarter on the steps of the office, while the operators were leisurely discussing and digesting their dinner. They came at last, just too late to enable me to stop the sending of a carriage eleven miles from Laporte to meet me at Westville; and I retraced my steps to the out-of-town depot, to see what chance remained or might turn up.

As quite a number had been deceived and left as I was, owing to the recent change in railroad arrangements, the agent said he would send out an extra train that afternoon, if he could procure an engine; but none came in that could be spared, and at four o'clock our extra train was adjourned to next morning at ten; and I returned to the telegraph office to apprise Laporte that I would speak there for Temperance the next (Sunday) evening, and then walked over to the Bramble House, and laid in a stock of sleep for future contingencies.

I was at the depot in ample season next morning; but the train that was to start at ten did not actually leave till noon, and then with a body entirely disproportioned to its head. Five cars closely packed with live hogs, five ditto with wheat, two ditto with lumber, three or four with live stock and notions returning from the Fair, and two or three cattle-cars containing passengers, formed entirely too heavy a load for our asthmatic engine, which had obviously seen its best days in the service of other roads, before that from New Albany to Michigan City was constructed. Still, we went ahead; crossed the Wabash; passed the Tippecanoe Battle-ground; ran our engine partly off the track, and got it back again; and by three o'clock had reached Brookston, a station fourteen miles from Lafayette, with a fair prospect of traversing our whole ninety-odd miles by the dawn of Monday morning.

But here we came to a long halt. The engine was in want of both wood and water; and, though woods and sloughs were in sight in various directions, neither were accessible. So our engine was detached, and ran ahead some five miles for water, and still farther for wood, and a weary two hours were tediously whiled away before its return.

It came at last, hitched on, and started us; but, before it had moved us another half-mile, the discharge-cock of the boiler flew out, letting off all our water and steam, and rendering us hopelessly immovable for hours to come.

We got out to take an observation. The village of Brookston consists of three houses and no barn, with a well (almost dry) for the use of the railroad; but neither of the houses is a tavern, nor more than one-story high; and their aggregate of accommodation fell far short of the needs of the hungry crowd so unexpectedly thrown upon their hospitality. Two or three more houses of like or inferior calibre were gleaming in the rays of the setting sun at various distances on the prairies; but these were already surfeited with railroad hands as boarders, not to speak of sick women or children in nearly every one; for disease has been very rife this season on these prairies. Still, a friend found an old acquaintance in one of the nearest residents, whose sick wife spread a generous table forthwith for as many of us as could sit around it; and, having supped, we turned out on the prairie to make room for a family party, including two women, one of them quite sick, — as she had been all the way up, and at Lafayette for some days before. Our conductor had started a hand-car back to Lafayette in quest of the only engine there, — a weak, old one, needing some repairs before it could be used. It was calculated that this engine would be up about eleven o'clock, and would then drag us back to Lafayette to spend the remainder of the night, and take a fair start in the morning. This I, for one, had resolved not to submit to, though the only alternative were a camp-fire on the prairie.

But now a bright thought struck the engineer, for which I think he was indebted to *my* good angel. He recollected that a good engine was stationed at a point named Culvertown, forty-three miles ahead; and he decided to take a hand-car and make for this, so that our bow should have two strings to it. The hand-car was dragged over the rough prairie around our long train, and launched, — I following with my carpet-bags, on the lookout for chances. In a trice, it was duly manned; I had coaxed my way to a seat upon it; and we were off.

The full moon rose bright over the eastern woods as, with the north star straight ahead, we bade adieu to the embryo City of Brookston.

We were seven of us on the hand-car; four propelling by twos, as if turning a heavy, two-handed grindstone; but we let off one passenger after traversing a few miles. The engineer and I made up the party; and the car — about equal in size to a wheelbarrow and a half — just managed to hold us and give the propellers working-room. To economize space, I sat a good part of the time facing backward, with my feet hanging over the rear of the car, knocking here and there on a tie or bridge-timber, and often tickled through my boots by the coarse, rank weeds growing up at intervals between the ties, and recently stiffened by the hard October frosts. As a constant effort to hold on was required, the position was not favorable to slumber, however it might be to cogitation. Our Irish steam was evolved from Yankee muscles, and proved of capital quality. We made our first five miles, heavily laden as we were, in twenty-five minutes; our first ten miles in an hour; but our propellers grew gradually weary; we stopped twice or thrice for oil, water, and perhaps one other liquid; so that we were five hours in making the forty-three miles, or from 7 P. M. till midnight. I only tried my hand at propelling for a short mile, and that experience sufficed to convince me that, however it may be as a business, this species of exercise cannot be conscientiously commended as an amusement. The night was chilly, though clear; the dead-ahead breeze, though light, was keen, and I, by no means dressed for such an airy ride, felt it most sensibly.

Our course lay across the east end of Grand Prairie, which stretches westward from the bank of the Wabash across Indiana and Illinois, to the Mississippi, and thence through Iowa and Nebraska, perhaps to Council Bluffs and the Rocky Mountains. The ground we traversed was nearly level, often marshy, and for the most part clear of wood; but we frequently crossed belts or spurs, on higher, dryer soil, of the great forest on our right, with occasional clumps of sturdy oaks, — islets of timber in the prairie sea, — to which the belts aforesaid served as promontories. Four prairie-fires, — two on either hand, — at intervals of miles, burned brightly but lazily; for the wind was not strong enough, nor the vegetation dry and crisp enough, to impel a rapid, roaring, sweeping fire.

Now a flock of geese flew by, murmuring subduedly; then a great heron rose before us, and flew heavily over the marshes; an opossum was ·frightened by our noisy approach, and fled eagerly into the prairie, under an evident mistake as to the nature of our business; and again an odorous skunk, keeping his carcass unseen, gave pungent evidence of his close proximity. Finally, a little after midnight, chilled and weary, we reached the one-horse village of Culvertown, and found the engine missing, — run down to Michigan City for repairs, — so that my companions had had their rugged ride for nothing. The landlady of the only house in sight got up and made a fire; the engineer decided to await the return of the fugitive engine; and I began to drum up the means of farther conveyance; for I was still twenty-odd miles from any public conveyance that would speed me on my way. Horses, I learned, were not easily to be had; and, even if I had a team, the roads across the great marsh and small river just north of us were rather shy. But the engineer lent me the hand-car which had already done such good service, and I evoked from slumber two Dutchmen, who were persuaded to act as my crew; and by 1 A. M. I was again under headway northward; the air keener, and I more vulnerable to its assaults in my loneliness, than when six of us were so closely huddled together. But my Dutchmen propelled with a will, and my good craft sped briskly onward.

From Culvertown, a prairie-marsh stretches thirteen miles northward, and I think no building, and hardly a cultivated acre, were visible through all that distance. The dense fog, beaten down by the cool air, lay low on this marsh, and was heavily charged with prairie-smoke for a part of the way. Three miles from C., we crossed, on a pokerish bridge of naked timbers, the slough-like bed wherein the Kankakee oozes and creeps sluggishly westward to join the Fox and form the Illinois. They say the Kankakee has a rapid current, and dry, inviting banks, from the point where it crosses the Illinois line, which might tempt one to regret that it did not cross that line forty miles higher up. Happily, the keen air had done for the mosquitoes, so that we had no more music than I had fairly bargained for; but Bunyan might have improved his description of the Slough of Despond had he been favored with a vision of the Kankakee marshes. At 4 A.M., my good craft brought up at Westville, and I was gratified by the sight of half a dozen houses at once for the first time since leaving Lafayette, seventy-eight miles below. I doubt that all the houses visible on that seventy-eight miles would amount to a hundred; and I am sure they would be dear at two hundred dollars each, on the average. Yet there are much fine timber and excellent land on that route, and he who passes over the railroad ten years hence will see a very different state of things. If efficient plans of drainage can but be devised and executed, that region will yet be one of the most productive in the world. Still, the financiering which conjured up the means of building that New Albany and Michigan City Railroad is worthy of a brazen monument. At Westville, I was but eleven miles from Laporte, and four from the crossing of the great Northern Indiana Road from Chicago: so, having accomplished sixty-four miles by hand-car since dark, and arrived within striking distance of a civilized railroad, I went to bed till breakfast-time; took passage by wagon at 7; was in Laporte by 9; spoke for Temperance at 1; took the railroad at 3; and came here to fulfil my engagement to lecture last evening; and thus, having reopened my communications, I close this hurried account of A Night Ride Across the Prairies.

A WINTER FLOOD IN ILLINOIS.

GALESBURG, ILLINOIS, February 7, 1857.

I LEFT the train from Chicago on this (the Burlington) Road at 7 A.M. yesterday at "Oquawka Junction," the last station this side of the Mississippi, and took the stage in due season for Oquawka (5½ miles north), on the bank of the great river, and the shire town of Henderson County. It had been raining and thawing for a day or so hereabout; and, though there was little snow to melt, the hard-frozen earth threw off the water like a glass roof. The creeks were all over their banks, wandering at their own sweet will, — "South Henderson," "Main Henderson," and "North Henderson" vying with each other in encroachments on the people's highway, and all the "sloughs" and depressions transformed into temporary lakes; but our stage crossed them all safely, — there being a solid frost bottom to each, — and reached Oquawka in due season.

But the rain poured harder as the day wore on, and the evening was as inclement and forbidding as could well be imagined. I said my say to a rather thin house, — yet a large gathering for such a night, — and then looked about for the means of making good my promise to be in Galesburg (only 33 miles distant, 27 of it railroad) this evening.

The prospect was not cheering. The rain was pouring, the wind howling, and the creeks rising. Already, the stage had been stopped by the creeks on its evening trip to the cars; and it was plain that to wait till morning was to prolong my stay indefinitely. Now, Oquawka is a nice place, as its melli-

fluous name would indicate, and has many excellent people
whose acquaintance I should have been glad to improve;
but the telegraph is not among its advantages, and I could
not let the people of Galesburg, and other towns to which I
was due, know what had become of me, nor why I disappointed them; so I resolved to dig out, if possible; and, as
the creeks were still rising rapidly, the only course was to
start at once. A council of wise friends decided that I could
not reach Oquawka Junction, if I were ever so bent upon it,
and should find no train there if I did; and that the only
hopeful course was to take the highest or eastern road, and
steer for Monmouth (half-way to Galesburg) at once. By
taking this course, I should turn several vicious creeks, leaving only " Main Henderson" really formidable. So a buggy
and capital span were procured from a livery-stable, with
their shrewd and capable owner as pilot, and, at a little past
10 o'clock, we put out into the storm, resolved to see Monmouth (18 miles, by our route) before daylight, if possible.
Though the clouds were thick, the wind blew, and the rain
poured, there was a good moon above all, which, though obscured, gave about all the light that was really necessary.

Though Oquawka is built on the sand, we crossed wide
stretches of water before we had cleared it; and, of the miles
of high sand-ridge that intervened between it and " Main
Henderson," I judge that fully a fourth lay under water.
Still, hoofs and wheels brought up on frost; and it was not
till we descended into the bottom of " Main Henderson " that
matters began to wear a serious aspect.

Forty rods west of the ordinary channel of the creek, we
plunged into the water, which grew gradually deeper, until
our boots and baggage had drunk of it to satiety. Just at
this point, the driver's quick and wary eye caught sight of
some plank or timber which had formed part of a bridge over
one of the ordinary side-cuts of the stream when over its
bank, — said plank or timber-head being even with the surface of the flood, with such an angle of inclination as indicated that the bridge was a wreck, and had probably in good

part floated off. He reined up his horses before reaching it, and turned them face about, and in a minute we were half-way back,—not to dry, but to unflooded land. Here we took sweet counsel together, and I offered to return to Oquawka if he considered it foolhardy to persist in going forward. He studied a moment, and concluded to make another attempt; which he did, and went through above the treacherous bridge, though I don't believe any man could have done it two hours later. We were soon in shallower water, found the main bridge all right, and no deep water east of it, though " Smith's Creek " (a tributary which enters " Main Henderson " just below the bridge) set back upon and covered our road with a swift current for perhaps a quarter of a mile. The driver was familiar with the road, and thought it had never been so covered before. Soon, however, we ascended a long, badly gullied hill of the very worst clay, and breathed more freely on the high, level prairie, covered in good part with water, and not pretty wheeling, but never threatening to float us bodily off, like that raving " Main Henderson."

Having reached " Stringtown," five or six miles on our way, the driver called up a wayside friend, and borrowed dry socks, while I made researches in my baggage for a like creature-comfort, but with very unsatisfactory results. " Main Henderson " had been there before me, and had made everything fit for his wear, and unfit for mine. I closed valise and leathern bag with a shiver, and we resumed our weary way.

I do like the prairies, though their admirers won't admit it; and I cheerfully certify that the best going we found was on the virgin turf. True, the " sloughs " were many and wide; yet, there was frost and ice at the bottom of them, which seldom cut through; but, whenever it did, it gave horses, buggy, and riders, a racking. My pilot picked our way with great judgment, and we were nevermore stopped, and hardly checked, until we came out on the main road westward from Monmouth, three miles distant.

That three miles of dense prairie was the heaviest travelling I ever underwent; and, if our jaded horses traversed it in an hour and a quarter, they did passing well. On the naked prairie, we felt little anxiety; for, if the slough seemed too deep straight ahead, we could sheer right or left *ad libitum*, only taking care to keep some landmark in view, if possible. But roads imply bridges over the water-courses; and these bridges were far more perilous than the water-courses themselves.

Still the wind blew, still the rain fell, in spite of our repeated predictions that it would soon hold up; and still our horses plodded slowly onward, until those three miles seemed to me interminable. Our main business was to watch the bridges just ahead, and see that they had not been washed out; and they generally seemed to stand remarkably well. At last, Monmouth was in sight; the last bridge was passed; no, not the last, for our horses were in a deep gully this instant. A second more, and they sprang out, and jerked the buggy in with a crash that is still audible. The nigh fore-wheel snapped its tire, and went down, an armful of oven-wood; the tongue split, but held on, and the driver was pitched across my knees head downward into the deep mortar-bed termed the road. I went forward on my face, but clung to the wreck, with my feet entangled in apron and blankets; and, as the horses started to run, the look ahead for an instant was not flattering.

Only for an instant, however. The idea of running with that wreck through such mud, after a heavy night-drag of eighteen miles, was so essentially ridiculous that no well-bred horse could have entertained it. Ours perceived this instinctively, and soon slacked up, while the driver recovered his feet and his reins, if he had ever fully lost the latter. I cannot say how I came out of the dilapidated vehicle, nor could the driver give me any light on the subject; but I soon found myself resuming the perpendicular, and facing rearward in quest of my hat, which I found in a wayside pond several rods back, two thirds full of water, but still floating. My blanket I fished out of the semi-liquid mud about midway between my goal and my starting-point, and, for the first time on my journey, found its company disagreeable.

Men never know when they are well off. Five minutes before, I had been industriously cherishing my cold, wet feet, fencing off the driving rain, and fancying myself an object of just compassion; now, I saw clearly that, so long as the carriage remained sound, I had been in an enviable state of ease and enjoyment. Throwing my soiled blanket over one arm, and taking my valise in the opposite hand, I pulled one foot after another out of the deep, tarry mud, losing both my well-fastened overshoes therein without knowing it, and pushed through to a tavern at the rate of a mile and a half per hour, in a state of general bedragglement and desperate jollity which Mark Tapley could not have bettered.

It was 4 A. M. when a hospitable roof overshadowed us. The house was full, and my petition for a pair of slippers, and a room with a fire in it, could not be granted. But a barroom fire was got up, and a bed in due time provided, though a ball that night in the village — no, city — had absorbed most of the accommodations. But our noble horses found what they needed, and we had an hour's sleep or more, though I did not incline to sleep at all. I got up to breakfast, and to find all as I expected about the railroad. The Chicago night-train went down nearly on time, but did not reach Oquawka Junction, finding the track all washed out at the crossing of "South Henderson," ten miles below. But its engine came back about 9 A.M., took on board half a dozen of us, and backed up to Galesburg (seventeen miles) in less than an hour; saving me another dreaded carriage-ride of at least six hours. We crossed one washed-out place, which threatened to throw us off, but did not. I guess I am the last person who will have left Oquawka for several days, and suspect Burlington (Iowa) has parted company with the world eastward of the Mississippi for at least as many.

MORAL. — We are none of us half grateful enough for the blessings of railroads, — when the trains run, and the cars don't fly the track.

MARRIAGE AND DIVORCE.

A DISCUSSION BETWEEN HORACE GREELEY AND ROBERT DALE OWEN.

DIVORCE. — WOMAN'S RIGHTS.*

OUR Legislature is again importuned to try its hand at increasing the facilities of divorce. We trust it will ponder long and carefully before it consents. That many persons are badly mated is true; but that is not the law's fault. The law of our State says plainly to all the unmarried, "Be very careful how you marry; for a mistake in this regard is irrevocable. The law does not constrain you to marry, does not hurry you to marry, but bids you be first *sure* that you know intimately and love devotedly the person with whom you form this irrevocable union. We rectify no mistakes; it. rests with you not to make any. If you do, bear the penalty as you ought, and do not seek to transfer it to the shoulders of the community." And this, we think, is, in the broad view, right, though in special cases it involves hardship.

The paradise of free-lovers is the State of Indiana, where the lax principles of Robert Dale Owen, and the utter want of principle of John Pettit (leading revisers of the laws), combined to establish, some years since, a state of law which enables men or women to get unmarried nearly at pleasure. A legal friend in that State recently remarked to us, that, at one County Court, he obtained eleven divorces one day before dinner; "and it was n't a good morning for divorces either." In one case within his knowledge, a prominent citizen of an Eastern manufacturing city came to Indiana, went through

---

* Editorial in The Tribune of March 1, 1860.

the usual routine, obtained his divorce about dinner-time, and, in the course of the evening was married to his new inamorata, who had come on for the purpose, and was staying at the same hotel with him. They soon started for home, having no more use for the State of Indiana ; and, on arriving, he introduced his new wife to her astonished predecessor, whom he notified that she must pack up and go, as there was no room for her in that house any longer. So she went.

How many want such facility of divorcing in New York ? We trust not one in a hundred. If we are right in this judgment, let the ninety-nine make themselves heard at Albany as well as the one. The discontented are always active ; the contented ought not to sleep evermore.

We favor whatever may be done to mitigate the hardships endured by mismated persons in perfect consistency with the maintenance of the sanctity and perpetuity of Marriage. Cases are constantly occurring in which a virtuous and worthy girl persists in marrying a dissolute scapegrace, in spite of the most conclusive demonstrations of his worthlessness. Five years hence, when he has become a miserable loafer and sot, she will wish herself divorced from him ; but the law says No, and we stand by it. But the law ought to allow her to earn for herself and her little ones, and not enable him to appropriate and squander her few hard-won shillings. This is asked for, and ought to be granted. So the law should allow the woman who is living wholly separate from her husband, by reason of his brutality, cruelty, or profligacy, to have the same control over her property and earnings as if she had never married. This is not now the case. Nay'; we know an instance in which a woman, long since separated from her worthless husband, and trying hard to earn a meagre living for their children, was disabled and crippled by a railroad accident ; yet the law gives her no right of action against the culpable company ; her broken ankles · are legally her runaway husband's, not her own ; and he would probably sell them outright for a gallon of good brandy, and let the company finish the job of breaking them at its convenience.

We heartily approve of such changes in our laws as would make this deserted wife the legal owner of her own ankles; but we would not dissolve the marriage obligation to constancy for any other cause than that recognized as sufficient by Jesus Christ.

MR. OWEN'S RESPONSE.*

To the Editor of the New York Tribune:—

Sir: Retired from political life, and now disposed to address the public, if at all, through a calmer medium than the columns of a daily paper, still, I cannot read the allusion in this morning's Tribune, made in connection with an important subject, to my adopted State and to myself by name, without feeling that justice to both, and, what is of more consequence, the fair statement of a question involving much of human morality and happiness, require of me a few words. You say:—

"The Paradise of free-lovers is the State of Indiana, where the lax principles of Robert Dale Owen, and the utter want of principle of John Pettit (leading revisers of the laws), combined to establish, some years since, a state of law which enables men and women to get unmarried nearly at pleasure."

You are usually, I think, correct in your statements of fact, and doubtless always intend to be so. That in this endeavor you sometimes fail, we have a proof to-day.

So far as I recollect, the Indiana law of divorce does not owe a single section to Mr. Pettit. Be that, however, as it may, it owes one of its provisions, *and one only*, to me. I found that law thirty-four years ago, when I first became a resident of the State, in substance nearly what it now is; indeed, with all its essential features the same. It was once referred to myself, in conjunction with another member of the Legislature, for revision; and we amended it in a single point; namely, by adding to the causes of divorce "habit-

* From The Tribune of March 5, 1860.

ual drunkenness for two years." In no other particular, either by vote or proposition, have I been instrumental in framing or amending the law in question, directly or indirectly.

Do not imagine, however, that I seek to avoid any responsibility in regard to that law as it stands. I cordially approve it. It has stood the test for forty or fifty years among a people whom, if you knew them as intimately as I do, candor would compel you to admit to be, according to the strictest standard of morality you may set up, not one whit behind those of sister States, perhaps of more pretensions. I approve the law, not on principle only, but because, for more than half a lifetime, I have witnessed its practical workings. I speak of its influence on *our own citizens.* It is much to be regretted that any one should ever be compelled to seek a divorce out of his own State. But, even in alluding to abuses which *have* occurred in this connection, you failed to tell your readers, what perhaps you did not know, that our law has of late years been so changed that the cases you state cannot possibly recur. No one can now sue for a divorce in Indiana, until he has been during one year, at least, a resident of the State; and the provision regarding timely notice to the absent party is of the strictest kind.

You speak of Indiana as "the Paradise of free-lovers." It is in New York and New England, refusing reasonable divorce, that free-love prevails; not in Indiana. I never even heard the name there. You locate the Paradise, then, too far west.

And does it not occur to you, when a million of men, — chiefly plain, hardy, industrious farmers, with wives whom, after the homely old fashion, they love, and daughters whose chastity and happiness are as dear to them as if their homes were the wealthiest in the land, — does it not occur to Horace Greeley that, when these men go on deliberately for half a century maintaining unchanged (or, if changed at all, made more liberal) a law of divorce which he denounces as breeding disorder and immorality, — that the million, with their long experience, may be right, and that Horace Greeley, without that experience, may be wrong?

You talk of my "lax principles." I think that, by my past life, I have earned the right to be believed when I say what *are* my principles and what are not.

On this subject, they go just so far as the Indiana law, and no further. I have given proof of this. I have had a hundred opportunities, and never used them, to move its amendment. I was chairman of the Revision Committee of our Constitutional Convention; but in our Constitution we incorporated nothing in regard to divorce, except a prohibition against all divorces by the Legislature. To that, I think you will not object. At the next session, I was chairman of the committee to revise the laws; but we merely reënacted the old divorce law, of which experience had taught us the benefits. It grants divorce for other causes than the one your law selects, — as for abandonment; for cruel treatment; for habitual drunkenness; and for any other cause for which the court may deem it proper that a divorce should be granted.

Are these "lax principles"? I claim to have them judged according to a Christian rule. "By their fruits ye shall know them." You have elopements, adultery, which your law, by rendering it indispensable to release, virtually encourages; you have free-love, and that most terrible of all social evils, prostitution. We, instead, have regulated, legal separations. You may feel disposed to thank God that you are not as other men, or even as these Indianians. I think that we are justified in His sight, rather than you.

Or is it, perhaps, the amendment I *did* propose and carry which seems to you lax in principle? — the provision, namely, that a wife should not be compelled to live with one who has been, for years, an habitual drunkard. You have told us that she ought to be so compelled. It constantly occurs, you say, that a "virtuous and worthy girl" marries a man who "becomes a miserable loafer and sot"; and you add: "She will wish herself divorced from him; but the law says No, and we stand to it."

Think, for a moment, what this actually involves! Let us take the "single captive," lest the multiplicity of images distract us. See the young creature, "virtuous and worthy," awaiting, late in the solitary night, the fate to which, for life, you consign her; and that for no sin more heinous than that her girl's heart, believing in human goodness, had trusted the vows and promises of a scoundrel. Is it her home where she is sitting? Let us not so desecrate the hallowed word. It is the den of her sufferings and of her shame. A bloated wretch, whom daily and nightly debauch has degraded below humanity, has the right to enter it. In what temper he will arrive, God alone knows, — all the animal within him, probably, aroused by drink. Will he beat her, — the mother of his children, the one he has sworn to love and protect? Likely enough. Ah! well if that be all! The scourge, though its strokes may cause the flesh to shudder, cannot reach the soul. But the possible outrages of this "miserable loafer and sot" 'may. He has the command of torments, legally permitted, far beyond those of the lash. That bedchamber is his, and the bed is the beast's own lair. It depends, too, on the brute's drunken will whether it shall be shared or not. Caliban is lord and master, by legal right. There is not a womanly instinct that he cannot outrage; not a holy emotion that he may not profane. He is authorized to commit what more resembles an infamous crime — usually rated second to murder, and often punished with death — than anything else.

And in this foul pit of degradation you would leave to a fate too horrible for infamy itself, a pure, gentle, blameless, Christian wife! Her cry thence may ascend to heaven; but, on earth, you think it should be stifled or contemned. She entreats for relief, — for escape from the pollution she abhors; you look down upon her misery, and answer her, "The law says No, and we stand to it."

God forgive you, Horace Greeley, the inhuman sentiment! I believe you to be a good man, desiring human improvement, the friend of what you deem essential to social morality. God send that you may never, in the person of a daughter of your own, and in the recital of her tortures, practically learn the terrible lesson how far you have strayed from the right !

Further to argue the general question would be an unwarrantable intrusion on your columns. Suffice it to say, that, if I differ from you as to the expediency of occasionally dissolving misery-bringing unions, it is precisely because I regard the marriage relation as the holiest of earthly institutions. It is for that very reason that I seek to preserve its purity, when other expedients fail, by the besom of divorce. No human relation ought to be suffered so to degenerate that it defeats the purpose of its institution. God imposes no laws on man merely to have the pleasure of seeing them obeyed ; but, on the contrary, with special reference to His creatures' welfare and improvement. Marriage itself, like the Sabbath, was made for man ; not man for marriage. It fulfils God's intentions so long as the domestic home is the abode of purity, of noble sentiment, of loving-kindness, or, at least, of mutual forbearance. But it defeats His purpose, and violates the Divine economy, when it becomes the daily cause of grievous words and heartless deeds, — of anger, strifes, selfishness, cruelty, ruffianism. That it should ever be thus degraded and perverted, all good men must lament ; and all ought earnestly to seek the most effectual remedy.

In no country have I found the marriage obligation so little binding as in the nation * near whose court, as minister, I recently spent five years, — a country where Marriage is a sacrament and Divorce an impossibility ; and where, indeed, on account of their "lax principles," the inhabitants neither need nor care for it. In no country have I seen marriage and its vows more strictly respected than in my adopted State, where the relation, when it engenders immorality, may be terminated by law. For the rest, divorces in Indiana are far less frequent than strangers, reading our divorce law, might be led to imagine. We find Jefferson's words to be as true of married persons as of the rest of man-

* Naples.

kind. They "are more disposed to suffer while evils are sufferable, than to right themselves by abolishing the forms to which they have been accustomed."

The question remains, whether it be more pleasing in the sight of God, and more conducive to virtue in man, to part decently in peace, or to live on in shameful discord.

I am, sir, your obedient servant,

ROBERT DALE OWEN.

NEW YORK, March 1, 1860.

REPLY BY MR. GREELEY.*

TO THE HON. ROBERT DALE OWEN, OF INDIANA : —

MY DEAR SIR: I had not expected to provoke your letter this day published; but the subject is one of the highest and widest importance, and I am very willing to aid in its further elucidation.

I do not think the issues of fact raised by you need long detain us. The country knows that you have for the last thirty years and more been a leading member of the generally dominant party in Indiana, — almost the only member who could with propriety be termed a political philosopher. As such, you have naturally exerted a very great influence over the legislation and internal policy of that State. Often a member of her Legislature as well as of Congress, and one of the revisers of her laws, you admit that the Law of Marriage and Divorce came at one time directly and distinctly under review before you, and that you ingrafted thereon a provision adding another — habitual drunkenness — to the pre-existing grounds on which divorce might legally be granted. As to "lax principles," I need not say more than that I cite your letter now before me as a sample and illustration.

But let me brush away one cobweb of your brain. You picture the case of a pure and gentle woman exposed to the

* From The Tribune of March 6, 1860.

brutalities and cruelties of a beastly sot of a husband. For such cases, *our* laws grant a separation from bed and board, — not a disruption of the marriage tie, with liberty to marry again. I think this is just right. I would not let loose such a wretch as you have depicted to delude and torture another " pure and virtuous girl." Let one victim suffice him.

Your reference to the " blameless *Christian* wife," and to what is " more pleasing in the sight of God," impels me to say that I must consider Jesus of Nazareth a better authority as to what is Christian and what pleases God than you are. His testimony on this point is express and unequivocal (Matt. xix. 9), that a marriage can be rightfully dissolved because of adultery alone. You well know that was not the law either of Jews or Romans in his day ; so that he cannot have been misled by custom or tradition, even were it possible for him to have been mistaken. I believe he was wholly right.

For what *is* Marriage ? I mind the Apostolic injunction, " Hold fast the form of sound words." Dr. Webster's great dictionary says : —

" MARRIAGE : The act of uniting a man and woman *for life ;* wedlock ; the legal union of a man and woman *for life. Marriage* is a contract both civil and religious, by which the parties engage to live together in mutual affection and fidelity *till death shall separate them.*"

So Worcester : —

" MARRIAGE : the act of marrying, or uniting a man and woman *for life* as husband and wife," &c., &c.

I surely need not quote to you the language of the marriage ceremony, — the mutual and solemn promise to " take each other for better, for worse," and " to live together *till death do part,*" &c., &c. You must be aware that the entire Christian, and I think most of the partially civilized pagan world, regard this solemn contract to cleave to each other *till death* as the very essence, the vital element, of Marriage.

Now it is not here necessary that I should prove this better than any possible substitute : suffice it that I insist that whoever would recommend a substitute should clearly, specifically, set forth its nature and conditions, and should call it by its distinctive name. There may be something better than Marriage ; but nothing *is Marriage* but a solemn engagement to live together in faith and love *till death.* Why should not they, who have devised something better than old-fashioned Marriage, give their bantling a distinctive *name,* and not appropriate ours ? They have been often enough warned off our premises ; shall we never be able to shame them out of their unwarrantable poaching ?

I am perfectly willing to see all social experiments tried that any earnest, rational being deems calculated to promote the well-being of the human family ; but I insist that this matter of Marriage and Divorce has passed beyond the reasonable scope of experiment. The ground has all been travelled over and over : — from Indissoluble Monogamic Marriage down through Polygamy, Concubinage, easy Divorce, to absolute Free Love, mankind have tried every possible modification and shade of relation between Man and Woman. If these multiform, protracted, diversified, infinitely repeated, experiments have not established the superiority of the union of one man to one woman for life — in short, Marriage — to all other forms of sexual relation, then History is a deluding mist, and Man has hitherto lived in vain.

But you assert that the people of Indiana are emphatically moral and chaste in their domestic relations. That may be ; at all events, *I* have not yet called it in question. Indiana is yet a young State, — not so old as either you or I, — and most of her adult population were born, and I think most of them were reared and married, in States which teach and maintain the Indissolubility of Marriage. That population is yet sparse ; the greater part of it in moderate circumstances, engaged in rural industry, and but slightly exposed to the temptations born of crowds, luxury, and idleness. In such circumstances, continence would probably be general, even were Marriage unknown. But let Time and Change do their work, and then see ! Given the population of Italy in the days of the Cæsars, with easy divorce, and I believe the result would be like that experienced by the Roman Republic, which, under the sway of easy divorce, rotted away and perished, — blasted by the mildew of unchaste mothers and dissolute homes.

If experiments are to be tried in the direction you favor, I insist that they shall be tried fairly, — not under cover of false promises and baseless pretences. Let those who will take each other on trial ; but let such unions have a distinct name as in Paris or Hayti, and let us know just who are married (old style), and who have formed unions to be maintained or terminated as circumstances shall dictate. Those who choose the latter will of course consummate it without benefit of clergy ; but I do not see how they need even so much ceremony as that of jumping the broomstick. " I 'll love you so long as I 'm able, and swear for no longer than this," — what need is there of any solemnity to hallow such a union ? What libertine would hesitate to promise that much, even if fully resolved to decamp next morning ? If man and woman are to be true to each other only so long as they shall each find constancy the dictate of their several inclinations, there can be no such crime as adultery, and mankind have too long been defrauded of innocent enjoyment by priestly anathemas and ghostly maledictions. Let us each do what for the moment shall give us pleasurable sensations, and let all such fantasies as God, Duty, Conscience, Retribution, Eternity, be banished to the moles and the bats, with other forgotten rubbish of bygone ages of darkness and unreal terrors.

But if — as I firmly believe — Marriage is a matter which concerns not only the men and women who contract it, but the State, the community, mankind, — if its object be not merely the mutual gratification and advantage of the husband and wife, but the due sustenance, nurture, and education of their children, — if, in other words, those who voluntarily incur the obligations of parentage can only discharge those obligations personally and conjointly, and to that end are bound to live together in love, at least until their youngest child shall have attained perfect physical and intellectual maturity, — then I deny that a marriage can be dissolved save by death or that crime which alone renders its continuance impossible. I look beyond the special case to the general law, and to the reason which underlies that law; and I say, — No couple can innocently take upon themselves the obligations of Marriage until they KNOW that they are one in spirit, and so must remain forever. If they rashly lay profane hands on the ark, theirs alone is the blame; be theirs alone the penalty ! They have no right to cast it on that public which admonished and entreated them to forbear, but admonished and entreated in vain.   Yours,

                                                    HORACE GREELEY.
NEW YORK, March 5, 1860.

MR. OWEN'S REJOINDER.*

TO THE HON. HORACE GREELEY : —

MY DEAR SIR : In one matter we shall not differ, and that is in the opinion that Jesus of Nazareth should be considered better authority as to what is Christian — and I will add as to what is conducive to public morals — than either you or I. The longer I live, the more I settle down to the conviction that *the* one great miracle of history is, that a system of ethics so far in advance as was the Christian System, not only of the semi-barbarism of Jewish life eighteen hundred years ago, but of what we term the civilization of our own day, should have taken root, and lived, and spread, where every opinion seemed adverse and every influence hostile. But, before we take Christ's opinion on the subject in hand, let us go a little further back.

You tell us that "the very essence of marriage" is, that

* From The Tribune of March 12, 1860.

the married should " cleave to each other till death." And, as a corollary, you insist that, if this condition is ever violated (as by the action of a divorce law), then it is *not* Marriage which prevails, but only a substitute. You add :—

" I insist that whoever would recommend such substitute should clearly, specifically set forth its nature and conditions, and should call it by its distinctive name. There may be something better than Marriage, but nothing *is Marriage* but a solemn engagement to live together *till death.* Why should not they who have devised something better than old-fashioned Marriage give their bantling a distinctive *name*, and not appropriate ours ? They have been often warned off our premises ; shall we never be able to shame them out of their unwarrantable poaching ? " [The Italics are yours.]

This is plain. If the law regards Marriage as a contract which, under any circumstances, may be terminated, then (you allege) men and women live together under what is but a substitute for marriage, — under what should go by the name of concubinage, or some similar term. Such is the state of things, you infer, under the present Indiana law.

I do not think you reflected what a sweeping assertion you were here making. For there is not a State in the Union — not even New York — which is without a divorce law. In every State of the Union, therefore, Marriage is a contract of such a nature that contingencies *may* arise under which the married may *not* " live together until death them do part." If, then, the possible contingency of separation, legally admitted, annuls " the very essence of marriage," and converts it into concubinage, in what condition, I pray you, are married people living throughout the United States ?

The same state of things prevails in all Protestant countries. Only in those which acknowledge the Pope as their religious head is Marriage an indissoluble sacrament. Is it your opinion that Catholics only are really married ?

But this is a mere instalment of the difficulties which inhere in your proposition. Moses, of whom we are told (Deuteronomy v. 31) that God said to him : " Stand thou here by me, and I will speak unto thee all the commandments, and the statutes, and the judgments which thou shalt teach my people," promulgated to the Jews a law of divorce. Our divorce-law in Indiana must be, even in your eyes, a moral statute, compared to that of the Jewish lawgiver; for the latter provided : "When a man hath taken a wife and married her, and it come to pass that she find no favor in his eyes, then let him write her a bill of divorcement, and give it in her hand, and send her out of his house. And when she is departed out of his house, she may go and be another man's wife." (Deuteronomy xxiv. 1.) This, unless you deny the record, you must admit to be God's own law. It was first declared, according to the usual chronology, about 1450 years before the Christian era. It remained unchanged till Christ's day. Joseph and Mary were married under it; and the former, when he doubted Mary's fidelity, was "minded to put her away privily." For fourteen centuries and a half, then, God's chosen people, living under His law, had, according to you, a mere substitute for marriage. What distinctive name the "bantling" deserves, I leave to your judgment. We have been accustomed to regard it as "old-fashioned marriage." It is certain, however, that the contract, under such a law, was, "I will be your husband just as long as you find favor in my eyes; and, as soon as you cease to do so, you shall have a bill of divorcement, and be sent out of my house. Then you may marry whom you please."

Jesus tells us that this law was given "because of the hardness of their hearts"; or, as we should now express it, because of the low grade of morality then existing in Judea. Nevertheless, if it really be God's own law, how can you allege that it is wrong in itself ? But, if it be not wrong, then divorce, even of the easiest attainment, must, in a certain state of society, be right. And hence results another important principle; namely, that there is no absolute right or wrong about this matter of divorce; but that it may properly vary in its details at different stages of civilization. It is certain that, under the Divine Economy, our modern sense of propriety and morality has been so developed, that we should not tolerate the Jewish statute giving uncontrolled license to the husband, but no right of relief whatever to the wife.

Jesus, discarding the old law, is stated to have proposed (as you remind us) to the people of his day a substitute where there was but a single cause for divorce, — the same recognized by the New York statute. But his idea of conjugal infidelity was not that entertained in our courts of law. He looked, beyond surface-morality, to the heart. In his pure eyes, the thought and the act were of equal criminality. His words were : " Whosoever looketh on a woman to lust after her hath committed adultery with her already in his heart." (Matthew v. 28.) The fair inference seems to be, that the proper cause for divorce is, not the mere physical act of infidelity, but that adultery of the heart which quenches conjugal love ; thus destroying that which, far more justly than your cohabitation till death, may be regarded as " the very essence of Marriage."

I do not allege that Jesus so connected his two teachings, — that regarding divorce and that defining adultery, — that the Jews of his day, gross-minded as they were, might detect the connection and perceive its inference. If the Hebrews, in Moses' time, were so steeped in barbarism that nothing better than the bill-of-divorcement privilege was suitable for them, we may readily imagine that, even after fourteen centuries had elapsed, enough of the hardness of heart would remain to justify a law, in advance of the other, indeed, but still only adapted to a hard, material race, — a race who had not learned that the letter killeth, but the spirit giveth life, — a race who cannot be supposed to have been capable of appreciating, hardly of comprehending, a morality of standard so exalted that the thought is brought to judgment though the deed disclose it not.

I will go further and admit that, if the words of Jesus, in the text quoted by you, have come down to us reported with strict accuracy, he may have intended the men of his day to put upon them, as best adapted to their social *status*, the lit-

erally material interpretation which seems to have suggested
itself to the framers of the New York divorce law.   Jesus
was not one who urged reform, as some modern innovators
do, rashly or prematurely.   Prudence was one of his distinguishing characteristics.   He said not all that was in itself
true and proper to be said at some time, but only all the
truths which the people to whom he addressed himself were
prepared to receive.   That he kept back a part, we have his
own words to prove: " I have yet many things to say unto
you, but ye cannot bear them now; howbeit, when He, the·
Spirit of Truth, is come, he will guide you into all truth."
(John xvi. 12, 13.)

Yet, even if your law-makers but received the same impression that was produced on the Jews by Jesus' words, it by no
means follows that it is the one adapted to our wants and
progress.   It by no means follows that *we* should not look beyond the dead letter to the living spirit.   If the divorce law
promulgated from Mount Sinai was no longer adapted to a
world grown fifteen hundred years older, are we to suppose
that eighteen hundred years more, passed away, have brought
with them no need for another advance and a more enlightened interpretation ?

Thus, I think, I have shown you : —

First. That it will not do to warn us who think Divorce a
moralizing engine, as poachers, off your self-enfeoffed premises; or to bid us seek some name other than Marriage wherewith to designate our legal unions.   The Bible tells us that
the ancestors of Christ were really married; and I never
heard this denied, till your doctrine denied it.

Second. That, according to the Old Testament, easy divorce
was expressly permitted, three thousand years ago, by the
Deity himself.

Third. That divorce laws may properly vary, in different
stages of civilization.   And

Fourth. That the language of Jesus, fairly construed, des-
ignates the proper cause of divorce to be, that infidelity of
the heart which defeats the true purpose of marriage.

In conclusion, permit me to say, as to the quasi-divorce to which, under the name of "separation from bed and board," you refer, and which you think "just right," that of all the various kinds of divorce it has been found, in practice, to be the most immoral in its tendency. The subjects of it, in that nondescript state which is neither married nor single, are exposed — as every person of strong affection must be who takes a vow of celibacy yet mixes with the world — to powerful temptations. Unable to marry, the chances are, that these law-condemned celibates may do worse. I think that those members of your bar with whom the procurement of legal separations is a specialty could make to you some startling disclosures on this subject.

But, be this as it may, what becomes of the "mutual and solemn vow to live together till death them do part"? What becomes of the dictionary definitions which you adduce about being "united for life," and about "affection and fidelity till death shall separate them"? Does not your policy of "separation from bed and board" as effectually extinguish these, and thus, according to your view, as completely convert Marriage into a concubinal substitute, as my remedy of Divorce?

I am, my dear sir, faithfully yours,

ROBERT DALE OWEN.

NEW YORK, March 6, 1860.

MR. GREELEY AGAIN.*

TO THE HON. ROBERT DALE OWEN OF INDIANA: —

DEAR SIR: In my former letter, I asserted, and I think proved, that

I. The established, express, unequivocal dictionary meaning of Marriage is *union for life*. Whether any other sort of union of man and woman be or be not more rational, more beneficent, more moral, more Christian, than this, it is cer-

* From The Tribune of March 17, 1860.

tain that *this is Marriage,* and that that other is something else.

II. That this is what we who are legally married — at all events, if married by the ministers of any Christian denomination — uniformly covenant to do. I distinctly remember that *my* marriage covenant was "for better, for worse," and "until death do part." I presume yours was the same.

III. That Jesus of Nazareth, in opposition to the ideas and usages current in his time, alike among Jews and Gentiles, expressly declared Adultery to be the only valid reason for dissolving a marriage.

IV. That the nature and inherent *reason* of Marriage inexorably demand that it be indissoluble except for that one crime which destroys its essential condition. In other words, no marriage can be innocently dissolved; but the husband or wife may be released from the engagement upon proof of the utter and flagrant violation of its essential condition by the other party.

And now, allow me to say that I do not see that your second letter successfully assails any of these positions. You do not, and cannot, deny that our standard dictionaries define Marriage as I do, and deny the name to any temporary arrangement; you do not deny that I have truly stated Christ's doctrine on the subject (whereof the Christian ceremonial of Marriage, whether in the Catholic or Protestant Churches, is a standing evidence); and I am willing to let your criticism on Christ's statement pass without comment. So with regard to Moses : I am content to leave Moses's law of divorce to the brief but pungent commentary of Jesus, and his unquestionably correct averment that "from the beginning, it was not so."

But you say that, if my position is sound, I make "a sweeping assertion" against the validity of the marriages now existing in Indiana and other divorcing States. O no, sir! Nine tenths of the people in those States — I trust, ninetynine hundredths — were married by Christian ministers, under the law of Christ. They solemnly covenanted to remain faithful until death, and they are fulfilling that promise.

Your easy-divorce laws are nothing to them; their conscience and their lives have no part in those laws. Your State might decree that any couple may divorce themselves at pleasure, and still those who regard Jesus as their Divine Master and Teacher, would hold fast to his Word, and live according to a " higher law " than that revised and relaxed by you.

I dissent entirely from your dictum that the words of Jesus relative to Marriage and Divorce may have been intended to have a local and temporary application. On the contrary, I believe he, unlike Moses, promulgated the eternal and universal law, founded, not in accommodation to special circumstances, but in the essential nature of God and man. I admit that he may sometimes have withheld the truth that he deemed his auditors unable to comprehend and accept, but I insist that what he *did* set forth was the absolute, unchanging fact. But I did not cite him to overbear reason by authority, but because you referred first to Christianity and the will of God, and because I believe what he said respecting Marriage to be the very truth. Can you seriously imagine that your personal exegesis on his words should outweigh the uniform tradition and practice of all Christendom ?

You understand, I presume, that I hold to separations " from bed and board "— as the laws of this State allow them — only in cases where the party thus separated is in danger of bodily harm from the ferocity of an insane, intemperate, or otherwise brutalized, infuriated husband or wife. I do not admit that even such peril can release one from the vow of continence, which is the vital condition of Marriage. It may possibly be that there is " temptation " involved in the position of one thus legally separated; but I judge this evil far less than that which must result from the easy dissolution of Marriage.

For here is the vital truth that your theory overlooks : The Divine end of Marriage is parentage, or the perpetuation and increase of the Human Race. To this end, it is indispensable — at least, eminently desirable — that each child should enjoy protection, nurture, sustenance, at the hands of a mother not only, but of a father also. In other words, the parents should be so attached, so devoted to each other, that they shall be practically separable but by death. Creatures of appetite, fools of temptation, lovers of change, as men are, there is but one talisman potent to distinguish between genuine affection and its meretricious counterfeit; and that is the solemn, searching question, " Do you know this woman so thoroughly, and love her so profoundly, that you can assuredly promise that you will forsake all others and cleave to her only until death ? " If you can, your union is one that God has hallowed, and man may honor and approve ; but, if not, wait till you can thus pledge yourself to some one irrevocably, invoking heaven and earth to witness your truth. If you rush into a union with one whom you do not thus know and love, and who does not thus know and love you, yours is the crime, the shame ; yours be the life-long penalty. I do not think, as men and women actually are, this law can be improved ; when we reach the spirit-world, I presume we shall find a Divine law adapted to its requirements, and to our moral condition. Here, I am satisfied with that set forth by Jesus Christ. And, while I admit that individual cases of hardship arise under this law, I hold that there is seldom an unhappy marriage that was not originally an unworthy one, — hasty and heedless, if not positively vicious. And, if people *will* transgress, God can scarcely save them from consequent suffering ; and I do not think you or I can.

Yours,
HORACE GREELEY.

NEW YORK, March 11, 1860.

A CORRECTION.*

TO THE EDITOR OF THE N. Y. TRIBUNE : —

SIR : Your paper of yesterday, 12th inst., contains a letter bearing the signature of Robert Dale Owen. After eulogizing

* From The Tribune of March 12, 1860.

the doctrine of the New Testament, which is carried out in the law of the State of New York, and which only permits divorce in case of adultery, the writer falls foul of that "semi-barbarous" people, the Jews, and their legislator, Moses, whose law of divorce Mr. R. D. Owen professes to quote *verbatim* from Deuteronomy xxiv. 1 : "When a man hath taken a wife and married her, and it come to pass that she find no favor in his eyes, then let him write her a bill of divorcement and give it in her hand, and send her out of his house." Now, I would respectfully ask of Mr. R. D. Owen, how is it, that, in transcribing these words out of the Bible, he has left out and altogether omitted the words "because he hath found some uncleanness in her," which form an integral part of the first verse in the twenty-fourth chapter of Deuteronomy, after the sentence, "find no favor in his eyes," and before the sentence, "then let him write," &c.

These words omitted by Mr. R. D. Owen form the gist of the whole law on Divorce. For the Hebrew word *ervah*, which the English version here renders "uncleanness," is throughout sacred Scripture invariably used to express illicit sexual intercourse. *Vide* Leviticus xviii., where the word occurs several times, and is rendered "nakedness."

Into the argument on Divorce it is not my intention to enter; and, as it is not parliamentary to impute motives, I must not say that Mr. R. Owen intentionally mutilated the text he quotes, leaving out words which fully prove that this Word of God, through Moses His servant, so cavalierly, not to say unfairly, treated by Mr. R. D. Owen, is identical with the law of our State, which he praises as derived from the New Testament. But I should like to know, and I ask you, Mr. Editor, what degree of confidence and consideration can be due to the assertions and opinions of a disputant who, professing to quote *verbatim* from a book so well known as the Bible, "somehow" contrives to omit the pith and marrow of a law against which he directs his assault?

Yours,

A SEMI-BARBAROUS RABBI.

REPLY BY MR. OWEN.*

To " A Semi–Barbarous Rabbi " : —

Sir : I omitted the words in the text from Deuteronomy, to which in to-day's Tribune you refer, intentionally. If they were at all essential to the true understanding of the text, you are right in taking me severely to task for their omission. A man who would garble a quotation from any book to suit his purpose ought to forfeit all claim to public confidence.

I omitted them from what you may term a weakness, or may pronounce to be mere fastidiousness. My studies never having gone beyond Greek, the Old Testament, in its original tongue, is a sealed book to me. The expression, " because he hath found some uncleanness in her," conveyed to my mind no idea except as a phrase, couched in terms less veiled than modern usage is wont to employ, to mean disgust produced by some personal habit or idiosyncrasy. If in this I was not mistaken, the words are clearly non-essential; and I might innocently consult my feelings by omitting them in the columns of a daily paper.

But if, as you assert, the Hebrew word rendered " uncleanness " means " adultery," the omission was a grave one, even if not wilfully committed.

Does it mean adultery ? If, without presumption, one who has never cultivated those roots of which that impudent fellow who indited Hudibras declared that they "flourish most on barren ground" may venture to argue the point with a Rabbi, I ask leave to take issue as to this interpretation. The subject, indeed, is a disagreeable one; but, in self-defence, I cannot now choose but follow whither you lead ; namely, to the chapter cited by you, Leviticus xviii., where, as you inform us, the same word rendered " uncleanness " in Deuteronomy occurs several times, and is translated " nakedness." The first verse in which this happens reads thus: " The nakedness

* From The Tribune of March 19, 1860.

of thy father and the nakedness of thy mother thou shalt not uncover." If, as you allege, the word *ervah*, here translated "nakedness," is "throughout Sacred Scripture invariably used to express illicit sexual intercourse," or, as in a wife's case it would be, adultery; and if in the above text we substitute the one word for the other (as, if you are right, we may properly do), we shall have a text which you may comprehend, but which, to my obtuser perceptions, becomes wholly unintelligible.

I, in what your learning may set down as my simplicity, have always interpreted the text in question as referring to that offence which Shem and Japheth avoided, and for which Canaan (Genesis ix. 25) was cursed.

The word "uncleanness" does, indeed, in another text (Numbers v. 19), mean adultery; but, to give it that meaning, other defining words are expressly added. The priest, in that text, thus addresses the woman suspected of infidelity, "If no man have lain with thee, and if thou hast not gone aside to uncleanness *with another instead of thy husband,* be thou free," &c. Even in this text, however, if we were to attempt to substitute "adultery" for "uncleanness," we should not only have flagrant tautology, but a phrase that would seem to favor the idea that a wife might commit adultery with her husband as well as with other men; a thing, I must confess, I never before heard of.

But, independently of all this, the very words of the text seem to preclude your reading. Those words are: "If it come to pass that she (the wife) find no favor in his eyes because of some uncleanness," &c. Now, a wife may be said to "find no favor" in a husband's eyes, if her person or her character become disagreeable to him; but who would ever select such a phrase for a graver occasion? What would you think of saying, "Mrs. Smith found no favor in Mr. Smith's eyes, because of some acts of adultery"?

Finally, a difficulty remains which, in my eyes, as in the eyes of all Christians it must be, is insuperable; though "A

Semi-Barbarous Rabbi," perhaps, may get over it. *Jesus did not interpret the text as you do.*

Your assertion is, that Moses' law " is identical with the law of your State " (New York) ; that is to say, that it allowed Divorce for no other cause except adultery. If that was so, why, I pray you, did Jesus say : " Moses, because of the hardness of your hearts, suffered you to put away your wives " ? And why did he add : " But in the beginning it was not so ; and I say unto you : Whosoever shall put away his wife, except it be for fornication, and shall marry another, committeth adultery " ? You make Moses' law and Jesus' law identical. Yet here we find Jesus discarding the one as a permission granted only because of the old Hebrews' hard hearts, and substituting the other. But was there nothing to discard ? Were the law discarded and the substitute inculcated one and the same ? That, as every reasonable man must see, is a sheer impossibility. For we cannot imagine Jesus' words to be meaningless, nor conclude that he was trifling with his audience, and recommending, for their adoption, the self-same thing he condemned.

We know, as well as we can know any historical fact, that, at the time when we are told that Jesus declared adultery to be the only valid cause for divorce, that declaration was, as Mr. Greeley, in his last letter, reminds us, " in opposition to the laws and usages alike among Jews and Gentiles."

I am not well informed as to how far Rabbis usually regard the words or the opinions of Jesus as authoritative. For myself, if I am in error, — if the ancient Jews, as you allege, were not permitted to divorce their wives " except it be for fornication," and if, in consequence, there was, in Christ's day, nothing to reform in the Jewish divorce law, — it is enough for me to know that, in adhering (as, after a careful survey of the whole ground, I do) to the opposite opinion, I am but adopting the views and sharing the interpretation put forth by the Author of the Christian religion.

ROBERT DALE OWEN.

NEW YORK, Saturday, March 17, 1860.

COMMENT BY MR. GREELEY.

ALL this strikes us as very absurd, and based on an unaccountable lack of perception. The fundamental idea of the Mosaic law is personal and perfect *purity.* Moses, therefore, permitted the husband who had been deceived as to the chastity, *prior to marriage,* of his wife, to put her away. This Jesus disallowed, as a temporary or local permission, based on grounds peculiar to the Hebrew economy, reëstablishing in its stead the law as it was "from the beginning," that only incontinence, *after marriage,* can afford a valid reason for divorce.

MR. OWEN IN RESPONSE.*

THE WORD "ERVAH."

TO THE EDITOR OF THE N. Y. TRIBUNE : —

SIR : Unwilling to rest under the imputation cast on me by you in to-day's "Tribune," namely, that my views in reply to a "Semi-Barbarous Rabbi" are "very absurd," and are "based on an unaccountable lack of perception," I have looked a little more closely into the philology of the question, and beg leave here to present to you the result.

Gesenius, than whom, you are aware, there is no better authority, in his Hebrew Lexicon, translates ERVAH, *turpitudo, fœditas;* and referring specially to the bill-of-divorcement text (Deuteronomy xxiv. 1), he renders it "*Macula aliquâ in muliere reperta*"; that is, "a blemish (or spot) found in the woman." You can consult this Lexicon in the Astor Library.

In Luther's Translation of the Bible (to be found in the same Library), at the text above referred to, that reformer, in explaining the word "uncleanness," parenthesises thus : (*um etwas das ihm misfällt, es sey an ihrem Leibe oder Gebärden oder Sitten, die sich aber sonst züchtig verhällt ;*) which, if you are familiar with German, you know to mean : ("in re-

* From The Tribune of March 24, 1860.

gard to something which displeases him, either in her person or in her demeanor, or in her conduct, without imputation, however, on her chastity.") The word *züchtig* means strictly, *chaste, modest.* One could hardly find anything more in accordance with my interpretation than this.

Again, the learned Ewald (in his "Geschichte des Volks Israel," Vol. II. of Anhang, page 185), commenting on the Jewish bill of divorcement, says : *Und sicher enthielte ein solcher Brief keinen weitern Tadel der Frau als wäre er ein Klagebrief gewesen ; sondern diente der Frau eher als ein Zeugniss dass ihrer Wiederheirath nichts im Wege stehe :* that is, "And such a document certainly imputed no further blame to the wife than if it had been a mere letter of complaint ; on the contrary, it rather served as a certificate in her hands, in proof that there was no obstacle to a second marriage."

I think you will no longer deny that, if my views are "very absurd," they are at least sustained by the best Hebrew Lexicon of the day, by a writer of the highest authority on Hebrew history, and, finally, that they are indorsed, beyond all possible doubt, by the Great Reformer himself. These learned men must all have shared my "unaccountable lack of perception."

Whence you disinterred your idea that incontinence in the wife *prior to marriage* was the Mosaic ground of permission to put her away I have no idea whatever. Certainly not from the Old Testament, so far as I am acquainted with its pages. As I read there, incontinence before marriage, unless disproved (Deuteronomy xxii. 20, 21), was, according to the Mosaic law, punishable, not by a bill of divorcement, but by a cruel death.

Yours,

ROBERT DALE OWEN.

NEW YORK, Monday, March 19, 1860.

MR. OWEN RESUMES.*

DIVORCE.

To the Hon. Horace Greeley : —

My dear Sir : You derive your arguments against Divorce from two sources :

1. From Scripture.
2. From the morality of the case.

I. If you regard the Old Testament as a portion of the Word of God, you must admit that the Jewish bill-of-divorcement law was framed, not by a fallible lawgiver, but by the Deity himself, Moses being only the medium of its promulgation.

If you accept the authority of Gesenius, of Ewald, and of Luther, you must further concede to me that that bill-of-divorcement law permitted a husband to put away a faithful wife in any case in which she became personally disagreeable, or in her deportment obnoxious to him, and that he was sole judge whether she found favor in his eyes or not.

These premises conceded, it follows, that, upwards of three thousand years ago, God sanctioned a law which permitted a husband to put away his wife when she displeased him, by means of a simple bill of divorcement, drawn up by the husband himself.

The New Testament informs us, and you remind us, that Jesus, fourteen centuries later, disallowed that law. But he did not condemn it as a law which ought never to have existed; he intimates that it was rendered necessary by the " hard hearts " of those for whose guidance it was framed.

Then the law of God, enacted thirty-two centuries ago, was declared by Jesus, eighteen centuries ago, to be no longer adapted to the state of human society.

What follows ? That there is no positive good or evil, — no absolute virtue or vice ? Far from it. There are principles permanent as the everlasting hills, immutable as the

* From The Tribune of March 28, 1860.

laws that hold the planets to their course; principles that depend not on times and seasons, that are the same yesterday, to-day, and forever. Such, to select an eminent example, is the declaration, "Love is the fulfilling of the law." It was true from the creation; it will be true until time shall be no more.

But the details of a law are one thing, and a great, eternal principle is another. Laws properly change as the world changes. But the master principles underlying laws — the "laws of the laws," to adopt Bacon's phrase — endure while the world lasts.

Beyond the general rule, however, we have, in this particular case, the direct authority of Jesus for it, that a divorce law adapted to one age may cease to be suitable in another.

But, if the details of a Divine law three thousand years old were properly rejected in a later stage of society, is it not certain that the same *may* be true in our age of other details put forth by Jesus as suitable for the Jews of his day? for men so low in the social scale that they found in his teachings nothing but blasphemy, and rewarded them by mockings and scourgings, and a death of torture on the cross?

It follows, past all denial, that while, as Christians, we should be guided by the great principles taught by the Author of our religion, we are *not* bound by the details of a law adapted for Judea in the days of Herod the King; provided our moral sense, moulded and quickened by Christian study, leads us to the conclusion that we — less hard of heart than those who cried out, "Crucify him!" — can bear other laws and greater liberty than they.

And thus, at last, we are thrown back, for guidance, to the second source whence your arguments are derived.

II. In other words: What is the true morality of the case?

"The Divine end of Marriage," you say, "is the perpetuation and increase of the human race."

Has civilization, in our day, reached no further than this? Do we find in the holiest of human relations no higher, nobler object — no end more divine — than the operation of that instinct (common to man with the lower races) which peoples the earth ? God has, indeed, ordained that, incidental to Marriage, and inseparable from it, shall be Reproduction. If, in any sense, it be true that this is *the* divine end of human marriage, it must be in the same sense which applies when the stag seeks his partner, or the dove submits to her mate. But, just in proportion as man is nobler than the bird of the air or the beast of the field, is his marriage removed to infinite distance above theirs. Woe to that bride, standing in her white robes before the altar, who is thought of, by the one at her side, only as the future bearer of his children ! Woe to her, if she has not chosen a spouse whose heart is swelled with aspirations that overmaster the sensual; in whose soul there burns not a light pure enough and bright enough to quench, in such a moment as that, the lurid flames of desire ?

It is one of the most beautiful and beneficent arrangements which mark the Divine economy, that an institution — a physical incident of which is the propagation of the race — should, in its higher and nobler results, be the means of calling forth all that is best and purest in the inner nature of man; love, in the broadest acceptation of that much profaned word, — love, that crushes man's innate selfishness, and teaches him the great lesson that the best happiness is to be found in cares for another, not in thoughts for himself; love that is heightened, indeed, by the warmth of earthly emotions, but has an existence above and apart from these ; to remain when age has quenched passion, — to endure beyond the term of our present stage of existence.

In that higher phase of wedded life which has its origin in sentiments and aspirations such as these, not in the results of our nature's lower instincts, will a cultivated mind, in its best moments, recognize " the Divine end of Marriage." If, some day, released from the daily round and deafening whirl of politics, you give to your better instincts, in quiet, fair scope and free voice, I think they will teach you this.

Meanwhile, we are here at issue. You have one conception of the Divine end of Marriage, I another. If yours be the correct idea, then it may be that nothing except that which casts doubt on the parentage of offspring should be valid cause for the dissolution of Marriage. If, on the contrary, I have more justly interpreted the higher purposes of that institution, then whatever violates these defeats the Divine end of Marriage, and supplies rightful cause why the relation, failing in its true intent, should be discontinued. It is a sound principle in jurisprudence, that, with the termination of the cause for a law, the law also should cease.

I do not merely say, in cases where the holiest purposes for which God ordained Marriage are frustrated, its divinest ends defeated, and its inmost sanctuary defiled, by evil passions, that the relation, thus outraged, *may* not improperly cease : I say that, for the sake of virtue and for the good of mankind, in all such demoralizing cases, it *ought* to cease. Household strife is immorality ; domestic hatred is immorality ; heartless selfishness is immorality ; inhuman treatment of the weak by the strong is terrible immorality. And that condition of things, degenerate from a noble purpose, which fosters evils such as these, has become itself immoral and demands abatement.

Why, in its vice-fostering perversion, should a life of bickering be dragged on, till death, at last, brings separation and peace ? In the interests of the children, perhaps ? But is that the atmosphere in which their young lives should expand ? Or, is it in order that that intangible generality called SOCIETY may be propitiated and appeased ? But how, I beg of you, can the true interests of Society be subserved by perpetuating immorality among its members ? What sort of Moloch is this Society that demands the immolation of its own offspring ?

What further objection do you interpose ? In substance, this, — that men and women about to marry, exercising deliberation and discrimination, ought never to select ill ; and that, if they do, "theirs is the crime and the shame, and theirs should be the life-long penalty."

If a lawgiver, directly or virtually, demands impossibilities, his laws will fail of their effect. In making his demands, then, he should have special reference to the powers likely to be at the disposal of those of whom these demands are made. It avails nothing to say that a thing ought to be, if, as a general rule, it cannot be.

But of all requirements, the most arduous — arduous even when mature thought has brought wisdom, and when age has conferred experience — is the decision whether a being, loved now, is the one of all others, intellectually, morally, physically, to whom, in a true home, we can impart permanent happiness, and from whom we are capable of receiving it. Mortal eyes, even the wisest, never fully penetrate the veil. There may be that beyond which no foresight could anticipate.

And, if such be the case, with wisdom and experience to guide, what shall we expect from unsuspicious faith, just entering a false world, serenely ignorant of its treacheries, an utter stranger to its guile ? Will its goodness be its protection ? The reverse. In such a trial, it is the noblest who are the most exposed. The better the nature, the more imminent the danger it encounters. The cold, the heartless, the calculating, have fair chance of escape; it is the warm, the trusting, the generous, who are the usual sufferers. What belief so blind as that of first, pure, young affection ? What so easily cheated as a fresh and faithful and innocent heart ?

And by what right, according to what principle, I pray you, do we decide that there is one mistake that is never to be corrected ; one error, the most fatal of all, which, once committed, we shall never be permitted to repair ?

A " life-long penalty " you would inflict. And for what heinous offence ? Say that an honest mistake were a crime ; say that a venial error were a career of shame. Even then, the sentiment would be Jewish, not Christian. " An eye for an eye, a tooth for a tooth," was the rule addressed to the hard hearts. Nowhere, in all Christ's teachings, will you find the like. The sin of your brother, sinning seven times, you would not forgive ; yet, as a Christian, you ought to forgive it, even to seventy times seventy. The entrance to the father's house you would bar against the returning prodigal. His, you would declare to him, was " the sin, the shame "; his should be " the life-long penalty." No rejoicing that he was dead and is alive again ; no weeping joy that he was lost and is found !

Let us dismiss abstractions, and stand face to face with the realities of life. The time may come when men and women (the eyesight of the affections opened) shall unfailingly distinguish and choose their own appropriate mates. I have heard enthusiasts argue that it will ; and that there is a future before mankind, even on earth, in which conjugal separation and divorce will be ·unknown terms. God send it ! But, meanwhile, it is with the present, and its errors, and its evils, and its sufferings, and its temptations to sin, that we have to deal. Where we fail to cure, it is our duty to alleviate. If we cannot make all the married virtuous and happy, let us do what we can, by humane laws of prevention, to relieve from immoral situations ; and thus to diminish domestic misery and arrest household vice.

I thank you, my dear sir, for the opportunity afforded to discuss this subject, and am

Faithfully yours,

ROBERT DALE OWEN.

NEW YORK, Tuesday, March 20, 1860.

MR. GREELEY'S REJOINDER.*

TO ROBERT DALE OWEN : —

DEAR SIR : As you have intimated your willingness that our discussion should here close, I will endeavor to introduce no new views into this letter. I will simply sum up the controversy as it stands.

I. I have hitherto shown, and you have not attempted to

* From The Tribune of April 7, 1860.

disprove, that Marriage is, according to every standard dictionary, *a union for life*, indissoluble at the pleasure of those married, or either of them. I have insisted that you have no right to use this important word in a vitally different sense from that given to it by the great lexicographers. What you favor may be ever so much better than Marriage (though I believe it far otherwise), but it is manifestly not the same thing, and you ought to give it a distinctive name. When I am told that two persons are married, I understand that they have covenanted to live together as husband and wife, not during pleasure, but during life. The dictionaries, the Christian religion, the general consent of my countrymen and of the civilized world, fully justify me in that conception. When, therefore, you apply the term Marriage to a very different compact, you not merely use words unjustifiably, but you virtually confess the badness of your cause. The tradesman who counterfeits another's trade-marks virtually confesses the inferiority of his own wares. I protest, then, against your using the word Marriage to designate any other union than one for life. If A and B have agreed, with ever so much ceremony, to live as man and wife until one or both of them shall see fit to separate and form new relations, they may be ever so wisely and rationally paired, but they are not married. I made this point as strongly before; our readers will judge whether you have or have not met it. At all events, I mind the Apostle's injunction to "Hold fast the form of sound words." We who stand by Marriage as Jesus Christ established and Noah Webster defines it, have a right to the word by which that relation has ever been characterized. What you advocate is quite another thing, — be pleased to give it a distinguishing name. Then, if we call our compact by your name, the public will understand that we admit your union to be more rational, honorable, ennobling, than ours. At all events, we warn you off our premises, and insist that you shall not lay your eggs in our nest. If you demand liberty to form temporary unions, we will consider that demand; but you must not call them marriages;

for, though they may be the same to you, they are far otherwise to us.

II. As to the religious or Christian view of the subject, I rest on the simple, explicit averment of Jesus of Nazareth, as universally understood and regarded by the Christian Church for eighteen centuries. We know what Hebrew, Greek, Roman laws and customs respecting the marital union were in Christ's day; we know that Jesus propounded and his disciples accepted a very different law, — that of Marriage indissoluble but by death, or by that crime which is death to all the sanctities of Marriage. We know that Orthodox and Heretic, Catholic and Protestant, literal and liberal, with barely exceptions enough to prove the rule, have understood the Saviour's doctrine of Marriage throughout the Christian centuries as I do to-day. That this Christian doctrine of Marriage is a chief .reason for the moral, intellectual, and even material, supremacy of Europe over Asia in our day, I do most firmly believe; *you* will regard it as you think fit. And, as to Moses and his law, with all you have to say of them, all the answer that seems to me needed is contained in the few words of Jesus on that very point: " Moses, for the hardness of your hearts," permitted easy divorce; " but from the beginning it was not so."

III. I have said that " the Divine end of Marriage is the perpetuation and increase of the human race." By that affirmation I abide. Of course, I did not say that Marriage has no other end than this ; so all your criticism seems to me ludicrously inapposite. I do not urge that, in a true sexual union, everything else but the production, nurture, and well-being of children, must be ignored. I *do* insist that there must be nothing incompatible or inconsistent with this. If required to say whether the union of this man with this woman is true, noble, and honorable, or sensual, selfish, and debasing, I must ask, " Would they gladly have children born of it ? Would they proudly acknowledge those children before the world, and undertake to fulfil toward them all the duties of parents ? "

If not, their union, though impelled by mutual admiration, and signalized by a lava-flood of passion, is shameful and un-blest. The sexual union which the immediate parties prefer should be childless has no right to be at all.

I was shocked when I heard an apostle of your faith say, some years since, "We hold that the parents are not to be *sacrificed* to the children." I hold, on the contrary, that the lives of true parents are filled with acts of self-sacrifice for their children, — that their lives have been well spent who have given to the world offspring nobler than themselves. And, while I admit that the conduct of a husband may be so outrageous, so brutal, as to justify the innocent wife in re-quiring a separation, I insist that one who truly comprehends the nature and purposes of Marriage will not seek to marry another while the father of her children is still living. I do not think she could look those children in the eye with all a mother's conscious purity and dignity while realizing that their father and her husband, both living, were different men. Nor do I feel that she could be to them all that a mother should be under such conditions.

IV. The vice of our age, the main source of its aberrations, is a morbid Egotism, which overrides the gravest social neces-sities in its mad pursuit of individual, personal ends. Your fling at that "intangible generality called SOCIETY" is direct-ly in point. You are concerned chiefly for those who, having married unfortunately, if not viciously, seek relief from their bonds; I am anxious rather to prevent, or at least to render infrequent, immoral, and unfit sexual unions hereafter. The miseries of the unfitly mated may be deplorable; but to make divorce easy is in effect to invite the sensual and selfish to profane the sanctions of Marriage whenever appetite and temptation may prompt. Here are a man and a woman who know absolutely nothing of each other but that they are re-ciprocally pleased with each other's appearance, and think Marriage would conduce to their mutual enjoyment, — so they form a connubial partnership. Next year — perhaps next month — they have tired of each other, — discovered incompatibilities of temper, — quarrelled, — in short, they hate each other, as they very well may ; so they are divorced, and ready to marry again.   Gibbon intimates that, under the Roman liberty of Divorce, by which Rome was debauched and ultimately ruined, a woman had eight husbands within five years.   Mr. Owen, whenever you shall have succeeded in appropriating our word Marriage as a fig-leaf for this sort of thing, you will cause us to invent or appropriate some other term to characterize what *we* mean by Marriage; and then you will very soon drop your own dishonored designation and come coveting ours again.   So please leave us what belongs to us, and choose a new term for *your* arrangement now.

" It is very hard," said a culprit to the judge who sentenced him, " that I should be so severely punished for merely stealing a horse."   " Man," replied the judge, " you are *not* so punished for merely stealing a horse, but *that horses may not be stolen.*"   The distinction seems to me clear and vital.   The wedded in soul may know each other if they will ; it is impossible that others should certainly know them.   To those who are thus wedded, the covenant to " take each other for better, for worse," and " to live together till death do part," has no terrors ; they enter upon it without hesitation, and fulfil its conditions without regret.   But to the libertine, the egotist, the selfish, sensual seeker of personal and present enjoyment at whatever cost to others, the Indissolubility of Marriage is an obstacle, a restraint, a terror ; and God forbid that it should ever cease to be !   Thousands would take a wife as readily, as thoughtlessly, as heartlessly, as they don a new coat or sport a new cravat, if it were understood that they might unmarry themselves whenever satiety, or disgust, or mutual dislike, should prompt to that step.   But it is not so, Mr. Owen, even in Indiana.   Men and women are married, even in Indiana, " for better, for worse," and under solemn covenant to " live together till death do part " ; and they cannot resort to Divorce, even there, without conscious shame or general reprobation.   That human laws may be everywhere conformed to the Divine, and no sexual union hallowed by

Church or State but that union for life which alone is true Marriage, is the ardent hope of

Yours,

HORACE GREELEY.

NEW YORK, March 31, 1860.

MR. OWEN'S CLOSING ARGUMENT.*

TO THE HON. HORACE GREELEY :——

MY DEAR SIR : Imitating your precaution, I shall, in summing up, avoid the introduction of new views ; I shall also study strictest brevity. Had your summing up fairly presented the question at issue, the public need not have been troubled with mine.

It is a besetting weakness of our nature to imagine itself unfailingly right, its opinions infallibly true, its rules of action the only morality. If, in a discussion of principles, we yield to this, the best thing is to close it ; because, conducted in such a spirit, it becomes useless, or worse.

The sole point of our discussion, and that which might be usefully, if dispassionately, debated, has been this : You advocate a divorce law with one only cause of divorce : I think it conducive to public morality that such a law should admit several causes. I took that position, and I took no other. I indorsed the divorce law of Indiana ; nothing more. But how, in summing up, do you state the case ? In substance, thus : Marriage under a single-cause divorce law, as in New York, *is* Marriage. There is no other Marriage. What goes by that name, under a divorce law admitting several causes, as in Connecticut or Indiana, is *not* Marriage, but concubinage. If those who are united under such laws call themselves married, they " use words unjustifiably " ; they " virtually confess the badness of their cause " ; they are as " tradesmen who counterfeit another's trade-marks " ;

* From The Tribune of April 21, 1860.

they are countenancing the Roman woman who had "eight husbands within five years," and appropriating Mr. Greeley's word Marriage "as a fig-leaf for this sort of thing." They must "choose a new term for *their* arrangement." Horace Greeley, armed with Noah Webster, declares to them, that "they may be ever so wisely and rationally paired, but they are not married," and he "protests against their using the word."

The law of Connecticut, the law of Indiana, declares, that Marriage, contracted under a divorce law admitting several causes, and by virtue of which the union *may*, in certain contingencies, terminate before death, *is* Marriage." Horace Greeley tells them it is "quite another thing." The law of Connecticut, the law of Indiana, provides, if a couple, legally divorced, contract a second marriage, such second marriage is legal. Horace Greeley insists that they "must not call that Marriage; for, though it may be the same to them, it is far otherwise to him."

Here is a conflict. The Revised Codes of Connecticut and Indiana (and of a dozen other States beside) declare one thing; Horace Greeley declares the opposite. The one or the other, it is evident, must be grievously in error.

Popes, from the Vatican, have, not unfrequently, assumed the power, as to certain laws enacted by duly constituted legal authority in various Catholic countries, by Papal Bull to override and annul them. But in our country we consider the law supreme; in force, and to be acknowledged and respected, until it be legally repealed.

This is not all. In your summing up, motives are imputed. Those who enact or approve a divorce law which admits more causes than one are told that "they are concerned chiefly for those who, having married unfortunately, if not viciously, seek relief"; and that this arises from a "morbid egotism, the vice of our age, which overrides the gravest social necessities in its mad pursuit of individual, personal ends."

Does it not occur to you, when men vote for or sanction reasonable divorce laws, they *may* do so from a conscientious motive ? Does it not occur to you, that when an opponent expresses the opinion, " in cases where the holiest purposes for which God ordained Marriage are frustrated, and its inmost sanctuary defiled by evil passions, it ought for the sake of virtue to cease," — that he *may* be sincere in that opinion ? Have you forgotten that there is One only who looks into the heart and reads its motives ; and that no human being has a right, setting himself up as judge and ruler, to usurp His place ?

The story of the horse-thief (told that he was punished not merely for his offence, but " *that horses may not be stolen* "), if it has any bearing on the subject at all, has an unfair one. Horse-stealing is a crime. To take it for granted that Divorce also is one is to prejudge the whole question under discussion. Again ; if the meaning be, that the unhappily married should suffer, not merely for their mistake, but *that divorces may not be granted*, then you fall into the same error as the Jews, when they, zealous without knowledge for their Sabbath, were reminded by Jesus, in the spirit of the truest philosophy, that human institutions are made for man, not man for human institutions.

Others may have argued that children ought to be sacrificed to parents. I hold, and ever have held, that there is no duty more sacred than that which we owe to those to whom we impart existence. It is a misfortune, and a great one, that a mother should look her children in the eye, and think that their father, then living, and her husband, are different men. But far greater is the misfortune when she looks upon them with the bitter consciousness that they are daily, hourly, learning to know in their father a sot, a brute, a ruffian, the desecrator of the domestic sanctuary ; far greater is the anguish to feel that that father never teaches them one lesson of virtue, never gives them one useful example, except it be such as the Helots furnished to the Spartan youth ; a terrible beacon, warning from the shame and the folly of intemperance.

If you conclude that divorce laws necessarily cause young people to marry as readily and heartlessly as they don a fresh hat or sport a new bonnet, you do your fellow-creatures great injustice; and a few years' residence in Indiana would convince you of your mistake. You might be reminded of what, even at our age, we ought not to have forgotten, — what manner of thing, namely, youthful affection is; how undoubtingly it believes, how wholly it trusts; how little it calculates laws or troubles itself about Divorce, or dreams of anything except that it shall always love as it loves now; constancy a pleasure even more than a duty, and change an impossible desire. We often err in ascribing to the restraining influence of faulty laws that which is due to the faithful impulses of our better nature.

You remind us, on Gibbon's authority, that the liberty of Divorce was grossly abused in debauched Rome. I remind you that the liberty of Republicanism was terribly abused in revolutionary France. But it would be a poor argument thence to conclude, that, in this country, we ought to forbid divorce and introduce a monarchy.

The moral and intellectual supremacy of Europe over Asia you ascribe mainly to Christian Marriage. To Christian Marriage, as opposed to Polygamy, it may justly be thus ascribed. This opinion I myself, in a recent work, expressed: "Under the system of Monogamy alone have man's physical powers and moral attributes ever maintained their ascendency; while weakness and national decadence follow in the train of Polygamy, whether openly carried out, as in Deseret and Constantinople, or secretly practised, as in London and New York."*

But this has no bearing on the Divorce question. You will not assert that the morals were better before the Reformation, in Catholic countries refusing divorce, than they were after Luther's time in Protestant countries permitting it.

Briefly summing up, I remind you : —

1. That I proved, and you have not attempted to disprove, that, according to the Old Testament, God promulgated, more than three thousand years ago, a divorce law permitting a

---

* Footfalls on the Boundary of Another World, page 42.

husband to put away a wife who found no favor in his eyes; that that law prevailed among His chosen people from the time of Moses till long after Joseph and Mary were united subject to its provisions; and, consequently, that if Marriage, determinable by Divorce, be no Marriage, there was not a married man or woman among the Jews for fifteen hundred years.

2. I have shown, and you have admitted, that Jesus disallowed that law; not denying that it was suitable at the period it was given, yet declaring that, in his day, it ought not to prevail. I thence deduced the inference, not assailed by you, that, according to Scripture, divorce laws may properly vary in different stages of civilization.

3. I have stated, what the best legal authority * indorses, that, of the various kinds of Divorce, none has been found, in practice, so immoral as that variety, unknown to our Indiana law, but known in New York as "separation from bed and board." You think it "just right." Let the public judge between us.

4. Referring to our modern state of civilization, I have argued, that the present age is prepared to see, in the holiest of human relations, purposes far higher, infinitely more worthy the epithet divine, than the mere operation of the instinct that peoples the earth; that Marriage was designed to be, and should be, the means of calling out all that is best and purest in the inner nature of man; and that, when it becomes the daily source of anger, strife, cruelty, brutality, it defeats God's purpose, violates the Divine economy, becomes itself immoral, and ought to cease. You dissent. Again be the public the judge in the premises.

But if in these I dissent, there are other points as to which, in concluding this controversy, I am glad to agree with you. I agree that every State has a direct interest in the private morals of its members. I agree that whatever policy is found, in the end, best calculated to promote these morals, ought to prevail. I agree that it is one of the greatest of earthly blessings, when a married couple dwell together in

* Bishop, on Marriage and Divorce, § 277.

unity till death. I agree that no light or transient cause should dissolve the conjugal union. I agree that men and women ought mutually to bear and forbear "while evils are sufferable," rather than to right themselves by resort to separation or divorce. I agree, further, that a state of things which leads to Divorce is to be deprecated and lamented, and that Divorce itself is a grave misfortune. And I but add that, when a long train of abuses and immoralities, pursuing invariably the same course, clearly shows that a union has become destructive of its holy ends, then it ought to be a right, and may become a duty, to select of two evils the lesser; to acquiesce in the necessity which indicates a separation, and legally to dissolve the bands which connect the ill-mated members together.

In taking leave of you, suffer me to correct an error which crept into my second letter. I there said that there was not a State of the Union without a Divorce law. I ought to have added, "except the State of South Carolina." She boasts that "within her limits, a divorce has not been granted since the Revolution." But suspend your approbation till you learn, as Bishop will inform you, what is the concomitant: "Not only is adultery not indictable there [in South Carolina], but the Legislature has found it necessary to regulate, by statute, how large a proportion a married man may give of his property to his concubine."*

You will admit that your system of Indissoluble Marriage is dearly paid for, under such a state of things; nor have you been in the habit of asserting that the morals of divorce-denying South Carolina are superior to those of Connecticut or Indiana.

I am, my dear sir,
Faithfully yours,
Robert Dale Owen.

Philadelphia, April 9, 1860.

* Marriage and Divorce, § 285.

MR. GREELEY CLOSES THE DISCUSSION.*

To the Hon. Robert Dale Owen : —

Sir : I understood from you that your concluding letter would be that to which I last replied ; · but, since you have deemed it necessary to write again, I necessarily, yet willingly, rejoin. As before, I shall confine myself strictly to the points made in your last.

I. You seem to complain that I consider my side of the question at issue the side of Morality and Right. But, if I did not, why should I so earnestly uphold it ? Do I complain of *your* holding your own side in similar regard ? Assuredly, I cannot change my convictions, and should not be required to conceal them. Indeed, since you admit that my conviction is grounded in a "besetting weakness of our nature," you surely cannot regard it with surprise, any more than I can deem it a reason for closing our discussion ; though I have at all times since you began it been willing to close it.

II. You think the difference between us to be simply this : I allow Divorce for a single cause (Adultery), you for several causes ; and you would thus reduce it, from a question of principle, to one of details. But you cannot deny that my one ground of Divorce is that expressly affirmed to be such by Jesus Christ, to the exclusion and negation of all others. Nor can you fail to see that if, as I hold, the paramount (not sole) Divine end of Marriage is Parentage, or the perpetuation and increase, under fit auspices, of the Human Race, then that crime which vitiates and confuses parentage may logically be deemed the sole sufficient reason for annulling a marriage. To my mind, therefore, our difference is clearly and emphatically one of principle. I do not hold that even Adultery justifies the dissolution of a marriage so far as the culpable party is concerned. It simply authorizes, but by no means requires, the faithful, exemplary husband or wife to procure a legal adjudication and declaration of the fact that

* From The Tribune of April 31, 1860.

this marriage has — solely through the infidelity of the adulterer — been dissolved, so far only as it imposes duties or obligations on the wronged and innocent party.

III. As to what constitutes Marriage, — what Marriage *is*, — I have quoted the standard lexicographers of our language, who unanimously pronounce it a union and consecration of one man to one woman *for life*, and deny the name to all other unions. Your quarrel on this point is not with me, but with the dictionaries, as well as with the Christian Church. I have made no new definitions; I have simply insisted that those which have stood unchallenged hitherto shall be recognized and respected. Not by me primarily, but by Jesus of Nazareth, and, following him, by Noah Webster and Dr. Worcester, have the definitions I rest on been set forth. If they truly define the term, then the mutual promise of a man and woman to live together until one of them shall have proved a sot, a termagant, a ruffian, or a beast, is *not* a marriage. If you insist that the authorities I quote mistake or misstate the true meaning and force of the term, why do you not quote lexicographers who favor *your* rendering? Is it not clear that you would have done so, had there been any? And, if there be none, how can you complain of me for insisting that the word Marriage shall be held to mean that, and that only, which our standard dictionaries say it *does* mean?

IV. And this disposes of your talk of "Horace Greeley" saying this or that, in opposition to your views. If any part of what I have urged rests on the naked dictum of Horace Greeley, it is, of course, of little moment; but, if it is correctly based on the explicit teachings of Jesus Christ, on the unbroken tradition and nearly universal affirmation of the Christian Church, on the lessons of Profane History (see Gibbon), the definitions of standard lexicographers, and the concurring judgment of a vast majority of the wise and good, why, then, you see, the case is bravely altered, and the fact that I reaffirm what all of these have constantly asserted, does not necessarily render it insignificant, nor subject it to ridicule.

V. You dwell on the fact that the codes of Indiana and of some other States permit Divorce for other cause than Adultery, as though this proved the people of those States not married, according to my understanding of the term. But I have already urged the fact that, in those States, as elsewhere, Christian Marriage is unqualifiedly a union for life, and that most of those who marry there are married by clergymen in a strict and open accordance with the Christian law. You know, as well as I do, that divorce, followed by another marriage, rarely fails to cover with odium the parties involved in it, or at least some of them. You may not know, however, as I do, that, in repeated instances, persons divorced under the State laws you glory in, and otherwise married, have been excommunicated therefor by Protestant churches, clergymen being silenced for the same cause. That no Catholic would even dream of contracting such second marriage, no matter in what State or under whatever permission of the secular authority, you, of course, fully understand. I must protest, then, against your inference, from the fact that the laws of certain States allow Divorce on various grounds, that their people are in verity generally educated and married, and afterward live, under the law as you would have it. The "higher law" is their safeguard.

VI. I am surprised that you could so mistake my application of the judge's remark, that he punished the horse-thief, "not for stealing a horse, but that horses may not be stolen."

My idea was, and is, that Marriage is rightfully made indissoluble, in order that unfit and unreal marriages may not be contracted. Say that a legal marriage may be nullified merely because the parties find or fancy themselves unsuited to each other, or unhappy in their union, and I defy you to guard against so-called marriages whereof the impulse is mere appetite or worldly convenience. Such unions, in fact, are made, and will be made, under whatever laws. But tens of thousands of libertines, lechers, egotists, who would take a new wife at least every Christmas, if they could legally and reputably rid themselves in season of the old one, are appalled and deterred by the stern exaction of a solemn promise to fulfil all the obligations of husband and wife "till death do part." We cannot, even thus, be sure that *all* marital unions will be genuine marriages; but I know no other touchstone which that "intangible something called Society" can apply half so searching as this.

VII. As to whatever discrepancy may exist between the teachings of Moses and of Jesus respectively, regarding Divorce, they present no difficulty to my mind. I hold the law of Moses (not the Decalogue, which says nothing of Divorce) to have been local and temporary in its application; while that of Jesus is permanent and universal. Hence my adhesion to the latter.

VIII. The vital difference between us seems to me to hinge just here: You regard primarily those who have made false marriages, — who have wedded hastily, giddily, carnally, viciously, — and seek to relieve them from the inevitable consequence of their errors. I, on the other hand, am more intent on dissuading and deterring others from following their bad example, and so plunging, like Dives, "into this torment." If you could unmarry every discordant pair to-morrow, and should thereby teach the yet single that they might marry in haste and get divorced at leisure, you would not diminish, but greatly increase, the aggregate of human woe; while, if I could convince the giddy millions of heedless youth that Marriage is the most important, serious, solemn incident of their lives, and that whoever contracts it on the strength of pleasing features and a six-weeks' acquaintance commits a crime which will assuredly and fearfully punish its perpetrators, I should do mankind the greatest service, even though I should thereby render it certain that no divorce be evermore granted. Believing that unhappy unions were mainly, in their outset, unworthy ones, and that none who marry truly and nobly ever need seek or wish for Divorce, I must continue to uphold the law given through the words of Jesus of Nazareth, which, I am happy to know, is substantially identical with the law of New York. The Puritan pioneers of New England, it is jocularly said, resolved to take the law of God for their guidance until they should find time to make a better. Lacking not merely the leisure to frame such better law, but the faith to anticipate or seek it, I propose to hold by what I clearly, undoubtingly, accord with Christendom in understanding to be the Law of Marriage as enunciated by Him who "spake as never man spake." In the hope that further reflection and observation may bring you to a realizing sense of its wisdom and benignity,

I remain, yours,

HORACE GREELEY.

NEW YORK, April 25, 1860.

NOTE.

INDIANA DIVORCE LAW, AS IN FORCE MARCH 1, 1860.

(*Revised Statutes of Indiana*, Vol. II. pp. 234 to 237.)

§ 6. Divorces may be decreed by the Circuit Courts of this State on petition filed by any person who, at the time of the filing of such petition, shall have been a *bona fide* resident of the State one year previous to the filing of the same, and a resident of the county at the time of the filing of such petition, which *bona fide* residence shall be duly proven by such petitioner to the satisfaction of the Court trying the same.

§ 7. Divorces shall be decreed, upon the application of the injured party, for the following causes : —

1. Adultery, except as hereinafter provided.
2. Impotency.
3. Abandonment for one year.
4. Cruel treatment of either party by the other.
5. Habitual drunkenness of either party, or the failure of the husband to make reasonable provision for his family.
6. The conviction, subsequent to the marriage, in any country, of either party of an infamous crime.
7. *Any other cause* for which the Court shall deem it proper that a divorce should be granted.

§ 8. Divorces shall not be granted for adultery in any of the following cases : —

1. When the offence has been committed with the connivance of the party seeking the divorce.

2. When the party seeking the divorce has voluntarily cohabited with the other, with knowledge of the fact ; or has failed to file his or her petition for two years after he or she had discovered the same.

3. When the party seeking the divorce has also been guilty of adultery, under such circumstances as would have entitled the opposite party, if innocent, to a divorce.

.   .   .   .   .   .

§ 21. The Court, in decreeing a divorce, shall make provision for the guardianship, custody, support, and education, of the minor children of such marriage.

.   .   .   .   .

§ 23. The divorce of one party shall fully dissolve the marriage contract as to both.

§ 24. A divorce decreed in any other State by a court having jurisdiction thereof shall have full effect in this State.

.   .   .   .   .   .

§ 27. Wherever a petition for divorce remains undefended, it shall be the duty of the prosecuting attorney to appear and resist such petition.

(The other sections refer to modes of procedure, legitimacy, property rights, etc. The Indiana law does not permit limited divorce.)

ANALYTICAL INDEX.